The Bible

The Biography

Other titles in the *Books That Shook the World* series:

AVAILABLE NOW:

Plato's *Republic* by Simon Blackburn

Darwin's *Origin of Species* by Janet Browne

Thomas Paine's *Rights of Man* by Christopher Hitchens

The Qur'an by Bruce Lawrence

Homer's *The Iliad and The Odyssey* by Alberto Manguel

On The Wealth of Nations by P. J. O'Rourke

Clausewitz's *On War* by Hew Strachan

Marx's *Das Kapital* by Francis Wheen

FORTHCOMING:

Machiavelli's *The Prince* by Philip Bobbitt

The Bible

The Biography

KAREN ARMSTRONG

Atlantic Books

LONDON

Published in Great Britain in hardback in 2007 by Atlantic Books.
Atlantic Books is an imprint of Grove Atlantic Ltd.

3 5 7 9 8 6 4 2

A CIP catalogue record for this book is available from the British Library

ISBN 978 1 84354 396 1
Export and Airside ISBN 978 1 84354 627 6

Designed by Richard Marston

Typeset by Avon DataSet Ltd, Bidford on Avon, Warwickshire

Printed in Great Britain by MPG Books Ltd, Bodmin, Cornwall

Atlantic Books
An imprint of Grove Atlantic Ltd
Ormond House
26–27 Boswell Street
London WC1N 3JZ

www.groveatlantic.co.uk

In Memory of Eileen Hastings Armstrong
(1921–2006)

CONTENTS

Introduction   1

1   Torah   9

2   Scripture   32

3   Gospel   55

4   Midrash   79

5   Charity   102

6   *Lectio Divina*   126

7   *Sola Scriptura*   155

8   Modernity   183

    Epilogue   222

    Glossary of Key Terms   231

    Notes   243

    Index   279

INTRODUCTION

Human beings are meaning-seeking creatures. Unless we find some pattern or significance in our lives, we fall very easily into despair. Language plays an important part in our quest. It is not only a vital means of communication, but it helps us to articulate and clarify the incoherent turbulence of our inner world. We use words when we want to make something happen outside ourselves: we give an order or make a request and, one way or the other, everything around us changes, however infinitesimally. But when we speak we also get something back: simply putting an idea into words can give it a lustre and appeal that it did not have before. Language is mysterious. When a word is spoken, the ethereal is made flesh; speech requires incarnation – respiration, muscle control, tongue and teeth. Language is a complex code, ruled by deep laws that combine to form a coherent system that is imperceptible to the speaker, unless he or she is a trained linguist. But language has an inherent inadequacy. There is always something left unsaid; something that remains inexpressible. Our speech makes us conscious of the transcendence that characterizes human experience.

All this has affected the way we read the Bible, which for both Jews and Christians is the Word of God. Scripture has been an important element in the religious enterprise. In nearly all the major faiths, people have regarded certain texts as sacred and ontologically different from other documents. They have invested these writings with the weight of their highest aspirations, most extravagant hopes and deepest fears, and mysteriously the texts have given them something in return. Readers have encountered what seems like a presence in these writings, which thus introduce them to a transcendent dimension. They have based their lives on scripture – practically, spiritually and morally. When their sacred texts tell stories, people have generally believed them to be true, but until recently literal or historical accuracy has never been the point. The truth of scripture cannot be assessed unless it is – ritually or ethically – put into practice. The Buddhist scriptures, for example, give readers some information about the life of the Buddha, but have included only those incidents that show Buddhists what they must do to achieve their own enlightenment.

Today scripture has a bad name. Terrorists use the Qur'an to justify atrocities, and some argue that the violence of their scripture makes Muslims chronically aggressive. Christians campaign against the teaching of evolutionary theory because it contradicts the biblical creation story. Jews argue that because God promised Canaan (modern Israel) to the descendants of Abraham, oppressive policies against the Palestinians are legitimate. There has been a scriptural revival that has intruded into public life. Secularist opponents of religion claim that scripture breeds violence, sectarianism and intolerance; that it prevents people from thinking for themselves, and encourages delusion. If religion preaches compassion, why is there so much hatred in sacred texts? Is it possible to be a 'believer' today when science has undermined so many biblical teachings?

Because scripture has become such an explosive issue, it is important to be clear what it is and what it is not. This biography of the Bible provides some insight into this religious phenomenon. It is, for example, crucial to note that an exclusively literal interpretation of the Bible is a recent development. Until the nineteenth century, very few people imagined that the first chapter of Genesis was a factual account of the origins of life. For centuries, Jews and Christians relished highly allegorical and inventive exegesis, insisting that a wholly literal reading of the Bible was neither possible nor desirable. They have rewritten biblical history, replaced Bible stories with new myths, and interpreted the first chapter of Genesis in surprisingly different ways.

The Jewish scriptures and the New Testament both began as oral proclamations and even after they were committed to writing, there often remained a bias towards the spoken word that is also present in other traditions. From the very beginning, people feared that a written scripture encouraged inflexibility and unrealistic, strident certainty. Religious knowledge cannot be imparted like other information, simply by scanning the sacred page. Documents became 'scripture' not, initially, because they were thought to be divinely inspired but because people started to treat them differently. This was certainly true of the early texts of the Bible, which became holy only when approached in a ritual context that set them apart from ordinary life and secular modes of thought.

Jews and Christians treat their scriptures with ceremonial reverence. The Torah scroll is the most sacred object in the synagogue; encased in a precious covering, housed in an 'ark', it is revealed at the climax of the liturgy when the scroll is conveyed formally around the congregation, who touch it with the tassels of their prayer shawls. Some Jews even dance with the scroll, embracing it like a beloved object. Catholics also carry the Bible in procession, douse it with incense, and stand up when it is recited, making the sign of the cross on forehead, lips and heart. In Protestant communities, the Bible reading is the high point of the service. But even more important were the spiritual disciplines that involved diet, posture and exercises in concentration, which, from a very early date, helped Jews and Christians to peruse the Bible in a different frame of mind. They were thus able to read between the lines and find something new, because the Bible always meant more than it said.

From the very beginning, the Bible had no single message. When the editors fixed the canons of both the Jewish and Christian testaments, they included competing visions and placed them, without comment, side by side. From the first, biblical authors felt free to revise the texts they had inherited and give them entirely different meaning. Later exegetes held up the Bible as a template for the problems of their time. Sometimes they allowed it to shape their world-view but they also felt free to change it and make it speak to contemporary conditions. They were not usually interested in discovering the original meaning of a biblical passage. The Bible 'proved' that it was holy because people continually discovered fresh ways to interpret it and found that this difficult, ancient set of documents cast light on situations that their authors could never have imagined. Revelation was an ongoing process; it had not been confined to a distant theophany on Mount Sinai; exegetes continued to make the Word of God audible in each generation.

Some of the most important biblical authorities insisted that charity must be the guiding principle of exegesis: any interpretation that spread hatred or disdain was illegitimate. All the world faiths claim that compassion is not only the prime virtue and the test of true religiosity but that it actually introduces us to Nirvana, God or the Dao. But sadly the biography of the Bible represents the failures as well as the triumphs of the religious quest. The biblical authors and their interpreters have all too often succumbed to the violence, unkindness and exclusivity that is rife in their societies.

Human beings seek *ekstasis*, a 'stepping outside' of their normal, mundane experience. If they no longer find ecstasy in a synagogue, church or mosque, they look for it in dance, music, sport, sex or drugs. When people read the Bible receptively and intuitively, they found that it gave them intimations of transcendence. A major characteristic of a peak religious insight is a sense of completeness and oneness. It has been called *coincidentia oppositorum:* in this ecstatic condition, things that seemed separate and even opposed coincide and reveal an unexpected unity. The biblical story of the Garden of Eden depicts this experience of primal wholeness: God and humanity were not divided but lived in the same place; men and women were unaware of gender difference; they lived in harmony with animals and the natural world; and there was no distinction between good and evil. In such a state, divisions are transcended in an *ekstasis* that is separate from the conflicted fragmentary nature of ordinary life. People have tried to recreate this Edenic experience in their religious rituals.

As we shall see, Jews and Christians developed a method of Bible study that linked together texts that had no intrinsic connection. By constantly breaking down barriers of textual difference, they achieved an ecstatic *coincidentia oppositorum*, which is also present in other scriptural traditions. It is, for example, essential to the proper interpretation of the Qur'an. From a very early period, the Aryans of India learned to apprehend the Brahman, the mysterious potency that held the diverse elements of the world together, when they listened to the paradoxes and riddles of the Rig Veda hymns, which fused apparently unrelated things. When Jews and Christians tried to find a unity in their paradoxical and multifarious scriptures, they also had intuitions of divine oneness. Exegesis was always a spiritual discipline rather than an academic pursuit.

Originally, the people of Israel had achieved this *ekstasis* in the Jerusalem temple, which had been designed as a symbolic replica of the Garden of Eden.[1] There they experienced *shalom*, a word that is usually translated 'peace' but is better rendered as 'wholeness, completeness'. When their temple was destroyed, they had to find a new way of finding *shalom* in a tragic, violent world. Twice their temple was burned to the ground; each time its destruction led to an intense period of scriptural activity, as they sought healing and harmony in the documents that would become the Bible.

CHAPTER 1

Torah

In 597 BCE, the tiny state of Judah in the highlands of Canaan broke its vassalage treaty with Nebuchadnezzar, ruler of the powerful Babylonian empire. It was a catastrophic mistake. Three months later, the Babylonian army besieged Jerusalem, Judah's capital. The young king surrendered immediately and was deported to Babylonia, together with some ten thousand of the citizens who made the state viable: priests, military leaders, craftsmen and metal workers. As they left Jerusalem, the exiles would have taken one last look at the temple built on Mount Zion by King Solomon (c.970–930 BCE), the centre of their national and spiritual life, sadly aware that in all likelihood they would never see it again. Their fears were realized: in 586, after yet another rebellion in Judah, Nebuchadnezzar destroyed Jerusalem and burned Solomon's temple to the ground.

The exiles were not ill-treated in Babylon. The king was comfortably housed with his entourage in the southern citadel, and the rest lived together in new settlements by the canals and were allowed to manage their domestic affairs. But they had lost their country, their political independence, and their religion. They belonged to the people of Israel and believed that their god Yahweh had promised that if they worshipped him exclusively, they would live in their land forever. The Jerusalem temple, where Yahweh had dwelt among his people, was essential to his cult. Yet here they were in an alien land, cast out of Yahweh's presence. This must be a divine punishment. Time and again, the Israelites had failed to keep their covenant agreement with Yahweh and had succumbed to the lure of other deities. Some of the exiles assumed that, as the leaders of Israel, it was up to them to rectify the situation, but how could they serve Yahweh without the temple that was their only means of making contact with their god?

Five years after his arrival in Babylon, standing beside the Chebar canal, a young priest called Ezekiel had a terrifying vision. It was impossible to see anything clearly because nothing in this stormy maelstrom of fire and tumultuous sound conformed to ordinary human categories, but Ezekiel knew that he was in the presence of the *kavod*, the 'glory' of Yahweh, which was usually enthroned in the inner sanctum of the temple.[1] God had left Jerusalem and, riding on what seemed to be a massive war chariot, had come to live with the exiles in Babylon. A hand stretched towards Ezekiel holding a scroll, which was inscribed with 'lamentations, wailing, and moanings'. 'Eat this scroll,' a divine voice commanded him, 'feed and be satisfied by the scroll I am giving you.' When he forced it down, accepting the pain and misery of his exile, Ezekiel found that 'it tasted sweet as honey'.[2]

It was a prophetic moment. The exiles would continue to long for their lost temple, because in the Middle East at this period, it was impossible to imagine religion without one.[3] But the time would come when Israelites would make contact with their God in sacred writings, rather than a shrine. Their holy book would not be easy to understand. Like Ezekiel's scroll, its message often seemed distressing and incoherent. Yet when they made the effort to absorb this confusing text, making it a part of their inmost being, they would feel that they had come into the presence of God – just as they did when they had visited his shrine in Jerusalem.

But it would be many years before Yahwism became a religion of the book. The exiles had brought a number of scrolls from the royal archive in Jerusalem with them to Babylon, and there they studied and edited these documents. If they were allowed to return home, these records of the history and cult of their people could play an important role in the restoration of national life. But the scribes did not regard these writings as sacrosanct and felt free to add new passages, altering them to fit their changed circumstances. They had as yet no notion of a sacred text. True, there were many stories in the Middle East about heavenly tablets that had descended miraculously to earth and imparted secret, divine knowledge. There were tales in Israel about the engraved stones that Yahweh had given to his prophet Moses, who had spoken with him face to face.[4] But the scrolls in the Judaean archive were not in this league, and did not play any part in the cult of Israel.

The Israelites, like most peoples in the ancient world, had always handed on their traditions by word of mouth. In the early days of their nation, in about 1200 BCE, they had lived in twelve tribal units in the Canaanite highlands but believed that they had a common ancestry and a shared history, which they celebrated in shrines associated with one of their patriarchs or an important event. Bards recited the epic stories of the sacred past and the people formally renewed the covenant agreement that bound them together as the *am Yahweh*, 'the family of Yahweh'. Already, at this very early stage, Israel had a distinctive religious vision. Most peoples in the region developed a mythology and liturgy that centred on the world of the gods in primordial time, but Israelites focused on their life with Yahweh in *this* world. From the very beginning, they thought historically, in terms of cause and effect.

From early fragments embedded in the later biblical narratives, we can infer that the Israelites believed their ancestors to have been nomads. Yahweh had led them to Canaan, and promised that one day their descendants would own the land. For many years they had lived as slaves under Egyptian rule, but Yahweh had liberated them with great signs and marvels, led them back to the Promised Land under the leadership of Moses, and helped them to conquer the highlands from the indigenous inhabitants.[5] But there was as yet no master-narrative: each tribe had its own version of the story, each region its local heroes. The priests of Dan, in the extreme north, for example, believed that they were descended from Moses; Abraham, the father of the whole nation, had lived in Hebron and was especially popular in the south. At Gilgal, the local tribes celebrated Israel's miraculous entry into the Promised Land, when the waters of the river Jordan had miraculously parted to let them through. The people of Shechem annually renewed the covenant that Joshua had made with Yahweh after his conquest of Canaan.[6]

By about 1000 BCE, however, the tribal system was no longer adequate, so the Israelites formed two monarchies in the Canaanite highlands: the kingdom of Judah in the south, and the larger, more prosperous kingdom of Israel in the north. The old covenant festivals were phased out in favour of royal rituals at the national shrines that centred on the person of the king. On his coronation day, the king was adopted by Yahweh, became a 'son of God', and a member of Yahweh's Divine Assembly of heavenly beings. We know almost nothing about the cult of the northern kingdom, because the biblical historians had a bias towards Judah, but many of the psalms later included in the Bible were used in the Jerusalem liturgy[7] and show that the Judahites had been influenced by the cult of Baal in neighbouring Syria, which had a similar royal mythology.[8] Yahweh had made an unconditional covenant with King David, the founder of the Judaean dynasty, and had promised that his descendants would rule in Jerusalem forever.

Now that the old tales had been liberated from the cult, they acquired an independent, literary life. During the eighth century, there was a literacy revolution throughout the Middle East and the eastern Mediterranean.[9] Kings commissioned documents that glorified their regime and housed these texts in libraries. In Greece, the epics of Homer were committed to writing at this time, and in Israel and Judah historians began to combine the old stories to create national sagas, which have been preserved in the earliest strata of the Pentateuch, the first five books of the Bible.[10]

From the multifarious traditions of Israel and Judah, the eighth-century historians built a coherent narrative. Scholars usually call the southern epic of Judah 'J' because the authors always called their God 'Yahweh', while the northern saga is known as 'E' because these historians preferred the more formal title 'Elohim'. Later these two separate accounts were combined by an editor to form a single story that formed the backbone of the Hebrew Bible. During the eighteenth century BCE, Yahweh had commanded Abraham to leave his home town of Ur in Mesopotamia and settle in the Canaanite highlands, where he made a covenant with him, promising that his descendants would inherit the whole country. Abraham lived in Hebron; his son Isaac in Beersheba, and his grandson, Jacob (also called 'Israel'), eventually settled in the countryside around Shechem.

During a famine, Jacob and his sons, the founders of the twelve Israelite tribes, migrated to Egypt, where they flourished initially but, when they became too numerous, were enslaved and oppressed. Finally, in about 1250 BCE, Yahweh liberated them under the leadership of Moses. As they fled, Yahweh parted the waters of the Sea of Reeds, so that the Israelites passed over in safety, but Pharaoh and his army were drowned. For forty years the Israelites wandered in the wilderness of Sinai, south of Canaan. On Mount Sinai, Yahweh had made a solemn covenant with Israel and gave them the law, which included the Ten Commandments inscribed on stone tablets in Yahweh's own hand. Finally, Moses's successor Joshua led the tribes across the Jordan river into Canaan; they destroyed all the Canaanite cities and villages, killed the native population and made the land their own.

However, Israeli archaeologists, who have been excavating the region since 1967, have found no evidence to corroborate this story: there is no sign of foreign invasion or mass destruction, and nothing to indicate a large-scale change of population. The scholarly consensus is that the story of the Exodus is not historical. There are many theories. Egypt had ruled the Canaanite city states since the nineteenth century BCE, and had withdrawn at the end of the thirteenth century, shortly before the first settlements appeared in the formerly uninhabitable highlands. We first hear about a people called 'Israel' in this region in about 1200 BCE. Some scholars argue that the Israelites were refugees from the failing city-states on the coastal plains. They may have been joined there by other tribes from the south, who brought with them their god Yahweh, who seems to have originated in the southern regions around Sinai.[11] Those who had lived under Egyptian rule in the Canaanite cities may have felt that they had indeed been liberated from Egypt – but in their own country.[12]

J and E were not modern historical accounts. Like Homer

and Herodotus, the authors included legends about divine figures and mythological elements that try to explain the meaning of what had happened. Their narratives are *more* than history. From the very beginning, there was no single, authoritative message in what would become the Bible. The J and E authors interpreted the saga of Israel very differently, and later editors made no attempt to iron out these inconsistencies and contradictions. Subsequently historians would feel at liberty to add to the JE narrative and make radical alterations.

In both J and E, for example, very different views of God were expressed. J used anthropomorphic imagery that would embarrass later exegetes. Yahweh strolls in the Garden of Eden like a Middle Eastern potentate, shuts the door of Noah's ark, gets angry and changes his mind. But in E there was a more transcendent view of Elohim, who scarcely even 'speaks' but prefers to send an angel as his messenger. Later Israelite religion would become passionately monotheist, convinced that Yahweh was the *only* God. But neither the J or E authors believed this. Originally Yahweh had been a member of the Divine Assembly of 'holy ones', over which El, the high god of Canaan, had presided with his consort Asherah. Each nation of the region had its own patronal deity, and Yahweh was the 'holy one of Israel'.[13] By the eighth century, Yahweh had ousted El in the Divine Assembly,[14] and ruled alone over a host of 'holy ones', who were warriors in his heavenly army.[15] None of the other gods could measure up to Yahweh in his fidelity to his people. Here he had no peers, no rivals.[16] But the Bible shows that right up to the destruction of the temple by Nebuchadnezzar in 586, Israelites also worshipped a host of other deities.[17]

Abraham, a man of the south, not Moses, was the hero of J's history. His career and the covenant God made with him looked forward to King David.[18] But E was more interested in Jacob, a northern character, and his son Joseph, who was buried in Shechem. E did not include any of the primeval history – the creation of the world, Cain and Abel, the Flood and the rebellion at the Tower of Babel – that was so important to J. E's hero was Moses, who was more widely revered in the north than the south.[19] But neither J nor E mentioned the law that Yahweh gave to Moses on Sinai, which would become so crucial later. There was as yet no reference to the Ten Commandments. Almost certainly, as in other Near Eastern legend, the heavenly tablets given to Moses originally contained some esoteric cultic lore.[20] For J and E, Sinai was important because Moses and the Elders had a vision of Yahweh on the mountaintop.[21]

By the eighth century, a small group of prophets wanted to make the people worship Yahweh exclusively. But this was not a popular move. As a warrior, Yahweh was unsurpassed, but he had no expertise in agriculture, so when they wanted a good harvest, it was natural for the people of Israel and Judah to have recourse to the cult of the local fertility god Baal and his sister-spouse Anat, practising the usual ritual sex to make the fields fertile. In the early eighth century, Hosea, a prophet in the northern kingdom, inveighed against this practice. His wife Gomer had served as a sacred prostitute of Baal and the pain he felt at her infidelity was, he imagined, similar to what Yahweh experienced when his people went whoring after other gods. Israelites must return to Yahweh, who could supply all their needs. It was no use hoping to appease him by temple ritual: Yahweh wanted cultic loyalty (*hesed*) not animal sacrifice.[22] If they continued to be unfaithful to Yahweh, the kingdom of Israel would be destroyed by the mighty Assyrian empire, their towns laid waste, and their children exterminated.[23]

Assyria had established unprecedented power in the Middle East; it regularly devastated the territories of recalcitrant vassals and deported the population. The prophet Amos, who preached in Israel in the mid-eighth century, argued that Yahweh was leading a holy war against Israel to punish its systemic injustice.[24] As Hosea condemned the widely respected cult of Baal, Amos turned the traditional cult of Yahweh the warrior on its head: he no longer reflexively took Israel's side. Amos also poured scorn on the temple rituals of the northern kingdom. Yahweh was sick of noisy chanting and devout strumming of harps. Instead he wanted justice to 'flow like water, and integrity like an unfailing stream'.[25] From this early date, the biblical writings were subversive and iconoclastic, challenging prevailing orthodoxy.

Isaiah of Jerusalem was more conventional; his oracles conformed entirely to the royal ideology of the House of David. He had received his prophetic commission in about 740 in the temple, where he saw Yahweh, surrounded by his Divine Assembly of celestial beings, and heard the cherubim crying 'holy [*qaddosh*] holy, holy!'[26] Yahweh was 'separate', 'other' and radically transcendent. Yahweh gave Isaiah a grim message: the countryside would be devastated and the inhabitants put to flight.[27] But Isaiah had no fear of Assyria. He had seen that Yahweh's 'glory' filled the earth;[28] as long as he was enthroned in his temple on Mount Zion, Judah was safe, because Yahweh, the divine warrior, was once again on the march, fighting for his people.[29]

But the northern kingdom enjoyed no such immunity. When the king of Israel joined a local confederacy to block Assyria's western advance in 732, the Assyrian king Tigleth-Pileser III descended and seized most of Israel's territory. Ten years later, in 722, after another rebellion, the Assyrian armies destroyed Samaria, Israel's beautiful capital, and deported the ruling class. The kingdom of Judah, which had become an Assyrian vassal, remained secure, and refugees fled to Jerusalem from the north, probably bringing with them the E saga and the recorded oracles of Hosea and Amos, who had foreseen the tragedy. These were included in Judah's royal archive where, at some later date, scribes combined the 'Elohist' tradition with J's southern epic.[30]

During these dark years, Isaiah was comforted by the imminent birth of a royal baby, a sign that God was still with the House of David: 'A young woman [*almah*] is with child and will soon give birth to a son whom she will call *Immanu-El* [God-with-us].'[31] His birth would even be a beacon of hope, 'a great light', to the traumatized people of the north, who 'walked in darkness' and 'deep shadow'.[32] When the baby was born, he was in fact named Hezekiah, and Isaiah imagined the entire Divine Assembly celebrating the royal child, who, like all the Davidic kings, would become a divine figure and a member of their heavenly council: on his coronation day he would be called 'Wonder-Counsellor, Mighty-God, Eternal-Father, Prince-of-Peace'.[33]

Although the biblical historians revere Hezekiah as a devout king who tried to outlaw the worship of foreign gods, his foreign policy was a disaster. After an ill-advised rebellion against Assyria in 701, Jerusalem was almost destroyed, the countryside brutally laid waste and Judah reduced to a tiny rump state. But under King Manasseh (687–42 BCE), who became a vassal of Assyria, Judah's fortunes improved. In an attempt to integrate with the empire, he reversed his father's religious jurisdiction, setting up altars to Baal, erecting an effigy of Asherah and statues of the divine horses of the sun in the Jerusalem temple, and instituting child sacrifice outside the city.[34] The biblical historian was horrified by these developments, but few of Manasseh's subjects would have been surprised, since most of them had similar icons in their own homes.[35] Despite Judah's prosperity, there was widespread unrest in the rural districts that had borne the brunt of the Assyrian invasion, and after Manasseh's death the smouldering discontent erupted in a palace coup, which deposed Manasseh's son Amon and put his eight-year-old son Josiah on the throne.

By this time, Assyria was in decline and Egypt in the ascendancy. In 656 the Pharoah forced Assyrian troops to withdraw from the Levant and the Judahites watched with astonishment, as the Assyrians vacated the territories of the former kingdom of Israel. While the great powers fought for supremacy, Judah was left to its own devices. There was a surge of national feeling and in 622 Josiah began to repair Solomon's temple, the symbolic memorial of Judah's golden age. During the construction, the high priest Hilkiah made a momentous discovery and hurried with the news to Shaphan, the royal scribe. He had found the 'scroll of the law' (*sefer torah*), which Yahweh had given to Moses on Mount Sinai.[36]

In the older stories, there was no mention of Yahweh's teaching (*torah*) being committed to writing. In the JE accounts, Moses had passed on Yahweh's directions by word of mouth and the people had responded orally.[37] The seventh-century reformers, however, added verses to the JE saga which explained that Moses 'put all the commands of Yahweh into writing' and read the *sefer torah* to the people.[38] Hilkiah and Shaphan claimed that this scroll had been lost and its teachings never implemented, but its providential discovery meant that Judah could make a new start. Hilkiah's document probably contained an early version of the book of Deuteronomy, which described Moses delivering a 'second law' (Greek: *deuteronomion*) shortly before his death. But instead of being an ancient work, Deuteronomy was an entirely new scripture. It was not unusual for reformers to attribute new ideas to a great figure of the past. The Deuteronomists believed that they were speaking for Moses at this time of transition. In other words, this was what Moses would say to Josiah if he were delivering a 'second law' today.

Instead of simply recording the status quo, for the first time an Israelite text was calling for radical change. After the scroll had been read aloud to him, Josiah tore his garments in distress and immediately inaugurated a programme that followed Yahweh's new *torah* to the letter. He burned down Manasseh's abominations in the temple and, because the Judahites had always regarded the royal shrines of the northern kingdom as illegitimate, demolished the temples of Bethel and Samaria, killed the priests in the rural sanctuaries and contaminated their altars.[39]

It is instructive that the Deuteronomists, who pioneered the idea of scriptural orthodoxy, introduced startlingly new legislation, which – had it been implemented – would have transformed the ancient faith of Israel.[40] To ensure purity of worship, they tried to centralize the cult,[41] create a secular judiciary independent of the temple, and strip the king of his sacral powers, making him subject to the *torah* like everybody else. The Deuteronomists actually changed the wording of earlier law codes, sagas and liturgical texts to make them endorse their proposals. In some ways, Deuteronomy, with its secular sphere, centralized state and constitutional monarchy, reads like a modern document. It was even more passionate about social justice than Amos and its theology more rational than the old cultic mythology of Judah:[42] you could not *see* God and he did not live in a humanly constructed building.[43] Israelites did not own their land because Yahweh dwelt on Zion, but because the people observed his commandments.

The reformers did not use their scripture to conserve tradition, as is often done today, but to introduce radical change. They also rewrote the history of Israel, adding fresh material that adapted the JE epic to the seventh century, paying special attention to Moses, who had liberated the Israelites from Egypt, at a time when Josiah hoped to become independent of Pharaoh. The climax of the Exodus story was no longer a theophany on Sinai, but the gift of the *sefer torah* and the tablets that Yahweh gave to Moses were now inscribed with the Ten Commandments. The Deuteronomists extended the Exodus story to include Joshua's conquest of the northern highlands – a blueprint for Josiah's reconquering of the northern territories.[44] They also wrote a history of the two kingdoms of Israel and Judah in the books of Samuel and Kings, arguing that the Davidic monarchs were the only legitimate rulers of the whole of Israel. Their story culminated in the reign of Josiah, a new Moses and a greater king than David.[45]

Not everybody was enamoured of the new *torah*. The prophet Jeremiah, who began his ministry at about this time, admired Josiah and agreed with many of the reformers' aims, but had reservations about a written scripture: the 'lying pen of the scribes' could subvert tradition by a mere sleight of the pen and a written text could encourage a superficial mode of thought that concentrated on information rather than wisdom.[46] In a study of modern Jewish movements, the eminent scholar Haym Soloveitchik argues that the transition from an oral tradition to written texts can lead to religious stridency by giving the reader an unrealistic certainty about essentially ineffable matters.[47] Deuteronomist religion was certainly strident. The reformers depicted Moses preaching a policy of violent suppression of the native Canaanites: 'You must destroy completely all the places where the nations you dispossess have served their gods ... you must tear down their altars, smash their pillars, cut down their sacred poles, set fire to the carved images of their gods and wipe out their name from that place.'[48] They described with approval Joshua massacring the people of Ai as though he were an Assyrian general:

> When Israel had finished killing all the inhabitants of Ai in the open ground and where they followed them into the wilderness, and when all to a man had fallen by the edge of the sword, all Israel returned to Ai and slaughtered all its people. The number of those who fell that day, men and women together, was twelve thousand, all people of Ai.[49]

The Deuteronomists had absorbed the violent ethos of a region that had experienced nearly two hundred years of Assyrian brutality. It was an early indication that scripture reflects the failures as well as the high points of the religious quest.

Although these texts were revered, they had not yet become 'scripture'. People felt free to alter older writings and there was no canon of prescribed sacred books. But they were beginning to express the community's highest aspirations. The Deuteronomists who celebrated Josiah's reform were convinced that Israel was on the brink of a glorious new era but in 622 he was killed in a skirmish with the Egyptian army. Within a few years, the Babylonians had conquered Nineveh, the Assyrian capital, and became the major power in the region. Judah's brief independence was over. For a few decades the kings veered in their allegiance between Egypt and Babylon. Many still believed that Judah would be safe as long as Yahweh dwelt in his temple, even though Jeremiah warned them that to defy Babylon was suicidal. Finally, after two futile rebellions, Jerusalem and its temple were destroyed by Nebuchadnezzar in 586.

In exile, the scribes pored over the scrolls in the royal archive. The Deuteronomists added passages to their history to account for the disaster, which they attributed to Manasseh's religious policies.[50] But some of the priests, who in losing their temple had lost their whole world, looked back to the past and found a reason for hope. Scholars call this priestly layer of the Penateuch 'P', though we do not know whether P was an individual or, as seems more likely, an entire school. P revised the JE narrative and added the books of Numbers and Leviticus, drawing upon older documents – genealogies, laws and ritual texts – some written down, others orally transmitted.[51] The most important of his sources was the 'Holiness Code'[52] (a collection of seventh-century laws) and the Tabernacle Document, a description of

Yahweh's tent shrine during the Israelites' years in the Sinai wilderness, which was central to P's vision.[53] Some of P's material was very old indeed, but he created an entirely new vision for his demoralized people.

P understood the Exodus story very differently from the Deuteronomists. The climax was not the *sefer torah* but the promise of God's continual presence during their desert years. God had brought Israel out of Egypt simply in order 'to live [*skn*] among them'.[54] The verb *shakan* meant: 'to lead the life of a nomadic tent dweller'. Instead of residing in a permanent building, God preferred to 'tent' with his wandering people; he was not tied to one place, but could accompany them wherever they went.[55] After P's revision, the book of Exodus ended with the completion of the tabernacle: the 'glory' of Yahweh filled the tent and the cloud of his presence covered it.[56] God, P implied, was still with his people in their latest 'wandering' in Babylonia. Instead of ending his saga with Joshua's conquest, P left the Israelites on the border of the Promised Land.[57] Israel was not a people because it dwelt in a particular country, but because it lived in the presence of its God.

In P's revised history, the exile was the latest in a sequence of migrations: Adam and Eve had been expelled from Eden; Cain condemned to a life of homeless vagrancy after murdering Abel; the human race had been scattered at the Tower of Babel; Abraham had left Ur; the tribes had emigrated to Egypt, and eventually lived as nomads in the desert. In their latest dispersal, the exiles must build a community to which the presence could return. In a startling innovation, P suggested that the entire people observe the purity laws of the temple personnel.[58] Everybody must live as though he were serving the divine presence. Israel must be 'holy' (*qaddosh*) and 'separate' like Yahweh,[59] so P crafted a way of life based on the principle of separation. The exiles must live apart from their Babylonian neighbours, observing distinctive rules of diet and cleanliness. Then – and only then – Yahweh would live among them: 'I will place my tabernacle in your midst,' God told them, 'and I will walk about among you.'[60] Babylonia could become another Eden, where God had walked with Adam in the cool of the evening.

Holiness also had a strong ethical component. Israelites must respect the sacred 'otherness' of every single creature. Nothing could be enslaved or possessed, therefore, not even the land.[61] Israelites must not despise the foreigner: 'If a stranger lives with you in your land, do not molest him. You must count him as one of your own countrymen and love him as yourself – for you were once strangers in Egypt.'[62] Unlike the Deuteronomists, P's vision was inclusive. His narrative of alienation and exile constantly stressed the importance of reconciliation with former enemies. Nowhere was this more apparent than in his most famous work, the first chapter of Genesis, in which P describes Elohim creating heaven and earth in six days.

This was not a literal, historically accurate account of creation. When the final editors put the extant biblical text together, they placed P's story next to J's creation narrative, which is quite different.[63] In the ancient world, cosmogony was a therapeutic rather than a factual genre. People recited creation myths at a sickbed, at the start of a new project, or at the beginning of a new year – whenever they felt the need for an infusion of the divine potency that had, somehow, brought all things into being. P's story would have been consoling to the exiles who felt that Yahweh had been ignominiously defeated by Marduk, god of Babylon. Unlike Marduk, whose creation of the world had to be repeated annually at New Year in spectacular rites in the ziggurat of Esagila, Yahweh was not obliged to fight other gods to create an ordered cosmos; the ocean was not a frightening sea-goddess like Tiamat, who fought Marduk to her bitter end, but simply the raw material of the universe; the sun, moon and stars were not deities but mere creatures and functionaries. Yahweh's victory did not have to be renewed: he finished his work in six days and rested on the seventh.[64]

This was no bombastic polemic, however; there was no taunting, no aggression. In the ancient Near East, gods usually created the cosmos after a series of violent, terrifying battles; indeed, the Israelites told stories of Yahweh slaying divine sea-monsters at the beginning of time.[65] But P's creation myth was non-violent. God simply spoke a word of command and one by one the components of our world came into being. After each day, God saw that all he had made was *tov*, 'good'. On the last day, Yahweh confirmed that everything was 'very good' and blessed his entire creation,[66] including, presumably, the Babylonians. Everybody should behave like Yahweh, resting calmly on the Sabbath, serving God's world and blessing every single one of his creatures.

But another prophet, who preached in Babylonia during the second half of the sixth century, espoused a more aggressive theology and could not wait to see the *goyim*, the foreign nations, marching behind Israel in chains. We do not know his name, but because his oracles were preserved in the same scroll as Isaiah's, he is usually known as the Second Isaiah. The exile was drawing to a close. In 539, Cyrus, king of Persia, defeated the Babylonians and became the master of the largest empire the world had yet seen. Because he promised to repatriate all deportees, Second Isaiah called him Yahweh's *meshiah*, his 'anointed' king.[67] For Israel's sake, Yahweh had summoned Cyrus as his instrument and caused a revolution of power in the region. Could any other god compete with him? No, Yahweh declared scornfully to the gods of the *goyim*, 'you are nothing and your works are nothingness.'[68] He had become the *only* God. 'I am Yahweh, unrivalled,' he announced proudly. 'There is no other god besides me.'[69] This is the first unequivocally monotheistic statement in what was becoming the Hebrew Bible. But its triumphalism reflected the more belligerent characteristics of religion. Second Isaiah relied upon a mythical tradition that had little connection with the rest of the Pentateuch. He revived the ancient tales of Yahweh slaying sea dragons to order primordial chaos, declaring that Yahweh was about to repeat this cosmic triumph by defeating the historical enemies of Israel.[70] He did not, however, reflect the views of the whole exiled community. Four 'Servant Songs' punctuated Second Isaiah's exuberant prophecies.[71] In these, a mysterious figure, who called himself Yahweh's servant, was entrusted with the task of establishing justice throughout the world – but in a non-violent campaign. He was despised and rejected, but his suffering would redeem his people. The servant had no desire to subjugate the *goyim*, but would become 'the light of the nations', and enable God's salvation to reach to the ends of the earth.[72]

Cyrus fulfilled his promise. Towards the end of 539, a few months after his coronation, a small party of exiles set out for Jerusalem. Most of the Israelites chose to stay in Babylon, where they would make an important contribution to the Hebrew scriptures. The returning exiles brought home nine scrolls that traced the history of their people from the creation until their deportation: Genesis, Exodus, Leviticus, Numbers, Deuteronomy, Joshua, Judges, Samuel and Kings; they also brought anthologies of the oracles of the prophets (*neviim*) and a hymn book, which included new psalms composed in Babylon. It was still not complete, but the exiles had in their possession the bare bones of the Hebrew Bible.

The Golah, the community of returning exiles, were convinced that their revised religion was the only authentic version of Yahwism. But the Israelites who had not been deported to Babylonia, most of whom lived in the territories of the former northern kingdom, could not share this vision and would resent this exclusive attitude. The new temple, a rather modest shrine, finally completed in 520 BCE, made

Yahwism a temple faith once again. But another spirituality began, very gradually, to develop alongside it. With the help of those Israelites who had remained in Babylonia, the Golah were about to transform their medley of texts into scripture.

CHAPTER 2

Scripture

Once the Judahites had completed their second temple on Mount Zion, they imagined that life would continue as before. But they were overcome by spiritual malaise. Many were disappointed with the new temple, which could not compete with the legendary splendour of Solomon's shrine; the Golah had encountered stiff opposition from foreigners who had settled in Judah during the exiles' absence in Babylonia; and they had received a less than cordial welcome from those Israelites who had not been deported by the Babylonians. The priests had become lazy and apathetic and provided no moral leadership.[1] But at the beginning of the fourth century, in about 398 BCE, the Persian king dispatched Ezra, his minister for Jewish affairs, to Jerusalem with a mandate to enforce the *torah* of Moses as the law of the land.[2] Ezra would make this set of hitherto miscellaneous teachings an absolute value, so that it became *the* Torah.

The Persians were reviewing the legal systems of all their subjects to make sure that they were compatible with the security of the empire. An expert in Torah, Ezra had probably worked out a satisfactory modus vivendi between Mosaic law and Persian jurisprudence. When he arrived in Jerusalem, he was appalled by what he found. The people were not maintaining the holy separation from the *goyim* that P had prescribed: some had even taken foreigh wives. For a whole day, the inhabitants of Jerusalem were dismayed to see the king's envoy tear his garments and sit in the public street in the posture of deep mourning. Then Ezra summoned the entire Golah to a meeting. Anybody who refused to attend would be cast out of the community and have his property confiscated.

On New Year's Day, Ezra brought the Torah to the square in front of the Water Gate. Standing on a raised wooden dais, he read the text aloud, 'translating and giving the sense, so that the people understood what was read', while Levites[3] versed in the Torah circulated among the crowds, supplementing this instruction.[4] We are not sure which laws were proclaimed on this occasion, but, whatever they were, the people had clearly never heard them before. They burst into tears, frightened by these unfamiliar demands. 'Do not weep!' Ezra insisted. They now 'understood the meaning of what had been proclaimed to them'. This was the season of Sukkoth, a festive time, and Ezra explained the law that commanded the Israelites to spend this sacred month in special 'booths' (*sukkoth*), in memory of their ancestors' forty years in the wilderness.[5] At once, the people rushed into the hills to pick branches of olive, myrtle, pine and palm, and leafy shelters appeared all over the city. There was a carnival atmosphere, as the people assembled each evening to listen to Ezra's exposition.

Ezra had begun to craft a spiritual discipline based on a sacred text. The Torah had now been elevated above the other writings and, for the first time, was called 'the law of Moses'. But, if it was simply read like any other text, the Torah could seem demanding and disconcerting. It must be heard in the contexts of rituals that separated it from ordinary life and put the audience in a different frame of mind. Because the people had begun to treat it differently, the Torah was becoming 'sacred scripture'.

Perhaps the most important element of this Torah spirituality was Ezra himself.[6] He was a priest, 'a diligent scribe in the Torah of Moses', and a guardian of tradition.[7] But he was also a new type of religious official: a scholar who 'set his heart to investigate (li-drosh) the Torah of Yahweh and to do and teach law and ordinance in Israel'.[8] He was offering something different from the usual priestly instruction about ceremonial lore. The biblical author makes a point of telling us that 'the hand of Yahweh rested upon him' – a phrase traditionally used to describe the weight of inspiration that had descended on the prophets.[9] Before the exile, priests had been wont to 'consult' (li-drosh) Yahweh, by casting lots with the sacred objects known as Urim and Thummim.[10] The new seer was not a fortune teller but a scholar who could interpret the scriptures. The practice of midrash (exegesis) would always retain this sense of expectant inquiry.[11] Torah study was not an academic exercise but a spiritual quest.

Yet Ezra's reading had been prefaced by the threat of expulsion and seizure of property. It was followed by a more sombre assembly in the square in front of the temple, during which the people stood shivering as the torrential winter rains deluged the city and heard Ezra command them to send away their foreign wives.[12] Membership of Israel was now confined to the Golah and those who submitted to the Torah, the official law code of Judah. There was always the danger that enthusiasm for scripture could foster an exclusive, divisive and potentially cruel orthodoxy.

Ezra's reading marks the beginning of classical Judaism, a religion concerned not merely with the reception and preservation of revelation but with its constant reinterpretation.[13] The law that Ezra read was clearly unknown to the people, who wept in fear when they heard it for the first time. When he expounded the text, the exegete did not reproduce the original *torah* imparted in the distant past to Moses but created something new and unexpected. The biblical writers had worked in the same way, radically revising the texts they had inherited. Revelation had not happened once and for all time; it was an ongoing process that could never end, because there were always fresh teachings to be discovered.

By this time, there were two established categories of scripture: the Torah and the Prophets (*Neviim*). But after the exile, another set of texts were produced that would become known as the *Kethuvim*, the 'Writings', which sometimes simply reinterpreted the older books. Thus Chronicles, a historical narrative written by priestly authors, was essentially a commentary on the Deuteronomic history of Samuel and Kings. When these two books were translated into Greek, they were called *paralipomena*: 'the things omitted'.[14] The authors were writing between the lines to make good what they regarded as deficiencies in the earlier accounts. They shared P's ideal of reconciliation and wanted to build bridges with the Israelites who had not gone into exile and were now resident in the north. They therefore omitted the Deuteronomists' harsh polemic against the northern kingdom.

A significant number of the Writings belonged to a school that was distinct from either the Law or the Prophets. In the ancient Near East, sages attached to the court as teachers or advisers tended to see the whole of reality as shaped by a vast, underlying principle of divine origin. The Hebrew sages called it *Hokhmah*, 'Wisdom'. Everything – the laws of nature, society, and events in the lives of individuals – conformed to this celestial blueprint, which no human being could ever grasp in its entirety. But the sages who devoted their lives to the contemplation of Wisdom believed that they occasionally had glimpses of it. Some expressed their insight in such pithy maxims as: 'A king gives a country stability by justice, an extortioner brings it to ruin', or 'The man who flatters his neighbour spreads a net for his feet'.[15] The Wisdom tradition had originally little connection with Moses and Sinai but was associated with King Solomon, who had a reputation for this type of acumen[16] and three of the *Kethuvim* were attributed to him: Proverbs, Ecclesiastes and the Song of Songs. Proverbs was a collection of common-sense aphorisms, similar to the two quoted above. Ecclesiastes, a flagrantly cynical meditation, saw all things as 'vanity', and appeared to undermine the entire Torah tradition, while the Song of Songs was an erotic poem with no apparent spiritual content.

Other Wisdom writings explored the insoluble problem of the suffering of innocent people in a world ruled by a just God. The book of Job was based on an ancient folktale. God gave Satan, the legal prosecutor of the Divine Assembly, permission to test Job's virtue by afflicting him with a series of wholly undeserved calamities. Job eloquently railed against his punishment and refused to accept any of the conventional explanations of the friends who tried to console him. Eventually Yahweh answered Job, not by referring to the events of the Exodus, but by forcing him to contemplate the underlying masterplan that governed creation. Could Job visit the place where snow was kept, fasten the harness of the Pleiades, or explain why a wild ox was willing to serve human beings? Job was forced to admit that he could not comprehend this divine Wisdom: 'I have been holding forth on matters I cannot understand, on marvels beyond me and my knowledge.'[17] The sage acquired Wisdom by meditating on the marvels of the physical world, not by studying Torah.

But by the second century BCE, some Wisdom writers were beginning to come closer to the Torah. Ben Sirah, a devout sage living in Jerusalem, no longer regarded Wisdom as an abstract principle but imagined her as a female figure and a member of the Divine Assembly.[18] He depicted her giving an account of herself before the other Counsellors. She was the Word by which God had called all things into being. She was the divine Spirit (*ruach*), which had hovered over the primal ocean at the beginning of the creative process. As God's Word and masterplan, she was divine and yet separate from her Maker, present everywhere on earth. But God had commanded her to pitch her tent with the people of Israel and she had accompanied them throughout their history. She had been in the pillar of cloud that had guided them in the wilderness and in the rituals of the temple, another symbolic expression of divine order. But above all, Wisdom was identical with the *sefer torah*, 'the law that Moses enjoined upon us'.[19] The Torah was no longer simply a legal code; it had become an expression of the highest wisdom and most transcendent goodness.

Another author, writing at about the same time, personified Wisdom in a similar way, as divine and yet separate from God's essence. 'Yahweh created me when his purpose first unfolded,' Wisdom explained, 'before the oldest of his works.' She was at his side – 'a master craftsman' – as he established the cosmos, 'delighting him day after day, ever at play in his presence, at play everywhere in the world, delighting to be with the sons of men'.[20] A new lightness and grace had entered Yahwism. The study of the Torah was beginning to arouse emotion and yearning that were almost erotic. Ben Sirah depicted Wisdom calling out to the sages like a lover: 'Approach me, you desire me, and take your fill of my fruits. For memories of me are sweeter than honey, inheriting me is sweeter than the honeycomb.'[21] There was no end to the quest for Wisdom: 'They who eat me will hunger for more, they who drink me will thirst for more.'[22] The tone and imagery of

Ben Sirah's hymn were very similar to the Song of Songs, which may explain why this love poem was eventually included in the Writings. It seemed to express the lyrically passionate experience of the *sefer* scholar when he studied the Torah and encountered a presence 'wider than the sea', whose designs were 'more profound than the abyss'.[23]

Ben Sirah described the *sefer* scholar delving into all categories of scripture: Torah, Prophets and Writings. He was not shut away from the world in an ivory tower but engaged in state affairs. His exegesis was wholly informed by prayer: 'At dawn and with all his heart he resorts to the Lord who made him', and, as a result, he received an influx of wisdom and understanding[24] that transformed him and made him a force for good in the world.[25] In a most important phrase, Ben Sirah claimed that the teachings of the sage were 'like prophecy, a legacy to all future generations'.[26] The scholar was not simply learning about the prophets; his exegesis had made him a prophet himself.

This becomes clear in the book of Daniel, which was written in Palestine during the second century BCE at a time of political crisis.[27] By this time, Judah had become a province of the Greek empires founded by the successors of Alexander the Great, who had conquered the Persian empire in 333 BCE. The Greeks introduced a diluted version of Athenian classical culture, known as Hellenism, into the Near East. Some Jews were enthalled by the Greek ideal but opposition to Hellenism became entrenched among the more conservative Jews after 167 BCE, when Antiochus Epiphanes, ruler of the

Seleucid empire in Mesopotamia and Palestine, violated the Jerusalem temple and introduced a Hellenistic cult there: Jews who opposed his regime were persecuted. Judas Maccabeus and his family led the Jewish resistance; in 164 they were able to oust the Greeks from the temple mount, but the war continued until 143, when the Maccabees were able to shake off Seleucid rule and establish Judah as an independent state, which was ruled by their Hasmonean dynasty until 63 BCE.

The book of Daniel was composed during the Maccabean war. It took the form of an historical novel, set in Babylon during the exile. In real life, Daniel had been one of the more virtuous exiles,[28] but in this fictional work he was an official prophet in the courts of Nebuchadnezzar and Cyrus. In the early chapters, written before Antiochus's sacrilege, Daniel was presented as a typical Middle Eastern court sage[29] with a special talent for 'interpreting every kind of vision and dream'.[30] But in the later chapters, composed after Antiochus's desecration of the temple but before the Maccabees' final victory, Daniel becomes an inspired exegete, whose study of scriptures endows him with prophetic insight.

Daniel experienced a series of perplexing visions. He saw a succession of four fearful empires (represented by fabulous beasts), each more terrible than the last. The fourth, a clear reference to the Seleucids, was of an entirely different order of wickedness, however. Its ruler would 'speak words against the Most High, and harass the saints of the Most High'.[31] Daniel foresaw 'the disastrous abomination' of Antiochus's

Hellenistic cult in the temple.[32] But there was a glimmer of hope. Daniel also saw 'coming on the clouds of heaven, one like a son of man', a figure representing the Maccabees, who was mysteriously human and yet more than human. The saviour entered the presence of God, who conferred upon him 'sovereignty, glory and kingship'.[33] These prophecies would later become very important, as we shall see in the following chapter. But what concerns us now is Daniel's inspired exegesis.

Daniel had another series of visions, which he was unable to understand. He sought enlightenment in scripture and was particularly preoccupied by Jeremiah's prediction of the number of years that must pass 'before the successive devastations of Jerusalem would come to an end, namely seventy years'.[34] The second-century author was clearly not interested in the original meaning of the text: Jeremiah had obviously prophesied, in a round figure, the length of the Babylonian exile. He wanted to find an entirely new significance in the ancient oracle that would bring comfort to the Jews who were anxiously awaiting the outcome of the Maccabean wars. This would become typical of Jewish exegesis. Instead of looking back to uncover its historical meaning, the interpreter would make the text speak to the present and the future. In order to seek out the hidden message in Jeremiah, Daniel put himself through a rigorous ascetic programme: 'I turned my face to the Lord God begging for time to pray and to plead with fasting, sackcloth and ashes.'[35] On another occasion, he said, 'I ate no rich food, touched no meat or wine, and did not anoint myself, until these three weeks were over'.[36] As a result of these spiritual disciplines, he became the recipient of a divine inspiration: Gabriel, the angel of revelation, flew towards him and enabled him to discover a new meaning in the problematic passage.

Torah study was becoming a prophetic discipline. The exegete now prepared himself to approach these ancient documents by purifying rituals, as if he were about to enter a holy place, putting himself into an alternative mental state that gave him fresh insight. The second-century author deliberately described Daniel's enlightenment in a way that recalled the visionary experiences of Isaiah and Ezekiel.[37] But where Isaiah had received his prophetic initiation in the temple, Daniel found his in the sacred text. He did not have to eat the scroll like Ezekiel; instead he lived with the words of scripture constantly in his mind, interiorizing them, and found himself transformed – 'purged, purified and made white'.[38] Finally the second-century author made Daniel predict the successful outcome of the Maccabean war by finding an entirely novel message in Jeremiah's words. In riddling, enigmatic verse, Gabriel indicated that whether it took 'seventy weeks' or 'seventy years', the Maccabees would win through! The text had proved its holiness and divine origin by speaking directly to circumstances that the original author could not have foreseen.[39]

Sadly, the Hasmonean dynasty founded by the Maccabees was a huge disappointment. The kings were cruel and corrupt; they were not descendants of David; and, to the horror of the more pious Jews, they violated the sanctity of the temple by assuming the office of High Priest, even though they were not of priestly descent. Outraged by this sacrilege, the historical imagination of the Jewish people projected itself into the future. At the end of the second century there was an explosion of apocalyptic piety. In new texts, Jews described eschatological visions in which God intervened powerfully in human affairs, smashed the present corrupt order and inaugurated an age of justice and purity. As they struggled to find a solution, the people of Judah split into myriad sects, each insisting that it alone was the true Israel.[40] This was, however, an extraordinarily creative period. The canon of the Bible had not yet been finalized. There was still no authoritative scripture and no orthodoxy and few of the sects felt bound to conform to traditional readings of the Law and the Prophets. Some even felt at liberty to write entirely new scriptures. The diversity of the Late Second Temple period was revealed when the library of the Qumran community was discovered in 1942.

Qumran manifested the iconoclastic spirit of this era. The sectarians had withdrawn from Jerusalem to the shore of the Dead Sea, where they lived in monastic seclusion. They revered the Law and the Prophets, but believed that they alone understood them.[41] Their leader, the Teacher of Righteousness, had received a revelation which convinced him that there were 'hidden things' in the scriptures that could only be uncovered by a special *pesher* (deciphering) exegesis. Every single word in the Law and the Prophets looked forward to their own community in these last days.[42] Qumran was the culmination of Jewish history, the true Israel. Soon God would usher in a new world order; and after the final victory of the children of light, a massive temple, not made with human hands, would be constructed and the Mosaic covenant would be rewritten. In the meantime, the Qumran community was a pure, symbolic temple that replaced the desecrated shrine in Jerusalem. Its members observed the priestly laws, purified their garments, and walked into the dining room as into the temple precincts.

Qumran was an extreme wing of the Essene movement, which had about four thousand members by the first century BCE.[43] Most Essenes also lived in tight-knit communities, but in towns and villages rather than the desert; they married and had children but conducted their lives as though the end time had already begun, observing the purity laws, eschewing private property, holding all things in common, and forbidding divorce.[44] They held communal meals, in which they looked forward to the coming kingdom, but though they anticipated the destruction of the temple, they continued to worship there.

The Pharisees, another sect which comprised about 1.2 per cent of the population,[45] were highly respected. Even though their approach to the Law and the Prophets was more conventional, they were open to such novel ideas as the general resurrection, when the righteous dead would rise from their tombs to share God's final triumph. Many of them were laymen, who made a dedicated effort to live like priests, observing the purity laws in their own homes as though they dwelt in the temple. They were opposed by the more conservative Saducees, who interpreted the written texts more stringently and did not accept the newfangled ideas about personal immortality.

People focused on the temple because it provided them with access to God; if it failed, religion lost its point. There was a desperate search for a new way of entering the divine presence, for new scriptures and new ways of being Jewish.[46] Some sects completely rewrote the older texts. The author of the First Book of Enoch imagined God rending the earth and the Mosaic revelation asunder on Mount Sinai to begin again with a clean slate. The author of Jubilees, which was widely read well into the second century CE, was distressed by the cruelty of some of the earlier writings and entirely revised the JEP narrative. Had God really tried to exterminate the human race in the Flood, commanded Abraham to kill his own son, and drowned the Egyptian army in the Sea of Reeds? He decided that God did not intervene directly in human affairs and that the suffering we see all around us was the work of Satan and his demons.

Before the first century CE, there was no widespread expectation that a messiah, an 'anointed one', would arrive to put the world to rights.[47] Despite occasional references to such a figure, this was still a peripheral, undeveloped idea. The apocalyptic scenarios of the Late Second Temple period usually imagined God establishing the new order, without human assistance. There were a few sporadic references to concepts that would later become crucial. There was mention of a Davidic king who would inaugurate the 'kingdom of God' and 'sit forever over the goyim in judgment'.[48] Another text spoke of a ruler who would 'be called son of God and . . . son of the most high and bring peace to the world'[49] – clearly a nostalgic harking back to Isaiah's prophecy of Immanu-El. But these isolated notions did not yet form a coherent vision.

This changed after Palestine was conquered by the Roman general Pompey in 63 BCE and became a province of the Roman empire. In some ways, Roman rule was beneficial. King Herod, the protégé of Rome who reigned in Jerusalem from 37 to 4 BCE, rebuilt the temple on a magnificent scale and pilgrims flocked there to celebrate the festivals. But the Romans were unpopular and some of the prefects, notably Pontius Pilate (26–36 CE), went out of their way to insult Jewish sensibilities. A number of prophets tried to mobilize the population to revolt.[50] A certain Theudas led four hundred men into the desert, promising that God would liberate them there. A prophet known as the 'Egyptian' persuaded thousands of people to congregate on the Mount of Olives in order to storm the Roman fortress that was positioned provocatively beside the temple. Most of these uprisings were savagely suppressed and on one occasion the Romans crucified as many as two thousand rebels outside Jerusalem. During the 20s CE, John the Baptizer, an ascetic prophet who may have belonged to the Essene movement, drew large crowds to the Judaean desert where he preached that the 'kingdom of heaven' was at hand.[51] There would be a great judgement for which Jews must prepare by confessing their sins, immersing themselves in the river Jordan, and vowing to live a blameless, honest life.[52] Even though John does not seem to have preached against Roman rule, he was executed by the authorities.

John seems to have been related in some way to Jesus of Nazareth, a Galilean healer and exorcist, who announced the imminent arrival of the kingdom of God at about the same time.[53] Anti-Roman feeling was especially rife during the great national festivals, and Jesus was executed by Pontius Pilate in about 30 CE when he went to Jerusalem to celebrate Passover there. But that did not end the Jesus movement. Some of his disciples were convinced that he had risen from the tomb; they claimed that they had seen him in visions and that his personal resurrection heralded the last days, when the righteous dead would rise from their graves. Jesus would soon return in glory to inaugurate the kingdom. Their leader in Jerusalem was Jesus's brother James, who was known as the *Tzaddik,* the 'Righteous One' and had good relations with both the Pharisees and the Essenes. But the movement also attracted Greek-speaking Jews in the diaspora and, most surprisingly, a significant number of 'God-fearers', non-Jews who were honorary members of the synagogues.

The Jesus movement was unusual in Palestine, where many of the sects were hostile to gentiles, but in the diaspora Jewish spirituality tended to be less exclusive and more open to Hellenistic ideas. There was a large Jewish community in

Alexandria in Upper Egypt, a city created by Alexander the Great, which had become a major centre of learning. Alexandrian Jews studied in the gynmnasium, spoke Greek and would achieve an interesting fusion of Greek and Jewish culture. But because few of them could read classical Hebrew, they could not understand the Torah. Indeed, even in Palestine, most Jews conversed in Aramaic rather than Hebrew, and needed a translation (*targum*) when the Law and the Prophets were read aloud in the synagogue.

Jews had started to translate their scriptures into Greek during the third century BCE on the island of Pharos, just off the coast of Alexandria.[54] This project was probably initiated by the Alexandrian Jews themselves but over the years it acquired a mythical aura. It was said that Ptolemy Philadelpus, the Greek king of Egypt, was so impressed by the Jewish scriptures that he wanted a translation for his library. So he asked the High Priest in Jerusalem to send six elders from each of the twelve tribes to Pharos. They all worked on the text together and produced a translation that was so perfect that everybody agreed that it must be preserved forever 'imperishable and unchanged'.[55] In honour of its seventy-plus translators, it was known as the Septuagint. Another legend seemed to have absorbed elements of the new Torah spirituality. The seventy translators proved to be 'prophets and priests of the mysteries': 'Sitting . . . in seclusion . . . they became as it were possessed, and under inspiration, wrote, not each several scribe something different, but the same word for word.'[56] Like the exegete, the translators were inspired and uttered the word of God in the same way as the biblical authors themselves.

This last story was told by the famous Alexandrian exegete Philo (70 BCE to 45CE), who came from a wealthy Jewish family in Alexandria.[57] Although Philo was a contemporary of John the Baptizer, Jesus and Hillel (one of the most distinguished of the early Pharisees), he inhabited a very different intellectual world. A Platonist, Philo produced a large number of commentaries on Genesis and Exodus, which transformed them into allegories of divine *logos* (reason). This was another species of *translatio*. Philo was trying to 'transfer' or 'carry over' the essence of the Semitic tales into another cultural idiom and place them in an alien conceptual framework.

Philo did not invent the allegorical method. The *grammatikoi* of Alexandria were already 'translating' Homer's epics into philosophical terms, so that Greeks who were trained in the rationalism of Plato and Aristotle could use the *Iliad* and *Odyssey* as part of their quest for wisdom. They based their *allegoria* on numerology and etymology. Besides its everyday connotation, every name had a deeper, symbolic meaning that expressed its eternal, Platonic form. By means of reflection and study, a critic could discover this deeper significance and thus transform the Homeric stories into allegories of moral philosophy. Jewish exegetes had already started to apply this method to the Bible, which seemed barbarous and incomprehensible to their Greek trained minds. They consulted manuals that gave Greek translations of Hebrew names. Adam, for example, became *nous* (natural reason); Israel, *psyche* (soul); and Moses, *sophia* (wisdom). This method threw an entirely new light on the biblical narratives. Did the characters live up to their names? What did a particular story reveal about the human dilemma? How could a reader apply it to his own search for insight?

In applying this method to the biblical narratives, Philo did not think he was distorting the original. He took the literal meaning of these stories very seriously,[58] but like Daniel he was looking for something fresh. There was more to a story than its literal meaning. As a Platonist, Philo believed that the timeless dimension of reality was more 'real' than its physical or historical dimension. So while the Jerusalem temple was undoubtedly an actual building, its architecture symbolized the cosmos; the temple was, therefore, also an eternal manifestation of the God who was Truth. Philo wanted to show that the biblical tales were what the Greeks called *mythos*. These events had happened in the real world at a particular moment, but they also had a dimension that transcended time. Unless they were liberated from their historical context and became a spiritual reality in the lives of the faithful, they could have no religious function. The process of *allegoria* 'translated' the deeper meaning of these stories into the inner life of the reader.

Allegoria was a term used by rhetoricians to describe a discourse that meant something different from its surface meaning. Philo preferred to call his method *hyponoia*, 'higher/deeper thought', because he was trying to reach a more fundamental level of truth. He also liked to speak of his exegesis as a 'conversion' of both the text and the interpreter. The text had to be 'turned around' (*trepain*).[59] When the interpreter was struggling with an obscure piece of writing, he had, as it were, to twist it this way and that, bringing it closer to the light to see it more clearly. Sometimes he had to change his own position in order to stand in a correct relation to the text and 'change his mind'.

Trepain revealed many different levels of a story, but Philo insisted that the exegete must find a central thread which ran through all his readings. He wrote four theses on the story of Cain and Abel in an attempt to discover its underlying philosophical significance. Eventually, he decided that its main theme was the battle between love of self and love of God. 'Cain' meant 'possession'. Cain wanted to keep everything for himself, and his chief aim was to serve his own interests. 'Abel' meant 'One who refers everything to God'. These qualities were present in every single individual and were constantly at war within him.[60] In another 'conversion', the story illustrated the conflict between true and false eloquence: Abel could not reply to Cain's specious arguments, but remained tongue-tied and helpless until his brother murdered him. This, Philo explained, was what happened when egotism got out of hand and destroyed the love of God within us. As mediated by Philo, Genesis gave to the Greek educated Jews of Alexandria a structure and symbolism that enabled them to contemplate difficult but basic truths about the spiritual life.

Philo also refined the biblical conception of God, which could seem hopelesly anthropomorphic to a Platonist. 'The apprehension of me is something more than human nature, yea, more even than the whole heaven and universe, will be able to contain,' he made God tell Moses.[61] Philo made the enormously important distinction between God's *ousia*, his essence, which was entirely incomprehensible to human beings, and his activities (*energeiaei*) and powers (*dynameis*) that we *can* apprehend in the world. There was nothing about God's *ousia* in the scripture; we only read about his powers, one of which was the Word or Logos of God, the rational design that structures the universe.[62] Like Ben Sirah, Philo believed that when we caught a glimpse of the Logos in creation and the Torah, we were taken beyond the reach of discursive reason to a rapturous recognition that God was 'higher than a way of thinking, more precious than anything that is merely thought'.[63]

It was, Philo argued, foolish to read the first chapter of Genesis literally and to imagine that the world had been created in six days. The number 'six' was a symbol of perfection. He noticed that there were two quite different creation stories in Genesis, and decided that P's account in Chapter One described the creation of the Logos, the masterplan of the universe that was God's 'first born',[64] and that J's more earthy account in Chapter Two symbolized the fashioning of the material universe by the *demiourgos*, the divine 'craftsman' in Plato's *Timaeus*, who had arranged the raw materials of the universe to establish an ordered cosmos.

Philo's exegesis was not simply a clever manipulation of names and numbers but a spiritual practice. Like any

Platonist, he experienced knowledge as remembrance, as known to him already at some profound level of his being. As he delved beneath the literal meaning of a biblical narrative and uncovered its deep philosophical principle, he experienced a shock of recognition. The story became suddenly fused with a truth that was a part of himself. Sometimes he struggled grimly with his books and seemed to make no progress, but then, almost without warning, he experienced rapture, like a priest in one of the ecstatic mystery cults:

> I . . . have suddenly become full, the ideas descending like snow, so that under the impact of divine possession, I have been filled with Corybantic frenzy and become ignorant of everything, place, people, past, present, myself, what was said and what was written. For I acquired expression, ideas, an enjoyment of life, sharp-sighted vision, exceedingly distinct clarity of objects such as might occur through the eyes as a result of clearest display.[65]

In the year of Philo's death, there were pogroms against the Jewish community in Alexandria. Throughout the Roman empire, there was widespread fear of Jewish insurgency, and in 66 CE a group of Jewish zealots orchestrated a rebellion in Palestine that, incredibly, managed to hold the Roman armies at bay for four years. Fearing that the rebellion would spread among the Jewish communities of the diaspora, the authorities were determined to crush it ruthlessly. In 70 the emperor Vespasian finally conquered Jerusalem. When the Roman soldiers broke into the temple's inner courts, they found six thousand Jewish zealots there, ready to fight to the death. When they saw the temple catch fire, a terrible cry arose. Some flung themselves on to the Romans' swords; others hurled themselves into the flames. Once the temple had gone, the Jews gave up and showed no interest in defending the rest of the city but watched helplessly as Titus's officers efficiently demolished what was left of the city.[66] For centuries, the temple had stood at the heart of the Jewish world and was central to Jewish religion. Once again it had been destroyed, but this time it would not be rebuilt. Only two of the Jewish sects that had proliferated during the Late Second Temple period were able to find a way forward. The first to do so was the Jesus movement, which was inspired by the disaster to write a wholly new set of scriptures.

CHAPTER 3

Gospel

We have no idea what Christianity would have been like if the Romans had not destroyed the temple. Its loss reverberates throughout the scriptures that comprise the New Testament, many of which were written in response to this tragedy.[1] During the Late Second Temple period, the Jesus movement had been just one of a multitude of fiercely competing sects. It had some unusual features, but, like several of the other groups, the first Christians regarded themselves as the true Israel, and had no intention of breaking away from Judaism. Even though we have little first-hand knowledge, we can make an educated guess about the history of the group during the forty years that had elapsed since Jesus was executed by Pontius Pilate.

Jesus himself remains an enigma. There have been interesting attempts to uncover the figure of the 'historical' Jesus, a project that has become something of a scholarly industry. But the fact remains that the only Jesus we really know is the Jesus described in the New Testament, which was not interested in scientifically objective history. There are no other contemporary accounts of his mission and death. We cannot even be certain why he was crucified. The gospel accounts indicate that he was thought to be the king of the Jews. He was said to have predicted the imminent arrival of the kingdom of heaven, but also made it clear that it was not of this world. In the literature of the Late Second Temple period, there had been hints that a few people were expecting a righteous king of the House of David to establish an eternal kingdom, and this idea seems to have become more popular during the tense years leading up to the war. Josephus, Tacitus and Suetonius all note the importance of revolutionary religiosity, both before and after the rebellion.[2] There was now keen expectation in some circles of a *meshiah* (in Greek, *christos*), an 'anointed' king of the House of David, who would redeem Israel. We do not know whether Jesus claimed to be this messiah – the gospels are ambiguous on this point.[3] Other people rather than Jesus himself may have made this claim on his behalf.[4] But after his death some of his followers had seen him in visions that convinced them that he had been raised from the tomb – an event that heralded the general resurrection of all the righteous when God would inaugurate his rule on earth.[5]

Jesus and his disciples came from Galilee in northern Palestine. After his death they moved to Jerusalem, probably to be on hand when the kingdom arrived, since all the prophecies declared that the temple would be the pivot of the new world order.[6] The leaders of their movement were known as 'the Twelve': in the kingdom, they would rule the twelve tribes of the reconstituted Israel.[7] The members of the

Jesus movement worshipped together every day in the temple,[8] but they also met for communal meals, in which they affirmed their faith in the kingdom's imminent arrival.[9] They continued to live as devout, orthodox Jews. Like the Essenes, they had no private property, shared their goods equally, and dedicated their lives to the last days.[10] It seems that Jesus had recommended voluntary poverty and special care for the poor; that loyalty to the group was to be valued more than family ties; and that evil should be met with non-violence and love.[11] Christians should pay their taxes, respect the Roman authorities, and must not even contemplate armed struggle.[12] Jesus's followers continued to revere the Torah,[13] keep the Sabbath,[14] and the observance of the dietary laws was a matter of extreme importance to them.[15] Like the great Pharisee Hillel, Jesus's older contemporary, they taught a version of the Golden Rule, which they believed to be the bedrock of the Jewish faith: 'So always treat others as you would like them to treat you; that is the message of the Law and the Prophets.'[16]

Like the Essenes, the members of the Jesus group seem to have had an ambiguous relationship with the temple. Jesus was said to have predicted that Herod's magnificent shrine would soon be laid waste. 'You see these great buildings?' he asked his disciples. 'Not a single stone will be left on another; everything will be destroyed.'[17] At his trial, it was claimed that he had vowed to destroy the temple and rebuild it in three days. But like the Essenes, Jesus's followers continued to pray in the temple and in this respect were in tune with other strands of Late Second Temple piety.

In other ways, however, Christianity was highly eccentric and controversial. There was no general expectation that the messiah would die and rise again. Indeed, the manner of Jesus's death was a source of embarrassment. How could a man who had died like a common criminal have been God's Anointed? Many regarded the messianic claims for Jesus as scandalous.[18] The movement also lacked the moral rigour of some of the other sects: it claimed that sinners, prostitutes and those who collected the Roman taxes would enter the kingdom ahead of the priests.[19] Christian missionaries preached the gospel or 'good news' of Jesus's imminent return in marginal and religiously dubious regions of Palestine, such as Samaria and Gaza. They also established congregations in the diaspora – in Damascus, Phoenicia, Cilicia and Antioch[20] – where they made an important breakthrough.

Even though the missionaries preached in the first instance to their fellow Jews, they found that they were also attracting gentiles, especially among the God-fearers.[21] In the diaspora, Jews welcomed these pagan sympathizers, and the huge outer court of Herod's new temple had been deliberately designed to accommodate crowds of gentiles who liked to participate in the Jewish festivals. The pagan worshippers had not become monotheists. They continued to worship other gods and participate in the local cults, and most Jews did not object to this, since God had only demanded exclusive worship of Israel. But if a gentile converted to Judaism, he had to be circumcised, observe the whole Torah and eschew idol worship. So the arrival of significant numbers of gentile converts in their congregations put the leaders of the Jesus sect in a quandary. Nobody seems to have felt that gentiles should be excluded, but there was considerable disagreement about the terms on which they could be admitted. Some believed that gentile Christians should convert to Judaism, take on the Torah and face the dangerous ordeal of circumcision, but others felt that, since the present world order was passing away, conversion was unnecessary. The debate became heated but eventually it was agreed that those gentiles who accepted Jesus as messiah need not convert to Judaism. They must simply shun idolatry and follow a modified version of the dietary rules.[22]

But instead of seeing these gentile converts as problematic, some enthusiasts were actually seeking them out and undertaking ambitious missions to the gentile world. Peter, one of the Twelve, had made converts in the Roman garrison town of Caesarea; Barnabas, a Greek-speaking Jew from Cyprus, had many gentiles in his *ekklesia* (church) in Antioch,[23] the city where those who believed that Jesus was the *christos* were first given the name of 'Christians'.[24] Somebody – we have no idea who – had even founded a church in Rome. Some of the Jerusalem congregation of Christians, especially Jesus's brother, James, found this disconcerting. These gentiles were showing a truly impressive commitment. Many Jews regarded pagans as chronically addicted to vicious habits:[25] the fact that so many of them were able to observe the high moral standards of their Jewish sect suggested that God must be at work among them. Why was he doing this? The gentile

converts were prepared to cut themselves off entirely from
the cults that were basic to social life in a pagan city and found
themselves in an unenviable limbo; they could eat no meat
that had been sacrificed to false gods, so socializing with
neighbours and relatives had become well-nigh impossible.[26]
They had lost their old world and did not feel wholly
welcome in the new. And yet gentile converts kept arriving.
What did this mean?

The Jewish Christians searched the scriptures for an
answer. Like the Qumran community, they developed their
own *pesher* exegesis, scouring the Torah and the prophets for
prophetic references to Jesus and gentiles in the end time.
They found that while some of the prophets had predicted
that *goyim* would be forced against their will to worship the
God of Israel, others believed that they would share in Israel's
triumph and voluntarily throw away their idols.[27] So, some of
the Christians decided, the presence of gentiles proved that
these were indeed the last days. The process foretold by the
prophets had begun; Jesus was truly the messiah and the
kingdom was really at hand.

One of the most forceful champions of this new eschatology was Paul, a Greek-speaking Jew from Tarsus in Cilicia,
who had joined the Christian movement some three years
after Jesus's death. He had never known Jesus personally, and
had initially been hostile to the sect, but had been converted
by a revelation, which convinced him the *christos* had
appointed him to be the apostle to the gentiles.[28] Paul travelled widely in the diaspora and founded congregations in

Syria, Asia Minor and Greece, determined to spread the gospel to the ends of the earth before Jesus returned. He wrote letters to his converts, answering their questions, exhorting them and explaining the faith. Paul did not think for a moment that he was writing 'scripture'; because he was convinced that Jesus would return in his own lifetime, he never imagined that future generations would pore over his epistles. He was regarded as a premier teacher, but was well aware that his explosive temperament meant that he was not universally popular. Nevertheless his letters to the churches in Rome, Corinth, Galatia, Philippi and Thessalonica[29] were preserved, and after his death in the early 60s, Christian writers who revered Paul wrote in his name and developed his ideas in letters to the churches in Ephesus and Colossae, and wrote supposedly posthumous letters addressed to Paul's associates, Timothy and Titus.

Paul insisted that his gentile converts renounce all pagan cults and worship only the God of Israel.[30] But he did not believe that they should convert to Judaism, because Jesus had already made them 'sons of God', without circumcision and the Torah. They must live as if the kingdom had already arrived: taking care of the poor and behaving with charity, sobriety, chastity and modesty. The fact that gentile Christians prophesied, performed miracles and, in the grip of ecstasy, spoke in strange tongues – all hallmarks of the messianic age[31] – proved that the spirit of God was alive in them and that the kingdom would arrive in the very near future.[32]

But Paul never suggested that Jews should cease to observe the Torah, because this would have put him outside the covenant. Israel had received the precious gift of the revelation of Sinai, the temple cult, and the privilege of being God's 'sons', enjoying a special intimacy with him, and Paul valued all this.[33] When he inveighed bitterly against 'Judaizers', he was not condemning either Jews or Judaism per se but those Jewish Christians who wanted the gentiles to be circumcised and observe the entire Torah. Like other sectarians in the Late Second Temple period, Paul was convinced that he alone was in possession of the truth.[34] In the messianic age, his mixed congregations of Jews and gentiles were the true Israel.

Paul also searched the scriptures, whose meaning, he believed, had changed since the coming of the *christos*. A psalm, which had seemed to refer to David, had actually been speaking of Jesus.[35] 'Indeed, everything that was written so long ago in the scriptures was meant to teach *us* something.'[36] The true significance of the Law and the prophets had only just come to light, so those Jews who refused to accept Jesus as the messiah no longer understood them. Sinai was no longer crucial. Hitherto, the people of Israel had not realized that the Mosaic covenant was only a temporary, interim measure, so their minds had been 'veiled' and they could not see what the scriptures had been about. The veil was still over their minds today, when they listened to the Torah in the synagogues. The Jews needed to be 'converted', turned around so that they saw correctly. Then they too would be transformed, their 'unveiled faces reflecting like mirrors the brightness of the Lord'.[37]

There was nothing heretical about this. Jews had been finding new meaning in older writings for a long time and the Qumran sect practised the same kind of *pesher*, finding a secret message in the scriptures that referrred to their own community. When Paul quoted biblical stories to instruct his converts, he interpreted them in a wholly novel way. Adam now prefigured Christ, but where Adam brought sin into the world, Jesus had put humanity into a correct relationship with God.[38] Abraham had now become not merely the father of the Jewish people but the ancestor of all the faithful. His 'faith' (Greek: *pistis,* a word which, it is important to note, should be translated as 'trust' rather than 'belief') had made him a model Christian, centuries before the coming of the messiah. When scripture praised Abraham's faith,[39] it was referring 'to *us* as well':[40] 'Scripture foresaw that God was going to use faith to justify the pagans, and proclaimed the Good News long ago, when Abraham was told: *In you all the pagans will be blessed.*'[41] When God commanded Abraham to abandon his concubine Hagar and their son Ishmael in the wilderness, this had been an *allegoria*: Hagar represented the Sinai covenant, which had enslaved Jews to the Law, while Sarah, Abraham's free-born wife, corresponded to the new covenant, which had liberated gentiles from Torah obligations.[42]

The author of the epistle to the Hebrews, who was probably writing at about the same time, was even more radical. He was trying to console a community of Jewish Christians who were beginning to lose heart by arguing forcefully that Christ had superseded the Torah, was more exalted than Moses [43] and that the sacrificial cult had simply foreshadowed Jesus's priestly act in giving his life for humanity.[44] In an extraordinary passage, the author saw the entire history of Israel as exemplifying the virtue of *pistis*, trust in 'realities that at present remain unseen'.[45] Abel, Enoch, Noah, Abraham, Moses, Gideon, Barak, Samson, Jephthah, David, Samuel and the prophets had all exhibited this 'faith': that had been their greatest, indeed their sole achievement.[46] But, the author concluded, 'they did not receive what was promised, since God made provision *for us* to have something better, and they were not to reach perfection except *with us*.'[47]

In this exegetical tour de force, the whole of Israelite history had been redefined, but in the process the old stories, which had been about far more than *pistis*, lost much of their rich complexity. Torah, temple and cult simply pointed to a future reality because God had always had something better in mind. Paul and the author of Hebrews showed future generations of Christians how to interpret the Hebrew Bible and make it their own. The other New Testament writers would develop this *pesher* and make it very difficult for Christians to see Jewish scripture as anything more than a prelude to Christianity.

The Jesus movement was becoming controversial even before the disaster of 70.[48] Christians, like all the other Jewish groups, were shocked to the core when they saw Herod's magnificent shrine reduced to a pile of burnt, stinking masonry. They may have dreamed of replacing Herod's temple but nobody had envisaged life without a temple at all. But the Christians also saw its destruction as an *apokalypsis*, a 'revelation' or 'unveiling' of a reality that had been there all along but had not been seen clearly before – namely that Judaism was finished. The temple ruins symbolized its tragic demise and were a sign that the end was approaching. God would now pull down the rest of the defunct world order and establish the kingdom.

The destruction of the first temple in 586 BCE had inspired an astonishing burst of creativity among the exiles in Babylon. The destruction of the second temple spurred a similar literary effort among the Christians. By the middle of the second century, nearly all the twenty-seven books of the New Testament had been completed. Communities were already quoting Paul's letters as though they were scripture,[49] and readings from one of the biographies of Jesus that were in circulation had become customary during Sunday worship. The gospels attributed to Matthew, Mark, Luke and John would eventually be selected for the canon, but there were many others. The Gospel of Thomas (*c*.150) was a collection of secret sayings of Jesus that imparted a redemptive 'knowledge' (*gnosis*). There were gospels, now lost, of the Ebionites, Nazarenes and Hebrews, that catered to Jewish-Christian congregations. There were many 'gnostic' gospels representing a form of Christianity that emphasized *gnosis* and distinguished a wholly spiritual God (who had sent Jesus as his envoy) from the *demiourgos*, who had created the corrupt material world.⁵⁰ Other writings did not survive: a gospel known to scholars as Q, because it was a source (German: *quelle*) for Matthew and Luke; various anthologies of Jesus's teachings; and an account of his trial, torture and death.

In the second century there was, however, no canon of prescribed texts because there was, as yet, no standard form of Christianity. Marcion (*c.*100–165), who held many gnostic ideas, wanted to sever the link between Christianity and the Hebrew scriptures, since he believed that Christianity was an entirely new religion. Marcion wrote his own gospel, based on the epistles of Paul and an expurgated reading of Luke. This made many Christians deeply uneasy about their relationship with Judaism. Irenaeus, bishop of Lyons (*c.*140–200) was appalled by both Marcion and the Gnostics and insisted on the link between the old scriptures and the new. He compiled a list of approved texts in which we see the future New Testament in embryo. It began with the gospels of Matthew, Mark, Luke and John – in that order – continued with the Acts of the Apostles (a history of the early church), included epistles by Paul, James, Peter and John, and concluded with two prophetic descriptions of the end: Revelation and the Shepherd of Hermas. But the canon was not fixed until well into the fourth century. Some of Irenaeus's chosen books, such as the Shepherd of Hermas, would be rejected and others, such as Hebrews and the epistle of Jude, would be added to Irenaeus's list.

The Christian scriptures were written at different times, in

different regions and for very different audiences, but they
shared a common language and set of symbols, derived from
the Law and the Prophets as well as the Late Second Temple
texts. They brought together ideas that originally had no connection with one another – son of God, son of man, messiah
and kingdom – into a new synthesis.[51] The authors did not
argue this logically but simply juxtaposed these images so
repeatedly that they merged together in the reader's mind.[52]
There was no uniform view of Jesus. Paul had called him the
'son of God', but had used the title in its traditional Jewish
sense: Jesus was a human being who had a special relationship to God, like the ancient kings of Israel, and had been
raised by him to uniquely high status.[53] Paul never claimed
that Jesus *was* God. Matthew, Mark and Luke, who are known
as the 'synoptics' because they 'see things together', also used
the title 'son of God' in this way, but they also implied that
Jesus was Daniel's 'son of man', which gave him an eschatological dimension.[54] John, who represented a different
Christian tradition, saw Jesus as the incarnation of the Word
and Wisdom of God which had existed before the creation of
the world.[55] When the final editors of the New Testament put
these texts together, they were not disturbed by these discrepancies. Jesus had become too immense a phenomenon in the
minds of Christians to be tied to a single definition.

The title of 'messiah' was crucial. Once Jesus had been
identified as God's 'anointed' (*christos*), the Christian writers
gave the term a radically new meaning. They read the Hebrew
scriptures in Greek and whenever they found a reference to a

christos – be it a king, prophet or priest – they immediately interpreted it as a coded reference to Jesus. They were also attracted to the mysterious figure of the servant in Second Isaiah, whose suffering had redeemed the world. The servant had not been a messianic figure, but by constantly comparing the servant with Jesus *christos*, using the same 'blurring' technique, they established for the first time the idea of a suffering messiah. Thus three separate figures – servant, messiah and Jesus – became inseparable in the Christian imagination.[56]

So thorough was the Christians' *pesher* exegesis that there is scarcely a verse in the New Testament that did not refer to the older scriptures. The four evangelists seemed to use the Septuagint as another source for the biography of Jesus. As a result it is difficult to disentangle fact from exegesis. Did his executioners really give Jesus vinegar to drink and cast lots for his garments or was this incident suggested by certain verses from the Psalms?[57] Did Matthew tell the story of the virgin birth of Jesus simply because Isaiah had prophesied that a 'virgin' would conceive and bear a son called Immanu-El (the Septuagint translated the Hebrew *almah*, 'young woman' as *parthenos*, 'virgin')?[58] Some scholars have gone so far as to suggest that it would be possible to construct an entire gospel from the Jewish scriptures, without quoting a single word by Jesus himself.[59]

We do not know who wrote the gospels. When they first appeared, they circulated anonymously and were only later attributed to important figures in the early church.[60] The authors were Jewish Christians,[61] who wrote in Greek and lived in the Hellenistic cities of the Roman empire. They were not only creative writers – each with his own particular bias – but also skilled redactors who edited earlier material. Mark wrote in about 70; Matthew and Luke in the late 80s, and John in the late 90s. All four gospels reflect the terror and anxiety of this traumatic period. The Jewish people were in turmoil. The war with Rome had divided families and communities and all the different sects had to rethink their relationship with the temple tradition. But the *apokalypsis* of the ruined shrine seemed so compelling to the Christians that they felt inspired to proclaim the messiahship of Jesus, whose mission, they believed, had been bound up with the temple.

Mark, who was writing immediately after the war, was especially preoccupied by this theme. His community was in deep trouble. Christians had been accused of rejoicing at the temple's destruction, and Mark shows that members of his *ekklesia* were being beaten in the synagogues, dragged before the Jewish elders and universally vilified. Many had lost faith.[62] Jesus's teachings seemed to fall on stony ground and Christian leaders seemed as obtuse as the Twelve, who, in Mark's gospel, rarely understood Jesus.[63] There was a grim sense of painful rupture with mainstream Judaism. You could not patch an old garment with new cloth, Jesus warned: 'the patch pulls away from it, the new from the old, and the tear gets worse. And nobody puts new wine into old wineskins; if he does, the wine will burst the skins, and the wine is lost and the skins too!'[64] Discipleship meant suffering and an endless struggle with demonic forces. Christians must stay awake; they must be perpetually vigilant![65]

Paul, who wrote while the temple was still standing, had scarcely mentioned it; but the temple was central to Mark's vision of Jesus.[66] Its destruction was only the first stage in the imminent apocalypse.[67] Daniel had already foreseen this 'desolating sacrilege' long ago so the temple had been doomed.[68] Jesus was not a renegade, as his enemies claimed, but deeply in tune with the great figures of the past. He quoted Jeremiah and Isaiah to show that the temple had been intended for all the nations as well as for the Jews.[69] Mark's *ekklesia*, which admitted gentiles, had fulfilled these ancient prophecies but the temple had not conformed to God's plan. No wonder it had been destroyed.

Jesus's death was not a scandal, but had been foretold in the Law and the prophets:[70] it had been foreseen that he would be betrayed by one of his own followers[71] and deserted by his disciples.[72] Yet the gospel ended on a note of terror. When the women went to anoint the body, they found that the tomb was empty. Even though an angel told them that Jesus had risen, 'the women came out and ran away from the tomb because they were frightened out of their wits; and they said nothing to a soul, for they were afraid'.[73] Mark's story ended here, epitomizing the sense of fearful suspension that Christians experienced at this time. Yet Mark's terse, brutal tale was 'Good News', because the kingdom had 'already arrived'.[74]

But by the time Matthew was writing in the late 80s, these hopes were beginning to fade. Nothing had changed: how could the kingdom have come? Matthew replied that it was coming unobtrusively, and was working silently in the world like yeast in a batch of dough.[75] His community was frightened and angry. They were accused by their fellow Jews of abandoning the Torah and the prophets;[76] they had been flogged in the synagogues, dragged before tribunals of elders,[77] and expected to be tortured and killed before the End.[78] Matthew was, therefore, especially anxious to show that Christianity was not only in harmony with Jewish tradition but was its culmination. Almost every single event in Jesus's life had happened 'to fulfil the scriptures'. Like Ishmael, Samson and Isaac, his birth was announced by an angel.[79] His forty days of temptation in the desert paralleled the Israelites' forty years in the wilderness; Isaiah had foretold his miracles.[80] And – most importantly – Jesus was a great Torah teacher. He proclaimed the new law of the messianic age from a mountaintop[81] – like Moses – and insisted that he had come not to abolish but to complete the Law and the prophets.[82] Jews must now observe the Torah more stringently than ever before. It was no longer sufficient for Jews to refrain from murder; they must not even get angry. Not only was adultery forbidden; a man could not even look at a woman lustfully.[83] The old law of retaliation – eye for eye, tooth for tooth – was superseded: Jews must now turn the other cheek and love their enemies.[84] Like Hosea, Jesus argued that compassion was more important than ritual observance.[85] Like Hillel, he preached the Golden Rule.[86] Jesus was greater than Solomon, Jonah and the temple.[87] The Pharisees of

Matthew's day claimed that Torah study would introduce Jews to the divine presence (*Shekhinah*) that they had formerly encountered in the temple: 'If two sit together and words of Torah are between them, the Shekhinah rests between them.'[88] But Jesus promised: 'where two or three meet in my name, I shall be there with them.'[89] Christians would encounter the Shekhinah through Jesus who had now replaced the temple and the Torah.

Luke was the author of some portions of the Acts of the Apostles as well as the gospel. He too was anxious to show that Jesus and his followers were devout Jews but he also emphasized that the gospel was for everybody: Jews and gentiles; women as well as men; the poor; tax collectors; the good Samaritan and the prodigal son. Luke gives us a precious glimpse of the spiritual experience that their *pesher* exegesis gave to early Christians. He told an emblematic story of two of Jesus's disciples, who were walking from Jerusalem to Emmaus three days after the crucifixion.[90] Like many of the Christians in Luke's own time they were distraught and despondent, but on the road they fell in with a stranger, who asked them why they were so troubled. They explained that they were followers of Jesus and had been certain that he was the messiah. But he had been crucified and, to make matters worse, the women in their company were spreading wild tales of an empty tomb and a vision of angels. The stranger gently rebuked them: had they not realized that the messiah must suffer before entering his glory? Starting with Moses, he began to expound 'the full message' of the prophets. When the disciples arrived at their destination that evening, they begged the stranger to lodge with them, and when he broke bread at dinner they suddenly realized that all along they had been in the presence of Jesus, but their 'eyes had been held' from recognizing him. As he vanished from their sight, they recalled how their hearts had 'burned' within them when he had 'opened the scriptures'.

Christian *pesher* was a spiritual discipline, rooted in grief and bewilderment, which spoke directly to the heart and set it alight. Christians would gather 'in twos and threes' and discuss the relationship of the Law and the prophets to Jesus. As they conversed together, the texts 'opened' and yielded a momentary illumination. This would pass, just as Jesus vanished as soon as he had been recognized, but afterwards apparent contradictions locked together in a numinous intimation of wholeness. The stranger played a crucial role. When they confided in somebody they had never seen before, the disciples made an act of trust *(pistis)*. In Luke's *ekklesia*, Jews and gentiles found that by reaching out to the 'other', they experienced the Shekhinah, which, increasingly, they identified with their *christos*.

A number of churches in Asia Minor were developing a different understanding of Jesus, represented by the gospel and three epistles attributed to John and the eschatological book of Revelation. All these 'Joannine' texts saw Jesus as the incarnate Logos who had descended to earth as God's ultimate revelation.[91] Jesus was the Lamb of God, a sacrificial victim who took away the sins of the world, like the lambs

ritually slaughtered in the temple at Passover.[92] They believed
that their most important duty was to love one another,[93] but
they did not reach out to the stranger. This community felt
beleaguered and clung together in opposition to 'the world'.[94]
The whole of existence seemed polarized into conflicting
opposites: light against darkness, world against spirit, life
against death, and good against evil. The churches had
recently suffered a painful schism: some of their members
had found their teachings 'intolerable' and 'stopped going
with Jesus'.[95] The faithful saw these apostates as 'antichrists',
filled with murderous hatred of the messiah.[96]

The members of this Christian sect were convinced that
they alone were right and that the whole world was against
them.[97] John's gospel in particular was addressing an 'in
group', which had a private symbolism that was incomprehensible to outsiders. Constantly Jesus had to tell 'the Jews'
that they would look for him and fail to find him: 'where I am
you cannot come'.[98] His audience was continually baffled but
because Jesus was God's ultimate revelation to the world, this
lack of acceptance was a judgement: those who rejected him
were the children of the devil and would remain in darkness.

For John, Judaism was well and truly over. He systematically depicted Jesus replacing every single one of God's major
revelations to Israel. Henceforth the risen Logos would be the
place where Jews would encounter the divine presence: Jesus
the Logos would take over the function of the ruined temple,
and become the place where Jews would encounter the divine
presence.[99] When he walked out of the temple, the Shekhinah

withdrew with him.[100] When he celebrated the festival of Sukkoth, during which water was ceremonially poured over the altar and the giant torches of the temple were set alight, Jesus – like Wisdom – cried aloud that *he* was the living water and the light of the world.[101] On the feast of Unleavened Bread, he claimed that *he* was the 'bread of life'. Not only was he greater than Moses[102] and Abraham, but he embodied the divine presence: he had the temerity to pronounce the forbidden name of God: 'before Abraham ever was, I Am [*Ani Waho*]'.[103] Unlike the synoptics, John never showed Jesus attracting non-Jewish converts. His *ekklesia* was probably entirely Jewish at the beginning and the apostates were probably Jewish Christians, who found the community's controversial and potentially blasphemous Christology 'intolerable'.[104]

The book of Revelation reveals the bitterness of Joannine Christianity. Here the dualism that was a recurrent motif in John's gospels became a cosmic battle against good and evil forces. Satan and his cohorts assailed Michael and his angelic army in heaven, while the wicked attacked the good on earth. It seemed to the troubled *ekklesia* that evil must prevail, but John of Patmos, the author of Revelation, insisted that God would intervene at the critical moment and vanquish their enemies. He had received a special 'revelation' (*apokalypsis*), which would 'unveil' the true state of affairs, so that the faithful would know how to conduct themselves during the last days. The apocalypse is informed, through and through, by fear: the church was terrified of the Roman empire, the local Jewish communities and rival Christian groups. But, the author assured them, eventually Satan would give his authority to a Beast, who would rise from the depths of the sea and demand universal obeisance. Then the Lamb would come to the rescue. Even though the Whore of Babylon arrived drunk with the blood of the Christian martyrs, angels would pour seven hideous plagues over the earth and the Word would ride into battle on a white horse, to fight the Beast and fling him into a pit of fire. For a thousand years, Jesus would rule the earth with his saints, but then God would release Satan from prison. There would be more destruction, more battles until peace was restored and the New Jerusalem descended from heaven like a bride to meet the Lamb.

Like all the Joannine writings, Revelation is deliberately obscure, its symbols unintelligible to outsiders. It is a toxic book and, as we shall see, would appeal to people who, like the Joannine churches, felt alienated and resentful. It was also controversial and some Christians were reluctant to include it in the canon. But when the final editors decided to place it at the end of the New Testament, it became the triumphant finale of their *pesher* exegesis of the Hebrew Scriptures. It transformed the historical story of the rise of Christianity into a future-oriented apocalypse. The New Jerusalem would replace the old: 'I saw no temple in the city, for its temple was the sovereign Lord God and the Lamb.' Judaism and its most sacred symbols had been replaced by a victorious, militant Christianity.[105]

A thread of hatred runs through the New Testament. It is inaccurate to call the Christian scriptures anti-Semitic, as the authors were themselves Jewish, but many of them had become disenchanted with Jewish religion. Paul did not share this hostility towards Judaism, but much of the New Testament reflected the widespread suspicion, anxiety and turbulence of the period immediately after the destruction of the temple, when the Jews were so bitterly divided. In their anxiety to reach out to the gentile world, the synoptics were too eager to absolve the Romans of their responsibility for Jesus's execution and claimed, with increasing stridency, that the Jews must shoulder the blame. Even Luke, who had the most positive view of Judaism, made it clear that there was a good Israel (represented by Jesus's followers) and a 'bad Israel', epitomized by the self-righteous Pharisee.[106] In the gospels of Matthew and John, this bias had become more entrenched. Matthew made the Jewish crowd cry aloud for Jesus's death: 'His blood be upon us and upon our children',[107] words that for centuries inspired the pogroms that made anti-Semitism an incurable disease in Europe.

Matthew was particularly incensed by the Pharisees: they were self-important hypocrites, obsessed with the letter of the law to the utter neglect of its spirit; they were 'blind guides', a 'brood of vipers', fanatically intent on the destruction of the Christian churches.[108] John too denounced the Pharisees as malicious, oppressive and chronically addicted to evil; it was the Pharisees who gathered information against Jesus and engineered his death.[109] Why this vitriolic hatred of Pharisees? After the destruction of the temple, the Christians had been the first to make a concerted effort to become the authentic Jewish voice and initially they seemed to have had no significant rivals. But by the 80s and 90s, Christians were becoming uncomfortably aware that something extraordinary was happening: the Pharisees were initiating an astonishing revival.

CHAPTER 4

Midrash

During the last days of the siege of Jerusalem, it was said that in order to get past the Jewish zealots who were guarding the gates, Rabbi Johanan ben Zakkai, leader of the Pharisees, was smuggled out of the city in a coffin. Throughout the war, he had repeatedly argued that rebellion against Rome was not only futile but self-destructive, and that the preservation of religion was more important than political independence. Once outside the city, he made his way to the Roman camp and asked Vespasian to spare the coastal city of Yavneh, south-west of Jerusalem, as a safe haven for Jewish scholars. After the destruction of Jerusalem and its temple, Pharisees, scribes and priests began to congregate at Yavneh, which for over sixty years became the centre of a remarkable religious synthesis. The story of Johanan's dramatic escape has obvious apocryphal elements, but the powerful image of the rabbi rising from the coffin outside the doomed city was prophetic, since Yavneh ensured the resurrection of a new version of temple Judaism from the ruins of the old.

We do not know very much about the Yavneh period, however.[1] The coalition of scholars was led by the Pharisees, initially by R. Johanan and his two gifted pupils, R. Eliezer and R. Joshua, and later by R. Akiba. Long before the tragedy of 70, the Pharisees had encouraged the laity to live as though they were serving in the temple, so that each hearth became an altar, each householder a priest. Yet the Pharisees had continued to worship in the real temple as well and never imagined that Jews would one day have to manage without it. Even during their years at Yavneh, they seem to have believed that Jews would be able to build a new temple, but their ideology was well suited to the post–70 world because they had, as it were, constructed their daily lives around a virtual temple which became the focus of their spirituality. Now R. Johanan and his successors would begin to build this imaginary shrine in more detail.

The first task of the rabbis at Yavneh was to collect and preserve all the available memories, practices and rituals of traditional religion, so that when the temple was rebuilt the cult could be resumed. Other Jews might plan new rebellions against the Roman empire; Christians could insist that Jesus had replaced the temple; but together with the scribes and priests who had joined them at Yavneh, the Pharisees would make a heroic effort to keep every single detail of the lost shrine in their minds, at the same time as they revised the Torah to meet the needs of their drastically altered world. It would take the Pharisees many years to become the undisputed leaders of the new Judaism. But by the late 80s and 90s, as we have seen, some of the Christians had begun to feel seriously threatened by Yavneh, whose vision seemed more compelling and authentic to many Jews than the gospel. Yet in fact the Pharisaic enterprise had much in common with early Christian churches. The Pharisees would also search the scriptures, invent another form of exegesis, and compose new sacred texts – even though they would never claim that these formed a 'New Testament'.

When two or three of the Pharisees studied the Torah together, they found – like the Christians – that the Shekhinah was in their midst. At Yavneh, the Pharisees pioneered a spirituality in which Torah study replaced the temple as the chief means of encountering the divine presence. But, unlike modern biblical scholars, they were not interested in recovering the original significance of a given scriptural passage. Like Daniel, they were looking for fresh meaning. In their view, there was no single authoritative reading of scripture. As events unfolded on earth, even God had to keep studying his own Torah in order to discover its full significance.[2] The rabbis called their exegesis *midrash,* which, as we saw in Chapter 2, derived from the verb *darash:* to investigate; to seek. The meaning of a text was not self-evident. The exegete had to go in search of it, because every time a Jew confronted the Word of God in scripture, it signified something different. Scripture was inexhaustible. The rabbis liked to point out that King Solomon used three thousand parables to illustrate every single verse of the Torah, and could give a thousand and five interpretations of each parable – which meant that there were three million, fifteen thousand possible expositions of each unit of scripture.[3]

Indeed, a text that could not be radically reinterpreted to meet the needs of the day was dead; the written words of scripture had to be revitalized by constant exegesis. Only then could they reveal the divine presence latent within God's Torah. Midrash was not a purely intellectual pursuit and study was never an end in itself: it had to inspire practical action in the world. The exegete had a duty to apply the Torah to his particular situation and make it speak to the condition of every single member of his community. The goal was never simply to clarify an obscure passage but to address the burning issues of the day. You did not understand a text until you had found a way of putting it into practice.[4] The rabbis called scripture *miqra:* a 'summons' that called the Jewish people to action.

Above all, midrash must be guided by the principle of compassion. In the early years of the first century, the great Pharisaic sage Hillel had come from Babylonia to Jerusalem, where he had preached alongside his rival Shammai, whose version of Pharisaism was more stringent. It was said that one day a pagan had approached Hillel and promised to convert to Judaism if he could summarize the entire Torah while he stood on one leg. Standing on one leg, Hillel replied: 'What is hateful to yourself, do not to your fellow man. That is the whole of the Torah and the remainder is but commentary. Go study it.'[5] This was an astonishing and deliberately controversial piece of midrash. The essence of Torah was the disciplined refusal to inflict pain on another human being. Everything else in the scriptures was merely 'commentary', a gloss on the Golden Rule. At the end of his exegesis, Hillel uttered a *miqra,* a call to action: 'Go study!' When they studied the Torah, rabbis should attempt to reveal the core of compassion that lay at the heart of all the legislation and narratives in the scriptures – even if this meant twisting the original meaning of the text. The rabbis of Yavneh were followers of Hillel. R. Akiba, the leading sage of the later Yavneh period, declared that the greatest principle of Torah was the commandment in Leviticus: 'Thou shalt love thy neighbour as thyself.'[6] Only one of the rabbis contested this, arguing that the simple words 'This is the roll of Adam's descendants' were more important because they revealed the unity of the entire human race.[7]

R. Johanan had been taught by the pupils of Hillel, and immediately after the catastrophe of 70 he applied this insight to the grim realities of the post-temple world. One day, he had walked past the burnt ruins of the temple with R. Joshua, who had cried out in distress: how could Jews atone for their sins now that they could no longer perform the sacrificial rituals there? R. Johanan consoled him by quoting words that God had spoken to Hosea: 'Grieve not, we have atonement equal to the temple, the doing of loving deeds, as it is said: "*I desire love* (hesed) *and not sacrifice*".'[8] The practice of compassion was a priestly act that would atone for sins more effectively than the old expiatory rites, and it could be performed by ordinary lay folk, instead of being the preserve of an exclusive priestly caste. But R. Johanan's exegesis would probably have surprised Hosea. If he had looked closely at the original context, the rabbi would have realized that God had not been speaking to Hosea of charitable deeds. *Hesed* should properly be translated as 'loyalty' rather than 'love'. God had not been concerned with the kindness that human beings should show to one another, but with the cultic fealty that Israel owed to *him*.

But this would not have disturbed R. Joshua, who was not attempting a historical exposition of the text, but seeking to console his traumatized community. There was no need to mourn the temple too extravagantly: practical charity could replace the old ceremonial ritual. He was building a *horoz*, a 'chain' that linked together quotations that originally had no connection to each other but which, once 'enchained', revealed their integral unity.[9] He began by citing a well-known maxim of Simeon the Just, a revered high priest of the third century BCE:[10] 'Upon three things the world is based: upon the Torah, upon the temple service, and upon the doing of loving deeds.'[11] Like the quotation from Hosea, this proved that practical compassion was as important as the Torah and temple worship. Loving kindness was, as it were, an essential leg of the tripod that supported the entire world, and now that the temple had gone, Torah and charity were more important than ever before. To back up this insight, R. Johanan quoted – or slightly misquoted – the psalmist: 'The world is built by love.'[12] In juxtaposing these three unrelated texts, R. Johanan had shown that, as Hillel claimed, charity was indeed central to scripture: it was the exegete's job to elucidate this hidden principle and bring it to light.

The *horoz* was essential to rabbinic midrash. It gave the

exegete an intuition of wholeness and completeness that was similar to the *shalom* that Jews had found in the temple and the *coincidenia oppositorum* that Christians experienced in their *pesher* exegesis. Like the Christians, the rabbis were reading the Law and the prophets differently, giving them a meaning that often bore little relationship to the original authors' intention. R. Akiba perfected this innovative midrash. His pupils liked to tell a story about him. The fame of R. Akiba's genius reached Moses in heaven, and one day he decided to come down to earth to attend one of his classes. He sat in the eighth row behind the other students, and to his dismay found that R. Akiba's exposition was incomprehensible to him, even though it was said to have been part of the revelation he had received on Mount Sinai. 'My sons have surpassed me,' Moses mused ruefully but proudly as he made his way back to heaven. But why, he asked, had God entrusted the Torah to him, when he could have chosen a man of Akiba's intellectual stature?[13] Another rabbi put it more succinctly: 'Matters that had not been disclosed to Moses were disclosed to R. Akiba and his colleagues.'[14] Revelation had not happened once and for all on Mount Sinai; it was an ongoing process and would continue for as long as skilled exegetes sought out the inexhaustible wisdom hidden in the text. Scripture contained the sum of human knowledge in embryonic form: it was possible to find 'everything in it.'[15] Sinai had just been the beginning. Indeed, when God had given the Torah to Moses, he knew that future generations would have to complete it. The written Torah was not a finished object; human beings were supposed to use their ingenuity to bring it to perfection, just as they extracted flour from wheat and weaved a garment from flax.[16]

Some of the rabbis thought that R. Akiba went too far. His colleague R. Ishmael accused him of imposing his own meaning on scripture: 'Indeed, you say to the text "Be silent until I interpret".'[17] A good midrash kept as close to the original meaning as possible and R. Ishmael contended that it should only be changed when absolutely necessary.[18] R. Ishmael's method was respected, but R. Akiba's carried the day because it kept scripture open. To a modern scholar, this method seems transgressive; midrash regularly goes too far, seems to violate the integrity of the text, and seeks meaning at the expense of the original.[19] But the rabbis believed that because scripture was the word of God, it was infinite. Any meaning that they discovered in a text had been intended by God if it yielded fresh insight and benefited the community.

When they expounded Torah, the rabbis regularly amended the words, telling their students, 'don't read this . . . but that.'[20] By altering the text in this way, they sometimes introduced into scripture a note of compassion that had been absent from the original. This happened when R. Meir, one of R. Akiba's most distinguished pupils, discussed a ruling in Deuteronomy:

> If a man guilty of a capital offence is put to death and you hang him on a tree, his body must not remain on the tree overnight; you must bury him the same day, for one who

has been hanged is accursed of God, [*qilelat Elohim*] and you must not defile the land that Yahweh your God has given you for your inheritance.[21]

There was self-interest in this legislation, because if the Israelites polluted the land they would lose it. But R. Meir suggested a new reading, based on a pun: 'Do not read *qilelat Elohim*,' he said, 'but *qallat Elohim* ("the pain of God")'. R. Meir explained that the new text revealed the pathos of God, who suffered with his creatures: 'When a person is in grave trouble, what does the Shekhinah say? It says, as it were: "My head is in pain, my arm is in pain".'[22] It was possible to find love and the Golden Rule in the most unlikely parts of the Torah. As a modern scholar remarks: 'the midrashic shuttle weaves a texture of compassion around a stern legal rule'; because the rabbi invited his pupils to change the text, they too became involved in the active process of endless reinterpretation.[23] The same applied to R. Judah's exposition of God's words to Zechariah: 'Whoever hurts you [i.e. Israel] is like one who hurts his own (*eyno*) eye.' 'Do not read *eyno* ("his"), but *eyni* ("my") eye,' R. Judah instructed his colleagues; the text now claimed that a loving God shared the pain of his own people: 'Whoever hurts Israel is like one who hurts My [*eyni*] eye.'[24]

There could be no definitive interpretation of scripture. This point was made in the very early days at Yavneh, when R. Eliezer was engaged in an intractable argument with his colleagues about a legal ruling (*halakha*) in the Torah. When they refused to accept his opinion, R. Eliezer asked God to back him up with some miracles, and – *mirabile dictu* – a carob tree moved four hundred cubits of its own accord; water in a conduit flowed uphill; and the walls of the house of studies shook so violently that the building seemed about to collapse. But the other rabbis were not impressed by this show of supernatural force. In desperation, R. Eliezer asked for a *bat qol* ('voice from heaven') to adjudicate and the divine voice obligingly declared: 'What have you against R. Eliezer? The Halakah is always as he says.' But Rabbi Joshua quoted a verse from Deuteronomy: 'It is not in heaven'.[25] The Torah was no longer confined to the celestial world; once it had been promulgated on Mount Sinai, it no longer belonged to God but was the inalienable possession of every single Jew. So, commented a later rabbi, 'We pay no attention to a heavenly voice.' And furthermore, it had been decreed at Sinai: 'By a majority you are to decide',[26] so R. Eliezer, a minority of one, could not override the popular vote. When God heard that his opinion had been overruled, he laughed and said: 'My children have conquered me.'[27]

Any limitations in a midrash were due to the weakness of the exegete, who lacked the ability to make sense of a text in a given situation or to find fresh meaning.[28] The Golden Rule also meant any midrash that spread hatred was illegitimate. A mean-spirited interpretation that poured scorn on other sages and sought to discredit them must be avoided.[29] The purpose of midrash was to serve the community, not to inflate the ego of the exegete, who should, R. Meir explained, study the Torah for 'its own sake', not for his own benefit. A good midrash, the rabbi continued, sowed affection rather than discord, because anyone who studied scripture properly was full of love and brought joy to others: he 'loves the Divine Presence and all creatures, makes the Divine Presence glad and makes glad all creatures'. Torah study transformed the exegete, robing him with humility and fear, making him upright, pious, righteous and faithful, so that everybody around him benefited. 'The mysteries of the Torah are revealed to him,' R. Meir concluded, 'he becomes like an overflowing fountain and ceaseless torrent . . . And it makes him great and lifts him above the entire creation.'[30]

'Does not my word burn like fire?' Yahweh had asked Jeremiah.[31] Midrash released the divine spark that lay dormant in the written words of the Torah. One day, R. Akiba heard that his pupil Ben Azzai was caught in a nimbus of flame that flashed around him while he was expounding the Torah. He hurried off to investigate and Ben Azzai told him that he had simply been practising *horoz:*

> I was only linking up the words of the Torah with one
> another and then with the words of the Prophets, and the
> Prophets with the Writings, and the words rejoiced, as when
> they were delivered at Sinai, and they were sweet, as at their
> original utterance.[32]

The Sinai revelation was renewed every time a Jew confronted the text, opened himself to it, and applied it to his own situation. Like Ezekiel, the midrashist found that when he had absorbed it and made it uniquely his own, the Word of God tasted sweet as honey and set the world aflame.

Like several of the early rabbis, Ben Azzai was a mystic. They liked to contemplate Ezekiel's account of his vision of God's 'glory' (*kavod*) while performing exercises – fasting, putting their heads between their knees, and whispering God's praises – that put them into an altered mental state. Then it seemed as though they flew through the seven heavens until they beheld the 'glory' on its heavenly throne. But this mystical journey was fraught with danger. A very early story tells how four of the sages tried to 'enter the *pardes*', a symbolic 'orchard' that recalled the paradisal garden of Eden. Ben Azzai managed to arrive at this spiritual state before his death, but two of the other mystics were spiritually and mentally damaged by the experience. Only R. Akiba had the maturity to emerge unscathed and live long enough to tell the tale.[33] R. Akiba himself found the Song of Songs especially conducive to this *ekstasis*; it not only signified but actually made the love that God felt for his people a burning reality in the heart of the mystic. 'The whole of time is not worth the day on which the Song of Songs was given to Israel,' R. Akiba declared. 'All the Writings (*Kethuvim*) are holy. The Song of Songs is the Holy of Holies.'[34] In R. Akiba's interior world, the Song had replaced the inner sanctum of the temple, where the divine presence had rested on its ancient throne.

Other rabbis experienced the Spirit of Yahweh as an

electrifying divine presence within and around them. On one occasion, when R. Johanan had discussed Ezekiel's vision with his pupils, a fire descended from heaven and a *bat qol* declared that he had a special mission from God.[35] But the Holy Spirit in the form of fire also descended upon R. Johanan and R. Eliezer – just as it descended upon Jesus's disciples at Pentecost – while they were engaged in *horoz*, linking the scriptural verses together.[36]

At this stage, the rabbis had not yet committed their insights to writing. It seems that they learned the traditions they were accummulating by heart and transmitted them orally, although R. Akiba and R. Meir arranged the material in blocks that made them easier to memorize.[37] It seemed risky to write down this precious lore. A book could be burned like the temple or fall into the hands of the Christians, and would be safer in the minds and hearts of the sages. But the rabbis also valued the spoken word for its own sake. Graduates of Yavneh, who had managed to learn these oral texts by rote, were called *tannaim*, 'repeaters'. They spoke the Torah aloud and developed their midrash in conversation. The House of Studies was noisy with lively discussion and clamorous debate.

But by 135 the rabbis felt the need for a more permanent written record. In an attempt to drag the Jews into the modern Graeco-Roman world, the emperor Hadrian announced that he intended to plough the ruins of Jerusalem into the ground and build a modern city on the sacred site. Circumcision, the training of rabbis and the teaching of Torah were all forbidden by law. The hard-headed Jewish soldier Simeon bar Koseba led a revolt against Rome and when he managed to oust the Tenth Legion from Jerusalem, R. Akiba hailed him as the messiah. R. Akiba himself refused to stop teaching and, it is said, was executed by the Roman authorities. Eventually Bar Koseba's rebellion was brutally quashed by Hadrian in 135.[38] Thousands of Jews had died; the new city was built, though the temple ruins remained; Jews were forbidden to reside in Judah and were confined to the north of Palestine. The academy at Yavneh was disbanded and the rabbinic cadre dispersed. But the situation improved under the emperor Antoninus Pius (158–161), who relaxed the anti-Jewish legislation, and the rabbis regrouped at Usha in Lower Galilee.

The disastrous outcome of the Bar Koseba rebellion had horrified the rabbis. A few radicals, such as the mystic R. Simeon ben Yohai, continued to campaign against Rome, but most withdrew from politics. The rabbis were now wary of messianism and discouraged the practice of mysticism, preferring a disciplined life of study to dangerous flights of the spirit. At Usha they settled the canon of the Hebrew Bible, by making a final selection of the Writings (*Kethuvim*) of the Second Temple period.[39] They chose the more sober historical works and rejected apocalyptic fantasies, selecting Chronicles, Esther, Ezra and Nehemiah; and from the Wisdom genre: Proverbs, Ecclesiastes, the Song of Songs and Job, but not Ben Sirah. The Bible, which now consisted of the *Torah*, *Neviim* ('Prophets') and *Kethuvim*, became known as the TaNaKh.

Between 135 and 160 the rabbis also started to create an
entirely new scripture, which they called the Mishnah, an
anthology of the traditions that the rabbis had collected at
Yavneh, arranged according to the scheme of R. Akiba and R.
Meir, which they now committed to writing.[40] The rabbis had
finally admitted to themselves that the temple would never
be rebuilt, so they added a mass of fresh material, most of
which was concerned with the cult and festivals. The Hebrew
term *mishnah* meant 'learning by repetition': even though it
took written form, the new scripture was still conceived as an
oral work and students continued to learn it by heart. The
Mishnah was completed by R. Judah the Patriarch in about
200 and became the rabbis' New Testament. Like the
Christian scriptures, it regarded the Tanakh as belonging to a
phase of history that had gone forever but which could be
used to legitimize post-temple Judaism. But there the resemblance ended. There was no history, no narrative and no the-
ology.The Mishnah was simply a formidable collection of
legal rulings, arranged in six *Sederim* ('Orders'.): *Zeraim*
('Seeds'), *Moed* ('Festivals'), *Nashim* ('Women'), *Niziqin*
('Damages'), *Qodeshim* ('Holy Things') and *Tohoroth* ('Purity
Rules'). These were then subdivided into sixty-three tractates.

Unlike the New Testament, which never missed an opportunity to cite the Hebrew scriptures, the Mishnah held
proudly aloof from the Tanakh, rarely quoting from the Bible
or appealing to its teaching. The Mishnah did not claim to
derive its authority from Moses, never discussed its origins or
authenticity, but loftily assumed that its competence was

beyond question.[41] The rabbis, who were living, breathing incarnations of Torah, were supremely capable of interpreting the will of God and did not need support from the Bible.[42] The Mishnah was not concerned with what Jews believed but with how they behaved. The temple had gone but the Shekhinah was still in the midst of Israel. The rabbis' task was to help Jews to live in holiness, as though the temple was still standing.

The six Orders were constructed like a temple.[43] The first and last Orders – *Zeraim* and *Tohoroth* – dealt respectively with the holiness of the land and the holiness of the people. The two innermost Orders – *Nashim* and *Niziqin* – legislated for the private, domestic lives of Jews and their business relationships. But the subject of the second and the fifth Orders – *Moed* ('Festivals') and *Qodeshim* ('Holy Things') was the temple. These two *Sederim*, which were compiled almost entirely at Usha,[44] were like two equidistant, load-bearing pillars on which the whole edifice depended. They lovingly recalled the homely details of life in the lost temple: what each room was used for and where the high priest kept his wine. How did the night-watch comport themselves? What happened if a priest fell asleep on duty? In this way, the temple would live on in the minds of Jews and would remain the centre of Jewish life. Studying the obsolete temple laws set forth in the Mishnah was equivalent to actually performing the rites.[45]

It had been one thing for the early Pharisees to live as priests while the temple was still standing, but quite another when all that remained were a few charred ruins. The new spirituality demanded a heroic exegetical denial. But the Mishnah did not simply look back to the past. Thousands of entirely novel rulings worked out the implications of the temple's virtual presence. If Jews were to live like priests, how should they deal with gentiles? What was the role of women, who now had the priestly task of supervising the purity rules in the house? The rabbis would never have been able to persuade the people to observe this formidable body of law if it had not given them a satisfying spiritual experience.

About fifty years after the Mishnah had been completed, a new text provided this oral tradition with a spiritual pedigree that went back to Mount Sinai.[46] The author of *Pirke Avoth* ('Chapters of the Fathers') traced the line of transmission from the rabbis of Usha and Yavneh, back to R. Johanan ben Zakkai, who had learned the Torah from Hillel and Shammai. He then showed how the teaching had passed through generations of distinguished sages of the Second Temple period, ending with the men of 'the Great Assembly',[47] who had received the Torah from the prophets; the prophets had been instructed by the 'elders' who had conquered the Promised Land,[48] the elders by Joshua, Joshua by Moses, and Moses, the source of the tradition, had received the Torah from God himself.

The genealogy was not intended to be factual; like all *mythos*, it was concerned with meaning rather than historically accurate information and described a religious experience. When Jews studied the Torah according to the Mishnah, they felt as though they were participating in an ongoing conversation with all the great sages of the past and with God himself. This would become the charter myth of rabbinic Judaism. There was not one Torah but two – written and oral. Both had been given to Moses on Sinai. The Torah could not be confined to a text; it had to be revivified by the living voices of the sages in each generation. When they studied the Torah, the rabbis felt as though they were standing beside Moses on Sinai. Revelation continued to unfold and the insights of all Jews past, present and to come derived from God as surely as the written Torah given to Moses.[49]

The position of Jews in the Roman empire deteriorated after the conversion of the emperor Constantine to Christianity in 312. After the Bar Koseba revolt, when the *christos* had so signally failed to return, Jewish Christianity had dwindled and the churches were now predominantly gentile. When Theodosius II (401–50) made Christianity the official faith of the empire, Jews were forbidden to hold civil or military posts, Hebrew was prohibited in the synagogues, and if Passover fell before Easter, Jews were not allowed to observe it on the correct date. The rabbis responded by obeying the instructions of the sages in *Pirke Avoth,* who had urged their disciples to 'build a fence for Torah'.[50] They produced more scriptures, which encircled the living Torah with learned, devoted commentary, shielding it from a hostile world as the temple courts had once protected the Holy of Holies.

The Tosefta, a 'supplement' to the Mishnah, was composed in Palestine between 250 and 350: it was a commentary on the Mishnah, gloss upon gloss. Sifra, also written in Palestine at about the same time, tried to reverse the trend that seemed to be taking Jews away from the Tanakh, and attempted, respectfully, to subordinate the Oral to the written Torah. But the two Talmuds made it clear that the Jewish people did not feel inclined to take this path. The Jerusalem Talmud, known as the *Yerushalmi,* was completed in the early fifth century in Palestine, at a very bad time for the Jewish community. *Talmud* means study; but the Yerushalmi studied the Mishnah not the Bible, though it mitigated the Mishnah's proud independence of the Tanakh.[51] The Yerushalmi quoted from the Bible more frequently, and often demanded scriptural proof for its legal rulings – though it never allowed the Bible to be the sole arbiter of legislation. Legal cases involve matters of fact as well as principle, and the Tanakh could not provide this necessary information. But one sixth of the Yerushalmi consisted of scriptural exegesis and anecdotes about the great rabbis, which helped to humanize the formidable legal corpus.

Poor conditions in Palestine may have prevented the completion of the Yerushalmi, which should, perhaps, be regarded as work in progress. But during the sixth century, the Jews of Babylonia produced a more satisfying and polished Talmud.[52] There had been constant interchange between the rabbis of Palestine and Babylonia. The Iranian rulers were more liberal than the Christian emperors, so the Jews of Babylonia had the freedom to manage their own affiars under an officially appointed exilarch. As Palestinian Jewry declined, Babylonia became the intellectual centre of the Jewish world and the Babylonian Talmud, known as the *Bavli*, has a quiet confidence that reflected these more favourable circumstances. It would become the key text of rabbinic Judaism. Like the Yerushalmi, it was a commentary (*gemara*) on the Mishnah, but did not ignore the Tanakh, which was used to support the Oral Torah. In some ways, the Bavli was similar to the New Testament in that its author-editors regarded it as the completion of the Hebrew Bible – a new revelation for a changed world.[53] Like the New Testament, the Bavli was highly selective in its treatment of the older scripture, choosing only those portions of the Tanakh that it found useful and ignoring the rest.

The commentary of the Bavli went systematically through the Mishnah, portion by portion. The gemara referred not only to the Bible but also to the opinions of the rabbis, legends, history, theological reflections and legal lore. This method compelled the student to integrate the written and oral traditions, so that they merged together in his mind. The Bavli included a good deal of material that was older than the Mishnah but much of its content was new, so the student gained a fresh perspective that changed his view of both the Mishnah and the Bible. The Bavli revered the older texts but saw neither as sacrosanct. In their commentary, the author-editors would sometimes reverse the legislation of the Mishnah, play off one rabbi against another, and point out serious gaps in the Mishnah's arguments. They did exactly the same with the Bible, noting lacunae in the biblical texts,[54] suggesting what the inspired authors *should* have said,[55] and even changing a biblical law to more congenial rulings of their own.[56] When read in conjunction with the Bavli, the Bible was transformed, in the same way as the New Testament altered the Christians' reading of the 'Old Testament'. If biblical texts were included in the gemara, they were never discussed on their own terms and in a biblical context, but were always read from the point of view of the Mishnah. As R. Abdini of Haifa explained, the rabbis were the new prophets: 'Since the day the temple was destroyed, prophecy has been taken from the prophets and given to the sages.'[57] The Torah was thus a transcendent reality embodied in two earthly forms: a written scripture and an oral tradition.[58] Both came from God; both were necessary, but the rabbis privileged the Oral Torah because a written text could encourage inflexibility and a backward-looking orientation, whereas the spoken word and the ever-shifting currents of human thought made the Word more sensitive to changing conditions.[59]

We hear many voices in the Bavli: Abraham, Moses, the prophets, the Pharisees and the rabbis. They were not confined to their historical period but brought together on the same page, so that they seemed to be debating with each other across the centuries – often disagreeing quite vehemently. The Bavli gave no definitive answers. If an argument ended in impasse, the students had to sort it out to their own satisfaction with their teachers. The Bavli has been described as the first interactive text.[60] Its method replicated the process of study used by the rabbis themselves and thus compelled the students to engage in the same discussion and make their own contribution. The layout of each page was crucial: the portion of the Mishnah under discussion was placed in the centre, and surrounded by the gemara of sages from the distant and more recent past. The prophets and patriarchs of the Bible were not regarded as superior to the rabbis because they had participated in the original revelation. As R. Ishmael had already explained: 'There is no anteriority or posteriority in scripture.'[61] On each page there was also space for the student to add his own commentary. When studying the Bible through the Bavli, the student learned that nobody had the last word, that truth was constantly changing, and that while tradition was numinous and valuable, it must not constrict his own powers of judgement. The student must add his own *gemara* to the sacred page, because without it the line of tradition would come to an end. 'What is Torah?' asked the Bavli, 'It is: the interpretation of Torah.'[62]

Torah study was not a solitary pursuit. R. Berachiah, a seventh-century Palestinian sage, compared rabbinic discussion to a shuttlecock: 'words fly back and forth when the wise come into a house of study and discuss Torah, one stating his view, still another stating another view, and another stating a different view'. Yet there was a fundamental unity, because the sages were not merely voicing their own opinions: 'The words of these and of the other sages all of them were given by Moses the Shepherd from what he received from the Unique One of the Universe.'[63] Even while he was embroiled in a heated debate, the truly engaged student was aware that both he and his opponent were in some way participating in a conversation that stretched back to Moses and would continue into the future and that what they both said had already been foreseen and blessed by God.

Even though they were now regarded as the enemies of Judaism, Christians were developing a similar spirituality.

CHAPTER 5

Charity

Before the conversion of Constantine in 312, it seemed unlikely that Christianity would survive, as Christians were subjected to sporadic but intense persecution by the Roman authorities. Once they had made it clear that they were no longer members of the synagogue, the Romans regarded the church as a *super-stitio* of fanatics, who had committed the cardinal sin of impiety by breaking with the parent faith. Romans were highly suspicious of mass movements that threw off the restraints of tradition. Christians were also accused of atheism because they refused to honour the patronal gods of Rome and thus endangered the empire. The persecutions were designed to stamp out the faith and could easily have done so. As late as 303, the emperor Diocletian began a war of annihilation against the Christians. This time of terror and anxiety left its mark. The martyr, who was ready to follow Jesus to the death, became the Christian hero par excellence.

Some Christians tried to persuade their pagan neighbours that Christianity was not a destructive break with past piety by writing *apologiae*, 'rational explanations', of their faith. One of their chief arguments was that Jesus's life and death had been predicted by the Hebrew prophets, an argument that the Romans, with their respect for augury and oracles, took very seriously. The evangelists had relished their *pesher* exegesis, but the apologists found it more difficult. Once Marcion had urged Christians to jettison the Hebrew scriptures, gentile converts felt increasingly uneasy about their Jewish heritage.[1] They no longer worshipped in the synagogues, so what had they to do with the Jewish god? Had God changed his mind about the old covenant? How could the sacred history of Israel be Christian history? What had the prophets really known about Jesus and how had they known it? Why had Isaiah and Zechariah been preoccupied by Jesus, the founder of a gentile religion?

One of the earliest of these apologists was Justin (100–160), a pagan convert from Samaria in the Holy Land who eventually died as a martyr. He had studied various Greek philosophies, but found what he was looking for in Christianity. The *logos* in the prologue to John's gospel reminded Justin of the fiery, divine breath that the Stoics believed organized the whole of reality and called *Logos* ('Reason'), *Pneuma* ('Spirit') or God. Evidently Christians and pagans had a set of common symbols. In his two *Apologiae*, Justin argued that Jesus was the incarnation of the Logos, which had been active in the world throughout history, inspiring Greeks and Hebrews alike. It had spoken through the prophets, who had thus been able to foretell the coming of the messiah. The Logos had taken many forms before its definitive revelation in Jesus. It had spoken through Plato and

Socrates. When Moses thought he heard God speaking from the burning bush, he had really been listening to the Logos. The oracles of the prophets had not been uttered 'by the inspired [prophets] themselves, but by the divine Word who moved them'.[2] Sometimes the Logos had foretold the future; at other times, it spoke in the name of God. But the Jews had imagined that God was talking to them directly and had not realized that it had been God's 'first-begotten Logos'.[3] In the Jewish scriptures, God had sent a coded message to humanity that the Christians alone had managed to decipher.

Justin's notion of the Logos became central to the exegesis of the theologians who are known as the 'fathers' of the church, because they created the seminal ideas of Christianity and adapted this Jewish faith to the Graeco-Roman world. From an early date, the fathers regarded the Tanakh as an elaborate sign system. As Irenaeus explained, the writings of Moses were really the words of Christ, the eternal Logos, who had been speaking through him.[4] The fathers did not see the 'Old Testament' as an anthology of writings but as a single book with a unified message, which Irenaeus called its *hypothesis*, the argument 'beneath' (*hypo*) the surface. The Hebrew scriptures did not mention Jesus directly but his life and death formed the coded subtext of the Bible and also revealed the secret of the cosmos.[5] Material objects, invisible realities, historical events and natural laws – indeed, everything that existed – formed part of a divinely organized system, which Irenaeus called the 'economy'. Everything had its proper place in the economy and connected with everything else to form a harmonious whole. Jesus was the incarnation of this divine economy. As Paul had explained, his coming had finally revealed God's plan: 'that the universe, everything in heaven and earth, might be brought into a unity [*anakephalaio-sis*] in Christ'.[6] Jesus was the reason, purpose and culmination of God's grand design.

Because Christ lay at the heart of the Hebrew scriptures, they also expressed the divine economy, but this subtext only became apparent if the Bible was interpreted correctly. Like the cosmos itself, scripture was a text (*textus*), a tissue made up of an infinite number of interconnecting entities that were 'woven together' to form an inextricable whole.[7] Contemplating the encoded *textus* of scripture helped people to understand that it was Jesus who held everything together and explained the deeper significance of the entire economy. The task of the exegete was to demonstrate this, fitting all the clues together like the interlocking pieces of a vast puzzle. Irenaeus compared the scriptures to a mosaic, composed of innumerable tiny stones which, once they had been placed together correctly, formed the image of a handsome king.[8]

The interpretation of scripture had to conform to the teaching of Jesus's apostles, which Irenaeus called the 'rule of faith', namely that the Logos, which had become incarnate in Jesus, had been implicit in the structure of creation from the very beginning:[9]

Anyone who reads the scriptures with attention will find in them a discourse about Christ, and a prefiguration of a new

calling. For Christ is *the treasure hidden in the field*, that is, in
this world, *for the field is the world*,[10] but he was also hidden in
the scriptures, since he was signified by types and parables
which could not be understood, humanly speaking, before
the consummation of those things that were prophesied as
coming, that is, the advent of Christ.[11]

But the fact that Christ was 'hidden' in scripture meant that
Christians had to make a strenuous exegetical effort if they
wanted to find him.

Christians could only make sense of the Tanakh by trans-
forming it into an *allegoria,* in which all the events and characters of the 'Old Testament' became types of Christ in the New.
The evangelists had already found 'types and parables' of
Jesus in the Hebrew scriptures, but the fathers were more
ambitious. '*Every* prophet, *every* ancient writer, *every* revolution of the state, *every* law, *every* ceremony of the old covenant
points *only* to Christ, announces *only* him, represents *only*
him,' insisted Eusebius, bishop of Caesarea (260–340).[12] Christ
the Logos had been present in Adam, the progenitor of the
race; in Abel the martyr; in Isaac the willing sacrificial victim;
and in the afflicted Job.[13] Christians were developing their own
distinctive *horoz*, 'linking' people, events and images that had
hitherto been separate, in order to reveal what they believed to
be the central reality of scripture. Like the rabbis, they were
not interested in discovering the intention of the biblical
author and seeing a text in its historical context. A good interpretation gave new insight into the divine economy.

Not everybody shared this enthusiasm for allegory. In Antioch, exegetes concentrated on the literal sense of scripture. Their aim was to find out what the prophets themselves had intended to teach – not what could be read into their words with the benefit of hindsight. The prophets often used metaphors and similes, but this figural language was part of the literal sense – essential to what the prophets and psalmists had meant to say. The Antiochenes saw no need for allegory. The late fourth-century preacher John Chrysostom showed that it was possible to derive sound moral lessons from the plain sense of the Bible. The Antiochenes could not discard all typological exegesis, because it had been used so copiously by the evangelists, but they urged scholars to stick to the allegories in the New Testament and not to go in search of new ones. Theodore, bishop of Mopsuestia from 392 to 428, could see no value in the Song of Songs, for example; it was just a love poem and could only be read as a sacred text if entirely alien meanings were superimposed upon it.

But in Alexandria, the Song was popular precisely because it offered such rich opportunities for *allegoria*. Versed in the same hermeneutic tradition as Philo, the Christians of Alexandria had developed an art of reading that they called spiritual interpretation – an attempt to reproduce the experience of the disciples on the road to Emmaus. Like the rabbis, they saw the Bible as an inexhaustible text, capable of yielding endlessly new meanings. They did not think that they were reading into scripture things that were not there but would have agreed with the rabbis that 'everything is in it'. The most brilliant Alexandrian exegete was Origen (185–254), the most influential and prolific author of the day.[14] Besides his biblical commentaries, he produced the *Hexapla* (an edition of the Bible that placed the Hebrew text beside five different Greek translations), and two monumental works: *Against Celsus*, an apologia to refute a pagan philosopher's critique of Christianity, and *On First Principles*, a comprehensive account of Christian doctrine.

For Origen, Jesus was the beginning and end of all exegesis:

> Jesus reveals the law to us when he reveals to us the secrets of the Law. For we who are of the catholic Church, we do not spurn the law of Moses but accept it, so long as it is Jesus who reads it to us. Indeed, we can only possess a correct understanding of the Law when he reads it to us, and we are able to receive his sense and understanding.[15]

For Origen, the Jewish scriptures were a midrash on the New Testament, which had itself been a commentary on the Tanakh. Without allegory, the Bible made no sense at all. How could you explain literally Christ's command: 'If your right eye should cause you to sin, tear it out and throw it away'?[16] How could a Christian accept the savage command that uncircumcised boys be killed?[17] What possible relevance to Christians were the lengthy instructions for the building of the tabernacle?[18] Did the biblical writer really mean that God 'walked' in the Garden of Eden?[19] Or insist that Christ's disciples should never wear shoes?[20] If you interpreted it literally it was 'a very difficult, not to say impossible task' to revere the Bible as a holy book.[21] Reading scripture was far from easy – a fact that Origen emphasized again and again. All too often heretics twisted the text for their own purposes or gave a facile interpretation of a highly complex passage. It was hard to find inspiration and sound teaching in some of the more problematic or unedifying biblical stories, but because the Logos spoke in scripture, 'We ought to believe that it is possible, even if we do not recognize the profit.'[22] So when Origen discussed Abraham's dubious behaviour in selling his wife to the Pharaoh, pretending that she was his sister,[23] he argued that Sarah was a symbol of virtue and that Abraham wanted to share this rather than keep it to himself.

A modern reader is likely to feel that Origen was as guilty of distorting the scriptures as the heretics he castigated. Like rabbinic midrash, his exegesis seems deliberately transgressive, a quest for meaning at the expense of the author's intention. Origen would have encountered Jewish midrash in Alexandria and later in Caesarea, where he set up his own academy. His methods were similar. In his commentary on Exodus, for example, Origen was not content with the big picture – seeing the Israelites' liberation from slavery as a type of the salvation brought by Christ – but was determined to find a reference to Christ in apparently insignificant details. All Christians had to leave the darkness of 'Egypt' behind, giving up their worldly ways to follow Jesus. On the first leg of their journey out of Egypt, scripture tells us that the

Israelites 'left Rameses for Succoth'.[24] Like Philo, Origen always researched the etymology of proper names, and discovered that *Rameses* meant 'the commotion of a moth'. He then found a 'chain' of scriptural quotations, which gave this seemingly inconsequential sentence entirely new meaning. The word 'moth' reminded him of Jesus's warning against attachment to earthly possessions that were vulnerable to moths and woodworm.[25] So every Christian had to 'depart from Rameses,'

> if you wish to come to the place where the Lord may be our leader and precede you *in the column of the cloud*[26] and the *rock* may follow you,[27] which offers you *spiritual food* and *spiritual drink,* no less.[28] Nor should you store treasure *there where the moth destroys or thieves dig through and steal.*[29] This is what the Lord says clearly in the Gospels: *If you wish to be perfect, sell all your possessions and give to the poor, and you will have treasure in heaven.*[30] This, therefore, is to depart from Rameses and follow Christ.[31]

Thus the Israelites' sojourn in Rameses looked forward to Christ's demand for total commitment. For Origen, scripture was a *textus,* a densely woven fabric of words, every one of which was spoken by Christ the Logos and summoned the reader to follow him. Origen did not believe that his exegesis was arbitrary, because God had planted the clues; his task was to solve them and make the divine voice audible in a way that had not been possible before the coming of Jesus.

Exegesis brought the interpreter and his students a moment of *ekstasis*, a 'stepping outside' of the mundane. Modern biblical scholarship seeks to place a text in the worldly economy of academe, treating it like any other ancient document.[32] Origen's goal was different. Central to early Christian spirituality was what has been called the 'perennial philosophy', because it has been found in almost every pre-modern culture. According to this mythical speculation, every earthly reality has its counterpart in the divine sphere.[33] It was an attempt to articulate the inchoate sense that our lives are somehow incomplete and fragmentary, separate from the more satisfying version that we can imagine so clearly. Because heaven and earth were linked together in the great chain of being, a symbol was inseparable from its unseen referent. The word 'symbol' comes from the Greek *symballein*, 'to throw together'. The archetype and its earthly replica were inextricably combined, like gin and tonic in a cocktail. To taste one, you must also taste the other. This was the basis of Christian ritual: when Christians drank wine and ate bread during the Eucharist, they encountered the Christ these objects represented. In the same way, when they struggled with the time-bound words of scripture, they encountered the Logos, the prototype of all human utterance. This was central to Origen's hermeneutics. 'The contents of scripture are outward forms of certain mysteries and the images of divine things,' he explained.[34] When he perused the New Testament, he was constantly 'amazed by the deep obscurity of the unspeakable mysteries contained therein'; at every turn, he came upon 'thousands of passages that provide, as if through a window, a narrow opening leading to multitudes of deepest thoughts'.[35]

But Origen did not neglect the literal sense of the Bible. His painstaking work on the *Hexapla* showed his determination to establish a dependable text. He learned Hebrew, consulted rabbis and was also fascinated by the geography, flora and fauna of the Holy Land. But the unsatisfactory surface meaning of so many of the teachings and narratives of the Bible compelled him to look beyond it. Scripture had a body and a soul. Our bodies shape our minds and thoughts. They caused us pain and constantly reminded us of our mortality. Our physical lives, therefore, provided us with a built-in ascetic, which, if we responded properly, led us to cultivate our spiritual, immortal nature.[36] In the same way, the glaring limitations in the body – the literal meaning – of scripture forced us to seek its soul, and God had planted these anomalies on purpose:

> Divine wisdom has arranged for certain stumbling blocks
> and interruptions of the historical sense . . . by inserting in
> the midst a number of impossibilities and incongruities, in
> order that the narrative might, as it were, present a barrier to
> the reader and lead him to refuse to proceed along the
> pathway of the ordinary meaning.[37]

These difficult pasages 'bring us, though the entrance of a narrow footpath, to a higher and loftier road precisely by "shutting us out and debarring us" from an acceptance of their plain sense'.[38] By means of the 'impossibility of the literal sense', God led us 'to an examination of the inner meaning'.[39]

Spiritual exegesis was hard work: we had to transform the scriptures in the same way as we transformed our recalcitrant selves. Biblical interpretation required 'the utmost purity and sobriety and ... nights of watching'; it was impossible without a life of prayer and virtue.[40] It was not like solving a mathematical problem, because it involved a more intuitive mode of thought. But if the scholar persevered, pondering the scriptures 'with all the attention and reverence they deserve, it is certain that, in the very act of reading and diligently studying them, his mind and feelings will be touched by a divine breath and he will recognize that the words he is reading are not the utterances of a man but the language of God'.[41]

This apprehension of the divine was acquired gradually, step by step. In the prologue to his commentary on the Song of Songs, Origen pointed out that the three books attributed to Solomon – Proverbs, Ecclesiastes and the Song of Songs – represented the stages of this journey. Scripture had a body, a psyche and a spirit that went beyond our mortal nature; these corresponded to the three different senses in which scripture could be understood. Proverbs was a book of the body. It could be comprehended without allegory, so it represented the *literal* sense of scripture, which the exegete had to master before he could progress to anything higher. Ecclesiastes worked at the level of the psyche, the natural powers of mind and heart. By pointing out that earthly things were vain and empty, Ecclesiastes revealed the futility of placing all our hope in the material world; it therefore exemplified the *moral* sense of scripture, because it showed us how to behave, using arguments that required no supernatural insight. In their reading of the Bible, most Christians rarely progressed beyond the literal and moral senses.

Only an exegete who had been properly initiated into the higher mysteries of scripture could tackle the Song of Songs, which was providentially placed after Proverbs and Ecclesiastes and represented the *spiritual,* allegorical sense. For those Christians who read the Bible in a purely literal way, the Song was just a love poem. But an allegorical interpretation revealed its deeper meaning: 'The love of the Bride for the celestial Bridegroom – that is, of the perfect soul for the Word of God.'[42]

Earthly love, which seems to promise so much, nearly always disappoints; it can be fulfilled solely by its archetype, the God who *is* love.[43] The Song depicted the drama of this ascent to the divine. Throughout, Origen interpreted the Song on three levels. When he expounded the opening verse, 'Let him kiss me with the kisses of his mouth,' he began with the *literal*, historical sense. This was the beginning of an epithalamium: the bride was waiting for her groom; he had sent her dowry but had not yet joined her, and she longed for his presence. *Allegorically*, however, the image of bride and groom referred to the relationship between Christ and the Church, as Paul had explained[44] and the verse symbolized the period before the coming of Christ. Israel had received the Law and the prophets as a dowry but was still waiting for the incarnate Logos, who would complete them. Finally, the text must be applied to the individual soul, whose 'only desire is to be united to the Word of God'.[45] The soul was already in possession of her dowry of natural law, reason and free will, but they could not satisfy her. So she prayed the opening words of the Song, in the hope that her purified 'pure and virginal soul may be enlightened by the illumination and the visitation of the Word of God himself'.[46] The *moral* sense of this verse showed that the bride was a model for all Christians, who must train themselves to yearn without ceasing to transcend their nature and achieve union with God.

Exegesis must always lead to action. For Origen this meant contemplation (*theoria*). Readers must meditate on the verse until they were 'capable of receiving the principles of truth'.[47] They would thus acquire a new orientation towards God. Origen's commentaries often seem to lack a firm conclusion, because his readers had to take the last and final step for themselves. Origen's commentary could only place them in the correct spiritual posture; he could not do the meditation for them. Without prolonged *theoria*, it was not possible to understand his exegesis fully.

Origen had longed to be a martyr as a young man. But after the conversion of Constantine, when Christianity became a legitimate religion in the Roman empire, there was no further opportunity for martyrdom and the monk became the chief Christian exemplar. During the early fourth century, ascetics started to retire to the deserts of Egypt and Syria to engage in a life of solitary prayer. One of the greatest of these monks was Antony of Egypt (250–356), who had felt unable to reconcile his wealth with the gospels. One day, he had heard read aloud in church the story of the rich young man who refused Jesus's invitation: 'go and sell what you own and give the money to the poor . . . then come, follow me'.[48] Like the rabbis, Antony experienced this scripture as a *miqra*, a 'summons'. That very afternoon, he gave all his possessions away and set off for the desert. Monks were revered as doers of the Word.[49] In their desert caves, the monks recited the scriptures, learned texts by heart and meditated on them. As these biblical passages became part of a monk's interior world, their original meaning became less important than this personal significance. Monks believed that Jesus showed them how to read the Bible: in the Sermon on the Mount, he had given scripture new meaning, emphasizing some portions of the Bible more than others. He also stressed the importance of charity. Monks were pioneers of a new Christian lifestyle, which required a different reading of the gospel. They had to allow the texts they had learned to reverberate in their minds, until they achieved the self-for-getfulness of *apatheia*, a lack of concern about their personal well-being that gave them the freedom to love. As a modern scholar explains:

> They could be ignored enough, invited outside themselves enough, to love and be loved in a way that met the deepest

social needs of the tension-filled world of late antiquity. Loving God, loving other people, loving the created world in which they were placed – this was the great and hoped-for conclusion of *apatheia* – the sublime indifference that ended in love.[50]

Origen had concentrated on the love of God in his commentary on the Song; the monks stressed love of neighbour. Living together in community, they had to dethrone themselves from the centre of their lives and put others there. Monks did not turn their backs on the world: literally thousands of Christians descended upon them from nearby towns and villages to seek their counsel. Living in silence had taught monks how to listen.

One of Antony's most ardent admirers was Athanasius of Alexandria (296–373), a central figure in the tumultuous fourth-century debate about the divinity of Christ. Now that Christianity was a gentile faith, people found it difficult to understand Jewish terms, such as 'Son of God' or 'Spirit'. Was Jesus divine in the same way as his Father? And was the Holy Spirit another God? The debate focused on a discussion of Wisdom's song in Proverbs which began:[51]'Yahweh created me when his purpose first unfolded, before the oldest of his works.' Did this mean that Christ was a mere creature, and, if so, how could he be divine? In a letter to Athanasius, Arius, a charismatic presbyter in Alexandria, insisted that Jesus was a human being who had been promoted by God to divine status. He was able to produce an armoury of scriptural texts to support his view. Arius argued that the very fact that Jesus had called God his 'Father' implied a distinction between them, since paternity involves prior existence; he also quoted gospel passages that stressed the humanity and vulnerability of Christ.[52] Athanasius took the opposite view: Jesus was divine in the same way as God the Father, an equally controversial idea at this time, which Athanasius backed up with his own proof texts.

At the beginning of the controversy, there was no orthodox teaching on the nature of Christ and nobody knew whether Athanasius or Arius was right. Discussion raged for over two hundred years. It was impossible to prove anything from scripture, since texts could be found to support either side. But the Greek fathers of the Church did not allow scripture to dominate their theology. In the creed he formulated after the Council of Nicaea, Athanasius used an entirely unscriptural term to describe Jesus's relationship with God: he was *homoousion*, 'of one substance' with the Father. Other fathers based their theology on religious experience rather than a detailed reading of the Bible, which could not tell us everything about a God who transcended all human words and concepts.

Basil of Caesarea in Cappadocia (329–79) argued that there were two kinds of religious teaching, both of which derived from Jesus: *kerygma* was the public teaching of the Church, based on the Bible, while *dogma* expressed everything that could *not* be said; it could be suggested only in the symbolic gestures of the liturgy or experienced in silent meditation.[53] Like Philo, Basil distinguished between God's essence (*ousia*), which lay beyond our understanding, and his operations (*energeiai*) in the world that are described in scripture. God's *ousia* was not even mentioned in the Bible.[54] This was central to the doctrine of the Trinity, which Basil formulated together with his brother Gregory of Nyssa (335–95) and their friend Gregory of Nazianzus (329–91). God had a single essence (*ousia*) which would always remain incomprehensible to us. But in scripture, God had made himself known to us in three *hypostases*, 'manifestations' (Father, Logos and Spirit), divine *energeiaei* that adapted the ineffable mystery of God to our limited intelligence.

The Cappadocian fathers were contemplatives; their daily *theoria* on scripture had introduced them to a transcendence that was beyond even the inspired language of the Bible. The same was true of the Greek father who wrote under the pseudonym Denys the Areopagite[55], whose work is almost as authoritative as scripture in the Greek Orthodox world. He promoted an apophatic theology of 'silence'. God had revealed some of his names to us in scripture, which tells us that God is 'good', 'compassionate', and 'just', but these attributes were 'sacred veils' that hid the divine mystery which lies beyond such words. When Christians listen to scripture, they must continually remind themselves that these human terms were too limited to apply to God. So God was 'good' and 'not-good'; 'just' and 'not-just'. This paradoxical reading would bring them 'into that darkness which is beyond intellect'[56] and into the presence of the indescribable

God. Denys liked the story of the cloud descending on Mount Sinai: on the summit, Moses was enveloped in a thick cloud of unknowing. He could see nothing but he was in the place where God was.

Scripture had not been able to settle the issue of Jesus's divinity, but the Byzantine theologian Maximus the Confessor (c.580–662) arrived at an explanation that became standard among Greek-speaking Christians, because it reflected their interior experience of Christ. Maximus did not believe that the Logos became human to make reparation for the sin of Adam; the incarnation would have occurred even if Adam had not sinned. Jesus was the first fully deified human being and we could all be like him – even in this life. The Word was made flesh in order that 'the whole human being would become God, deified by the grace of God become man – whole man, soul and body, by nature, and becoming whole God, soul and body, by grace'.[57]

The Latin-speaking fathers of Western Europe and North Africa were more down to earth. It is significant that in the West, *theoria* came to mean a rational construct and *dogma* expressed everything that *could* be said about religion. This was a frightening time in the West, where the Roman empire was falling to the barbarian tribes from Germany and Eastern Europe. One of the most influential Western exegetes was Jerome (342–420), who was born in Dalmatia, studied literature and rhetoric in Rome and, fleeing the invading tribes, travelled in Antioch and Egypt before settling in Bethlehem where he founded a monastery. Jerome had initially been attracted to the allegorical hermeneutics of Alexandria, but as a gifted linguist, unique in his day for his mastery of both Greek and Hebrew, his chief contribution was his translation of the entire Bible into Latin. This was called the Vulgate ('vernacular') and it remained the standard text in Europe until the sixteenth century. At first Jerome, who had a great respect for what he called *Hebraica veritas* ('the truth in Hebrew'), wanted to exclude the Apocrypha, books which had been excluded from the Canon by the rabbis, but at the request of his colleague Augustine he agreed to translate them. As a result of his work on the text, Jerome tended increasingly to concentrate in his commentaries on the Bible's literal, historical sense.

His friend Augustine, bishop of Hippo in North Africa (354–430), had studied rhetoric and was at first disappointed in the Bible, which seemed inferior to the great Latin poets and orators. Yet the Bible played a crucial role in his conversion to Christianity after a long, painful struggle. At a moment of spiritual crisis, he had heard a child in the next garden singing a refrain: *'tolle, lege'* ('Pick it up and read it') and he remembered that Antony had decided to embrace the monastic life after a reading from the gospel. In great excitement, he snatched up a copy of Paul's epistles and read the first words that caught his eye: 'no drunken orgies, no promiscuity or licentiousness, and no wrangling or jealousy. Let your armour be the Lord Jesus Christ; forget about satisfying your bodies with all their cravings.'[58] In one of the first recorded 'born-again' conversions that would become a feature of Western Christianity, Augustine felt all his doubts fall away: 'It was as if the light of steadfast trust poured into my heart, and all the shadows of hesitation fled away.'[59]

Augustine later realized that his earlier difficulties with the Bible were due to pride: scripture was only accessible to those who had emptied themselves of conceit and self-importance.[60] The Logos had descended from heaven in order to share our human frailty; and in the same way, when God revealed his Word in scripture, he had to come down to our level and use time-bound images that we could understand.[61] We could never know the whole truth in this life; even Moses could not gaze upon the divine essence directly.[62] Language was inherently defective: we rarely convey our thoughts adequately to others and this makes our relationships with other people problematic. So our struggle with scripture should remind us of the impossibility of expressing the divine mystery in human speech. Bitter, angry disputes about the meaning of scripture were, therefore, ridiculous. The Bible expressed a truth that was infinite and beyond the comprehension of every single person, so nobody could have the last word. Even if Moses appeared in person to explain what he had written, some people would be unable to accept his interpretation of the Pentateuch, because each of us could hold only a tiny facet of the entire revelation in our minds.[63] Instead of engaging in uncharitable controversies, in which everybody insisted that he alone was right, a humble acknowledgement of our lack of insight should draw us together.

The Bible was about love; everything that Moses had

written 'was for the sake of love', so to quarrel about scripture was perverse: 'There are so many meanings to be extracted from these words; so how foolish it is, then, to be in a hurry to assert which of them Moses really meant, and with destructive controversies to offend against the spirit of love – when it was for the sake of love that Moses said all the things that we are trying to elucidate.'[64] Augustine had arrived at the same concluson as Hillel and the rabbis. Charity was the central principle of Torah and everything else was commentary. Whatever else Moses had written, his chief purpose was to preach the dual commandment: love of God and love of neighbour. This had also been the central message of Jesus.[65] So if we insult others in the name of the Bible, 'we *make the Lord a liar*'.[66] People who quarrelled about scripture were full of pride; they 'know not Moses' meaning, but love their own, not because it is true but because it is theirs'.[67] So 'let no one be filled with pride against his brother over what is written,' Augustine begged his congregation, 'But let us love the Lord our God with all our heart, with all our soul, and with all our mind, and our neighbours as ourselves.'[68]

As a Platonist, it was natural for Augustine to elevate the spiritual above the literal meaning. But he had a strong sense of history, which enabled him to steer a middle course. Instead of rushing to give a figurative interpretation of an unedifying story, Augustine was more inclined to point out that moral standards were culturally conditioned. Polygamy, for example, was common and permissible among primitive peoples. Even the best of us fall into sin, so there was no need to allegorize the story of David's adultery, which had been included in the Bible as a warning to us all.[69] Righteous condemnation is not only unkind but smacks of the self-satisfaction and self-congratulation that is a major impediment to our understanding of scripture. So 'we must meditate on what we read, until an interpretation be found that tends to establish the reign of charity,' Augustine urged. 'Scripture teaches nothing but charity, nor condemns anything except cupidity, and in this way shapes the minds of men.'[70]

Irenaeus had insisted that exegesis must conform to the 'rule of faith'. For Augustine, the 'rule of faith' was not a doctrine but the spirit of love. Whatever the author had originally intended, a biblical passage that was not conducive to love must be interpreted figuratively, because charity was the beginning and end of the Bible:

> Whoever, therefore, thinks that he understands the divine scriptures or any part of them so that it does not build the double love of God and of our neighbour does not understand it at all. Whoever finds a lesson there useful to the building of charity, even though he has not said what the author may be shown to have intended in that place, has not been deceived.[71]

Exegesis was a discipline that trained us in the difficult art of charity. By habitually seeking a charitable explanation of disturbing texts, we could learn to do the same in our daily lives. Like the other Christian exegetes, Augustine believed that

Jesus was central to the Bible: 'Our whole purpose when we hear the Psalms, the Prophets and the Law,' he explained in a sermon, 'is to see Christ there, to understand Christ there.'[72] But the Christ he found in scripture was never simply the historical Jesus, but the whole Christ, who, as St Paul had taught, was inseparable from humanity.[73] After finding Christ in scripture, the Christian must return to the world and learn to seek him in loving service to the community.

Augustine was not a linguist. He knew no Hebrew and could not have encountered Jewish midrash, but he had come to the same conclusion as Hillel and Akiba. Any interpretation of scripture that spread hatred and dissension was illegitimate; all exegesis must be guided by the principle of charity.

CHAPTER 6

Lectio Divina

In 430, the last year of his life, Augustine had watched the Vandals besieging the city of Hippo, as the western provinces of the Roman empire fell helplessly before the invading barbarian tribes. A deep sadness pervades Augustine's work during these final years, and is especially evident in his interpretation of the fall of Adam and Eve. The tragedy of Rome's collapse had convinced Augustine that this original sin had sentenced the human race to eternal damnation. Even after our redemption by Christ, our humanity was impaired by concupiscence, the irrational desire to take pleasure in creatures rather than in God. The guilt of original sin was transmitted to Adam's descendants through the sexual act: when our reasoning powers were swamped by passion, God was forgotten, and men and women revelled shamelessly in one another. The image of rationality dragged down by a chaos of sensation reflected the plight of Rome, source of order in the West, brought low by the barbarians. This interpretation of the third chapter of Genesis is unique to Western Christianity; neither the Jews nor the Greek Orthodox, who did not experience the fall of Rome, have subscribed to this tragic vision. The collapse of the empire plunged Western Europe into centuries of political, economic and social stagnation and the trauma convinced the more educated Christians that men and women were indeed permanently damaged by Adam's sin. They could no longer hear what God said to them, and this made it well-nigh impossible to understand the scriptures.

Europe had become a pagan wilderness. From the fifth to the ninth centuries, the Christian tradition was confined to the monasteries, the only places that could provide the stability and quiet necessary for the study of the Bible. The monastic ideal had been brought to the West by John Cassian (360–435). He had also introduced Western Christians to Origen's threefold interpretation of scripture according to the literal, moral and allegorical senses, but added a fourth: the *anagogical* or mystical sense, which revealed a text's eschatological significance. When, for example, the prophets had described the future glories of Jerusalem, this referred anagogically to the heavenly Jerusalem in Revelation. Cassian taught his monks that the study of scripture was a lifelong task. In order to appreciate the ineffable realities that lay hidden behind the veil of human words, they must rectify their fallen nature – training their powers of concentration, disciplining their bodies in fasts and vigils, and cultivating a habit of inwardness.[1]

Lectio divina ('sacred study') was also central to the Rule of St Benedict of Nursia (AD 480–543). Benedictine monks spent at least two hours every day studying the scriptures and the

writings of the fathers. Scripture, however, was not experienced as a book: many of the monks would never have seen
the Bible as a single volume but read it in separate manuscripts; much of their biblical knowledge came to them at
second hand in the liturgy or the works of the fathers. The
Bible was read aloud during meals and the Psalter chanted at
regular intervals throughout the day in the Divine Office. The
rhythms, imagery and teaching of the Bible became the
substratum of their spirituality, built up incrementally and
undramatically day by day, year by year, in silent, regular
meditation.

There was nothing formal or systematic about *lectio divina*.
Monks were not obliged to cover a given number of chapters
per session. *Lectio* was a peaceful, leisurely perusal of the text
in which the monk learned to find a quiet place in his mind
that enabled him to hear the Word. The biblical story was not
studied as a historical event but experienced as a contemporary reality. Monks were encouraged to enter the action imaginatively – visualizing themselves beside Moses on Sinai, in
the audience when Jesus delivered the Sermon on the Mount,
or at the foot of the cross. They were supposed to consider the
scene according to each of the four senses in turn, moving
from literal to spiritual in a process that marked an ascent to
mystical union with God.[2]

A formative influence in the West was Gregory the Great
(540–604), a Benedictine monk who was elected Pope.
Gregory was steeped in the discipline of *lectio divina* but his
biblical theology revealed the shadow that haunted the

Western spirit in the aftermath of Rome's fall. He had fully absorbed the doctrine of original sin, and saw the human mind as irreparably damaged and twisted. God was now difficult to access. We could know nothing about him. It took a massive mental effort to experience a momentary joy in contemplation before falling back into the darkness that was our natural element.[3] In the Bible, God had condescended to our sinfulness, and come down to the level of our puny minds, but human language had splintered under the divine impact. That was why the grammar and vocabulary of Jerome's Vulgate departed from classical Latin usage and why, on first reading, it was hard to find any religious value in some of the biblical stories. Unlike Origen, Jerome and Augustine, Gregory wasted no time on the literal meaning. Studying the plain sense of scripture was like looking at somebody's face without seeing what was in his heart.[4] The literal text was like a flat expanse of land surrounded by mountains that represented the 'spiritual senses that would take us beyond the broken human words'.[5]

By the eleventh century, Europe had started to emerge from the Dark Ages. The Benedictines of Cluny, near Paris, initiated a reform to educate the laity, whose knowledge of Christianity was woefully inadequate. Uneducated layfolk could not read the Bible, of course, but were taught to experience the Mass as a complex allegory that symbolically re-enacted Jesus's life: the readings from scripture in the first part of the liturgy recalled his ministry; during the offering of the bread and wine, they meditated on his sacrificial death, and the communion represented his resurrection in the lives of the faithful. The fact that lay people could no longer follow the Latin added to the mystique: much of the Mass was recited by the priest in an undertone, and the silence and the sacred language transported the ritual into a separate space apart, introducing the congregation to the gospel as a *mysterium,* a power-filled act. By enabling them to enter imaginatively into the gospel story, Mass was the laity's *lectio divina.*[6] The Cluniacs also encouraged lay people to make pilgrimages to places associated with Jesus and the saints. Not many could make the long trip to the Holy Land, but, it was said, some of the apostles had travelled to Europe and were buried there: Peter in Rome; Joseph of Arimathea in Glastonbury, and James at Compostela in Spain. During the journey, pilgrims learned Christian values, living for a while like monks: they left secular life behind, were celibate during the journey, lived in community with other pilgrims, and were forbidden to fight or bear arms.

But Europe was still a dangerous, desolate place. People were barely able to farm the land, there was famine and sickness and constant warfare, as the nobility engaged in ceaseless battles with one another, devastating the countryside and wrecking entire villages. The Cluniacs tried to impose a periodic truce and some tried to reform the barons and kings. But the knights were soldiers and wanted an aggressive religion. The first communal, cooperative act of the new Europe, as she crawled out of the Dark Ages, was the First Crusade (1095–99). Some of the Crusaders began their journey to the

Holy Land by attacking the Jewish communities in the Rhine Valley; at its conclusion, the Crusaders massacred some thirty thousand Jews and Muslims in Jerusalem. The crusading ethos was based on a literal interpretation of Christ's warning in the gospel: 'Anyone who does not carry his cross and come after me cannot be my disciple.'[7] Crusaders sewed crosses on their clothes and followed in Jesus's footsteps to the land where he had lived and died. With tragic irony, crusading was preached as an act of love.[8] Christ was the Crusaders' feudal lord, and as loyal vassals they were duty-bound to recover his patrimony. In the Crusades, Christianity absorbed and baptized the feudal violence of Europe.

While some Europeans were fighting Muslims in the Near East, others were studying with Muslim scholars in Spain, who helped them to recover much of the culture they had lost during the Dark Ages. In the Muslim kingdom of al-Andalus, Western scholars discovered the medicine, mathematics and science of classical Greece that had been preserved and developed in the Islamic world. They read Aristotle for the first time in Arabic, and translated his work into Latin. Europe embarked on an intellectual renaissance. Aristotle's rational philosophy, which was more down to earth than the Platonism that they had imbibed from the fathers of the Church, filled many Western scholars with excitement and encouraged them to use their own reasoning powers.

This inevitably affected the study of the Bible. As Europe became more organized and the rational ideal took hold, scholars and monks tried to impose some kind of system on the somewhat chaotic traditions they had inherited. The text of the Vulgate had been corrupted by the compounded errors of generations of monk-copyists.[9] The copyists had usually prefaced each book of the Bible with a commentary by Jerome or one of the other fathers. By the eleventh century, the most popular books were accompanied by several prefaces, which often contradicted each other. So a group of French scholars put together a standard commentary, known as the *Glossa Ordinaria*. Anselm of Laon (d. 1117), who began this work, wanted to provide teachers with a clear explanation of each verse of the Bible. If the reader encountered a problem, he could look at the notes written in the margins or between the lines of the manuscript, which provided him with explanations by Jerome, Augustine or Gregory. The *Glossa* was little more than a crib: the notes were necessarily brief and basic and there was no space for an elaborate exploration of the finer points. But it provided scholars with a rudimentary knowledge on which they could build. Anselm completed the commentary on the most popular books: Psalms, Paul's letters and John's gospel. He also collected *Sententiae*, anthologies of the fathers' 'opinions', arranged according to topic. Anselm's brother Ralph tackled Matthew's gospel, while his students, Gilbert of Poitiers and Peter Lombard, completed the project.

In the classroom, the master would read the glossed text to his students, who would then have the opportunity to ask questions and engage in further discussion: later, as the number of queries accumulated, a separate session was devoted to *quaestiones*. Discussion became more intense, as students began to experiment with Aristotelian logic and dialectic. Others applied the new science of grammar to the biblical text: why did the Latin of the Vulgate break basic rules of classical Latin? Gradually a rift developed between the monasteries and the cathedral schools. In the monasteries, masters concentrated on *lectio divina*: they wanted their novices to read the Bible meditatively and develop their spirituality. But in the cathedral schools, masters were more interested in the new learning and objective biblical criticism.

There was also a dawning interest in the literal sense of the Bible, which had been initiated by the rabbis of northern France. *Rabbi Sh*lomo *Yi*tzhak, known as RaSHI (1040–1105), had no interest in Aristotle. His passion was for philology, and he was concerned above all with the plain meaning of scripture.[10] He wrote a running commentary on the text of the Hebrew Bible, concentrating on individual words in a way that threw new light on the text. He noticed, for example, that *bereshit,* the first word of the first chapter of Genesis, could mean 'In the beginning *of'*, so the sentence should read: 'In the beginning of God's creation of heaven and earth, the earth was a formless void (*tohu bohu*).' This implied that the raw materials of the earth were already in existence when God started his creative work, and that he simply brought order to *tohu bohu*. Rashi also noted that in one midrashic interpretation, *bereshit* was understood to mean: 'because of the beginning' and that the Bible called both Israel and the Torah 'the beginning'. Did this mean that God had created the world in order to give Israel the Torah? Rashi's method forced the reader to look at the text closely before he imposed his own midrash upon it: his commentary would become one of the most important and influential guides to the Pentateuch.

Rashi saw his literal exegesis as complementary to traditional midrash but his successors were more radical. Joseph Kara (d. 1130) argued that anybody who did not concentrate on the plain sense was like a drowning man clutching at a straw. Rashi's grandson, **R. Sh**emuel **b**en **M**eir, known as the RaSHBaM (d. 1174), was more tolerant of midrash, but still favoured a more rational explanation. Rashi's method of literal exposition was proceeding at a feverish place in his circle, he said, 'new examples come up every day'.[11] Joseph Bekhor Shor, a pupil of the Rashbam, always tried to find a natural explanation for the more fantastic biblical stories.[12] There was no mystery about the death of Lot's wife, for example; she had simply been enveloped by the volcanic lava that destroyed Sodom and Gomorrah. Joseph had dreamed of future greatness simply because he was an ambitious young man, and had needed no help from God when he interpreted Pharaoh's dreams: anybody with a modicum of intelligence could have done the same.

Despite the Crusades, relations between Jews and Christians in France were still reasonably good, and scholars from the Abbey of St Victor on the left bank of the Seine, who were also becoming interested in the literal sense, began to consult the local rabbis and learn Hebrew. The Victorines tried to combine traditional *lectio divina* with the more academic scholarship of the cathedral schools. Hugh of St Victor, who taught at the abbey until his death in 1141, was a committed contemplative but did not find that this conflicted with his rational powers. Aristotelian grammar, logic, dialectic and natural science could help students to understand the Bible. Hugh was convinced that the study of history was the foundation of what he called 'the house of exposition'. Moses and the evangelists had all been historians, and students should start their study of the Bible with the historical books. Without a correct literal understanding of the Bible, allegory was doomed to failure. Students must not run before they could walk. They must begin by examining the Vulgate's syntax and vocabulary in order to discover what the biblical author had intended to say. 'We must not read our own meaning (*sententia*) into scripture, but must make the sentence of scripture ours.'[13]

Andrew of St Victor (1110–75), Hugh's gifted pupil, was the first Christian scholar to attempt a wholly literal interpretation of the Hebrew Bible.[14] He had nothing against allegory, but it did not interest him. He learned a great deal from the rabbis and found that scripture read 'more clearly in the Hebrew'.[15] His academic commitment to the literal never failed, even when the rabbis discounted interpretations that were essential to the Christian understanding of the Old Testament. After discovering that the Hebrew text did not support the traditional Christian interpretation, which saw the verse as a prophecy of Jesus's virgin birth, Andrew accepted Rashi's exegesis of Isaiah's oracle: 'Behold a young woman (*almah*) shall conceive and bear a child.' (Rashi thought that Isaiah had referred to his own wife.) In his exposition of the Servant Songs, Andrew did not even bother to mention Christ, but accepted the Jewish view that the servant symbolized the people of Israel. Instead of seeing the figure in Ezekiel's vision that was 'like a son of man' as a prediction of Jesus, Andrew simply wanted to know what this imagery had meant to Ezekiel and the exiles. He decided that because the 'son of man' was the only human element in a very weird and frightening theophany, the exiles would have been reassured that God was interested in their own predicament.

Andrew and his Jewish friends had taken a first step towards modern historical criticism of the Bible, but Andrew, a morose, uncharismatic man, had few followers in his own day. During the twelfth century, the men of the hour were the philosophers, who were beginning to develop a new kind of rationalistic theology in which they used reason to sustain their faith and clarify what had hitherto been deemed ineffable. Anselm of Bec (1033–1109), who would become Archbishop of Canterbury in 1189, thought that it was possible to prove anything.[16] As a monk, *lectio divina* was essential to his spiritual life but he wrote no commentaries on scripture and seldom quoted the Bible in his theological writing. But religion, like poetry or art, requires an intuitive rather than a purely rational approach and Anselm's theology shows its limitations. In his treatise *Cur Deus Homo,* for example, he attempted a logical account of the Incarnation that bore no relation at all to scripture: any biblical quotations simply carried the argument along. The Greek Orthodox had also produced a theology that was independent of scripture, but Anselm's forensic explanation of the incarnation lacks the spiritual insight of Maximus. He argued that the sin of Adam required atonement; because God was just, a human being must atone; but because the fault was so serious, only God could make reparation. Therefore God had to become man.[17] Anselm makes God weigh the matter up as if he were a mere human being. It is not surprising that at this time the Greek Orthodox feared that Latin theology was too anthropomorphic. Anselm's theory of the atonement, however, became normative in the West, while the Greek Orthodox continued to prefer Maximus's interpretation.

The French philosopher Peter Abelard (1079–1142) developed a different account of the redemption, which again owed little to scripture but came closer to the spirit of the fathers.[18] Like some of the rabbis, he believed that God suffered with his creatures and argued that the crucifixion showed us one moment in the eternal pathos of God. When we contemplate the flayed figure of Jesus we are moved to pity, and it is the act of compassion that saves us – not Jesus's sacrificial death. Abelard was the intellectual star of his generation; students flocked to his lectures from all over Europe. Like Anselm, he rarely quoted scripture and raised questions without appearing to offer solutions. In fact, Abelard was more interested in philosophy and his theology was rather conservative. But his iconoclastic, aggressive manner made it sound as though he was arrogantly pitting his human reason against the mystery of God and this brought him into head-long collision with one of the most powerful churchmen of the day.

Bernard (1090–1153), abbot of the Cistercian monastery of Clairvaux in Burgundy (1090–1153), dominated Pope Eugene II and King Louis VII of France and was as charismatic in his own way as Abelard. Scores of young men had followed him into the new Cistercian Order, a reformed branch of Benedictine monasticism. He accused Abelard of 'attempting to bring the Christian faith to naught because he supposes that human reason can comprehend all that is God'.[19] Quoting Paul's hymn to charity, he claimed that Abelard 'sees nothing as an enigma, nothing as in a mirror, but looks on everything face to face'.[20] In 1141, Bernard summoned Abelard, who by this time was suffering from Parkinson's disease, to the Council of Sens, and attacked him so ferociously that he collapsed and died the following year.

Even though Bernard could not be described as a charita-ble man, his exegesis and spirituality were based on the love of God. His most famous work was his exposition of the Song of Songs, eighty-six sermons delivered to the monks of Clairvaux between 1135 and 1153, which mark the apogee of *lectio divina*.[21] 'It is desire that drives me,' he insisted, 'not reason.'[22] In the incarnation of the Logos, God had descended to our level so that we could ascend to the divine. In the Song, God shows us that we make this ascent in three stages. When the bride cried: 'The king has brought me into his chambers', this referred allegorically to the senses of scripture. There were three 'chambers': the garden, the storeroom and the bedchamber. 'Let the garden ... represent the plain, unadorned sense of scripture,' Bernard suggested, 'the storeroom its moral sense, and the bedroom the mystery of divine contemplation.'[23] We began by reading the Bible as a simple story of creation and redemption but we must then progress to the storerooms, the moral sense which teaches us to modify our behaviour. In the 'storerooms', the soul was refined by the practice of charity. She became 'pleasant and temperate' to others; 'an earnest zeal for the works of love' leads her 'to forgetfulness of self and indifference of self-interest'.[24] When the bride looked for her groom 'by night' in her bedchamber, she showed us the importance of modesty. It was better to avoid ostentatious piety and pray in the privacy of one's cell because 'if we pray when others are present, their approbation may rob our prayer of . . . its effect'.[25] There would be no sudden illumination; by dint of regular *lectio divina* and the practice of charity, monks would make steady, unobtrusive and incremental progress.

Eventually, the soul might be permitted to enter the groom's 'bedchamber' and attain the vision of God, though Bernard admitted that he had only had momentary intimations of this final state. The Song could not be understood rationally. Its meaning was a 'mystery' that was 'hidden' in the text[26] – an overwhelming transcendence that would always elude our conceptual grasp.[27] Unlike the rationalists, Bernard constantly quoted scripture: his commentary on the Song has 5,526 quotations ranging from Genesis to Revelation.[28] And instead of seeing the Bible as an objective academic challenge, Bible study was a personal, spiritual discipline. 'Today the text we are to study is the book of our experience,' he told his monks, 'you must therefore turn your affections inwards, each one must take note of his own particular awareness of things.'[29]

During the thirteenth century, the new Order of Preachers, founded by the Spaniard Dominic Guzman (1170–1221), managed to marry the old *lectio divina* with the rationalism of the schools. The Dominicans were the intellectual heirs of both the philosophers and the scholars of St Victor.[30] They did not abandon spiritual exegesis, but gave more serious attention to the literal sense and they were systematic academics, whose aim was to adapt Aristotelian philosophy to Christianity. The fathers had compared allegory to the 'soul' or 'spirit' of scripture, but for Aristotle the soul was inseparable from the body; it defined and shaped our physical development and relied on the evidence of the senses. So for the Dominicans, the 'spirit' of scripture was not hidden beneath the text but found within the literal and historical meaning.

In his *Summa Theologica*, Thomas Aquinas (1225–74) reconciled the older spiritual method with the new philosophy. According to Aristotle, God was the 'First Mover' who had set the cosmos in motion; Thomas extended this idea, pointing out that God was also the 'First Author' of the Bible. The human authors who made the divine Word an earthly reality, were God's instruments. He had set them in motion too, but they were solely responsible for the style and literary form of the text. Instead of disregarding the plain sense, the exegete could discover a great deal about the divine message by studying the work of these writers in a methodical and scientific way. Like the twelfth-century rationalists, the scholastics, as these schoolmen were called, felt sufficiently confident of their reasoning powers to liberate their theological speculation from exegesis. But Aquinas himself took a more conservative position. God was not like a human author, who could merely convey his message in words. God also had the power to orchestrate historical events in order to reveal the truths of salvation. The literal sense of the 'Old Testament' could be found in the words used by the human authors, but its spiritual meaning could be discerned in the events of the Exodus and the institution of the Paschal Lamb, which God had used to prefigure the redemptive work of Christ.

Meanwhile, Jews who lived in the Islamic world had also tried to apply the rationalism of classical Greek culture to the Bible and found it difficult to square the revealed God of scripture with the deity described by Aristotle and Plato, which was timeless and impassable, took no notice of mundane events, had not created the cosmos – which, like God itself, was eternal, – and would not judge it at the end of time. Jewish philosophers insisted that the most anthropomorphic passages of the Bible must be interpreted allegorically. They could not accept a God who walked and talked, sat on a throne, was jealous, became angry and changed his mind.

They were particularly worried by the idea that God had created the world *ex nihilo,* 'out of nothing'. Saadia ibn Joseph (882–942) insisted that because God lay beyond all speech and concepts, one could only say that he existed.[31] Saadia felt obliged to accept creation *ex nihilo* because it was now deeply rooted in Jewish tradition, but argued that if you accepted a divine Creator, you could logically make other statements about him. Because the world he made was intelligently planned and had life and energy, it followed that the Creator must have the attributes of Wisdom, Life and Power. In an attempt to explain rationally how the material world had derived from a wholly spiritual God, other Jewish philosophers imagined creation as an evolutionary process of ten emanations from God that became progressively more material. Each emanation had generated one of the spheres of Ptolemy's universe: the fixed stars, then Saturn, Jupiter, Mars, Sun, Venus, Mercury and finally the Moon. Our sublunary world, however, had developed in the opposite direction: it had begun as inanimate matter, and progressed through plants and animals to humans, whose souls participated in the divine reason, but whose bodies derived from the earth.

Maimonides (1135–1204) tried to reassure Jews who were perturbed by the conflict between Aristotle and the Bible.[32] In *The Guide of the Perplexed,* he argued that since truth was one, scripture must be in harmony with reason. He had no problem with creation *ex nihilo,* because he did not find Aristotle's argument for the eternity of matter convincing. Maimonides agreed that anthropomorphic descriptions of

God in the Bible must not be interpreted literally, and tried to find rational reasons for some of the more irrational biblical laws. But he knew that religious experience transcended reason. The intuitive knowledge of the prophets, which was accompanied by tremulous awe, was of a higher order than the knowledge we acquire by our rational powers.

Abraham ibn Ezra (1089–1164), one of the great poets and philosophers of Spain, was another medieval forerunner of modern historical criticism.[33] Exegesis must give priority to the literal sense; while legend (*aggadah*) had spiritual value, it must not be confused with fact. He found discrepancies in the biblical text: Isaiah of Jerusalem could not have composed the second half of the book attributed to him because it referred to events that occurred long after his death. He also cautiously and elliptically hinted that Moses was not the author of the entire Pentateuch: he could not, for example, have described his own death and since Moses never entered the Promised Land, how could he have written the opening verses of Deuteronomy, which positioned the site of his final address '*on the other side* of the Jordan river'.[34] This must have been written by somebody who lived in the land of Israel after its conquest by Joshua.

Philosophical rationalism inspired a mystical backlash in Spain and Provence. Nahmanides (1194–1270), an outstanding Talmudist and an influential member of the Jewish community in Castile, believed that Maimonides's rationalistic exegesis did not do justice to the Torah.[35] He wrote an influential commentary on the Pentateuch, which rigorously elucidated its plain meaning, but in the course of his study he had encountered a numinous significance that entirely transcended the literal sense. In the late thirteenth century, a small group of mystics in Castile took this further. Their study of scripture had not merely introduced them to a deeper level of the text but to the inner life of God. They called their esoteric discipline *kaballah* ('inherited tradition'), because it had passed from teacher to pupil. Unlike Nahmanides, these kabbalists – Abraham Abulafia, Moses de Leon, Isaac de Latif and Joseph Gikatilla – had no expertise in Talmud but they had all been interested in philosophy before deciding that its attenuated God was empty of religious content.[36] Instead, they explored a hermeneutic method, which they may have learned from their Christian neighbours.

Their mystical midrash was based on the Talmudic story of the four sages who entered the 'orchard' (*pardes*).[37] Because R. Akiba alone had survived this perilous spiritual experiment, the kabbalists claimed that their exegesis, which they called *pardes*, derived from him and was the only safe form of mysticism.[38] They found that their method of studying Torah carried them daily to 'paradise'.[39] *PaRDeS* was an anagram for the four senses of scripture: *peshat*, the literal sense; *remez*, allegory; *darash*, the moral, homiletic sense; and *sod*, the mystical culmination of Torah study. *Pardes* was a rite of passage which began with *peshat* and rose to the ineffable heights of *sod*. As the original *Pardes* story made clear, this journey was not for everybody but only for a properly initiated elite. The first three forms of midrash – *pardes, remez* and *darash* – had all been used by Philo, the rabbis and the philosophers, so the kabbalists implied that their new spirituality was in line with tradition, while at the same time suggesting that their own speciality – *sod* – was its fulfilment. Their experience probably seemed so self-evidently Jewish that they may have been entirely unaware of any conflict with the mainstream.[40]

The kabbalists created a powerful synthesis.[41] They revived the mythical element in ancient Israelite tradition, which the rabbis and the philosophers had downplayed or tried to eradicate. They were also inspired by the Gnostic tradition, which had surfaced again in various mystical movements in the Muslim world with which they were probably familiar. Finally, the kabbalists drew upon the ten emanations envisaged by the philosophers in which every element in the chain of being was connected. Revelation no longer had to bridge an ontological abyss, but occurred continuously within each individual, and creation had not happened once in the distant past but was a timeless event in which we could all participate.

Kabbalah was probably more scripturally based than any other form of mysticism. Its 'bible' was the *Zohar*, 'The Book of Splendour', which was probably the work of Moses of Leon, but took the form of a second-century novel about the mystical revolutionary R. Simeon ben Yohai, who wandered around Palestine, meeting with his companions to discuss the Torah, which, as a result of their exegesis 'opened' directly on to the divine world. By studying scripture, the kabbalist descended into the text and into himself, layer by layer, and found that he was at the same time ascending to the source of all being. The kabbalists agreed with the philosophers that words could not convey the incomprehensible transcendence of God, but believed that even though God could not be known, he could be experienced in the symbols of scripture. They were convinced that God had left hints about his inner life in the biblical text. In their mystical exegesis, kabbalists built on these, creating mythical stories and dramas which broke the *peshat* text open. Their mystical interpretation found an esoteric meaning in every single verse of scripture that described the mysteries of the divine being.

The kabbalists called the innermost essence of God *En Sof* ('without end'). En Sof was incomprehensible and was not even mentioned in the Bible or the Talmud. It was not a personality, so it was more accurate to call En Sof 'it' rather than 'he'. But the incomprehensible En Sof had revealed itself to humanity at the same time as it had created the world. It had emerged from its impenetrable concealment like a massive tree sprouting a trunk, branches and leaves. The divine life spread in ever wider spheres until it filled everything that is, while En Sof itself remained hidden. It was the root of the tree, source of its stability and vitality but forever invisible. What the philosophers called God's attributes – his Power, Wisdom, Beauty and Intelligence – thus became manifest, but the kabbalists transformed these abstract qualities into dynamic potencies. Like the philosophers' ten emanations, they revealed aspects of the unfathomable En Sof and became more concrete and more comprehensible as they approached the material world. The kabbalists called these ten potencies, the inner dimensions of the divine psyche, *sefiroth* ('numerations'). Each *sefirah* had its own symbolic name and represented a stage in En Sof's unfolding revelation, but they were not 'segments' of God but together formed one great Name not known to human beings. Each *sefirah* encapsulated the entire mystery of God under a particular heading.

The kabbalists interpreted the first chapter of Genesis as a parable of the emergence of the *sefiroth*. *Bereshit* ('the beginning'), the very first word of the Bible, revealed the moment when Kether Elyon (the 'Supreme Crown'), the first *sefirah*, broke through the unfathomable mystery of En Sof as a 'dark flame'. As yet nothing had been revealed, because there was nothing about this first *sefirah* that human beings could understand. 'It could not be recognized at all,' the *Zohar* explained, 'until a hidden, supernal point shone forth under the impact of the final breaking through.' This 'point' was the second *sefirah*, Hokhmah ('Wisdom'), the divine masterplan of creation that represented the limit of human understanding. 'Beyond this nothing can be known,' the *Zohar* continued. 'Therefore is it called *reshit*, beginning.' Next Hokhmah penetrated the third *sefirah*, Binah, the divine Intelligence whose 'unknowable radiance' was of a slightly 'lesser subtility and translucency than the primal point'. After this 'beginning', the seven 'lower' *sefiroth* followed, one after the other, 'extension upon extension, each constituting a vesture to the one before, as a membrane to the brain'.[42]

This *mythos* was designed to throw light on the indescribable process in which the unknowable God made itself known to human beings and brought the cosmos into being. There was always a strong sexual element in Kabbalah. Binah was also known as the Supernal Mother, whose womb, once penetrated by the 'primal point' gave birth to the lower *sefiroth*, which reflected aspects of the divine that were more accessible to human beings and, in the first chapter of Genesis, were symbolized by the seven days of creation. Human beings could discern these 'powers' of God in the world and in scripture: *Rakhamin* (Compassion) – also called *Tifereth* (Grace); *Din* (Stern Judgement) which should always be balanced by *Hesed* (Mercy); *Netsakh* (Patience), *Hod* (Majesty), *Yesod* (Stability) and finally *Malkuth* (Kingdom), also called *Shekhinah*, whom the kabbalists imagined as a female personality.

The *sefiroth* should not be seen as a ladder linking the Godhead with humanity. They informed our world and enclosed it, so that we were embraced and pervaded by this dynamic, multifarious divine activity. Because they were also present in the human psyche, the *sefiroth* also represented the stages of human consciousness through which the mystic ascended to the Godhead. The emanation of the *sefiroth* depicted the process whereby impersonal En Sof became the personal God of the Bible. As the three 'higher' *sefiroth* emerged, the 'it' of En Sof became 'he'. In the next six *sefiroth*, 'he' became 'you', a reality to whom human beings could relate. In the Shekhinah, the divine presence in our world, 'you' became 'I', because God was also present in each individual. In the course of the *pardes* exegesis, kabbalists gradually became aware of the divine presence in the deepest recesses of the psyche.

Kabbalists took the doctrine of creation *ex nihilo* very seriously, but turned it on its head. This 'nothing' could not be outside the Godhead which constituted the whole of reality. The abyss was within En Sof and was – somehow – overcome in creation. The kabbalists also called the first *sefirah*, the dark flame that started the revelatory/creative process, 'Nothing', because it did not correspond to any reality that we could conceive. Creation was truly *ex nihilo*. The kabbalists noticed that there were two accounts of the creation of Adam. In Chapter One of Genesis, God created *adam* ('humankind'), which, the mystics decided, was primordial humanity (*adam kadmon*), the climax of the creative process, made in God's image: the divine became manifest in the archetypal human being, the *sefiroth* forming his body and limbs.

In Chapter Two, when God created Adam from dust, he brought earthbound humanity as we know it into being. This mundane Adam was supposed to contemplate the entire mystery of the Godhead on the first Sabbath, but he took the easier option and meditated only on the Shekhinah, the nearest and most accessible *sefirah*. This – not the act of disobedience – was the reason for Adam's fall, which shattered the unity of the divine world, separating the Tree of Life from the Tree of Knowledge, and tearing the fruit from the tree to which it was supposed to cling. The Shekhinah was ripped away from the tree of *sefiroth* and has remained in exile from the divine world.

The kabbalists, however, had the power to reunite the Shekhinah with the rest of the *sefiroth* by performing the task assigned to Adam. In their *pardes* exegesis, they could contemplate the entire divine mystery in all its complexity and the whole of scripture became a coded reference to the interaction of the *sefiroth*. Abraham's binding of Isaac showed how *Din* and *Hesed* – Judgement and Mercy – must act together, each tempering the other. The story of Joseph, who resisted sexual temptation and rose to power as the provider of food in Egypt, showed that in the divine psyche, restraint (*Din*) was always balanced by grace (*Tifereth*). The Song of Songs symbolized the yearning for harmony and unity that throbs through all levels of existence.[43]

Just as En Sof devolved, exteriorized and constricted itself in the progressive emanation of the *sefiroth*, so too the Godhead expressed itself in the limited human words of the Torah. The kabbalists learned to explore the different levels of the Bible in the same way as they contemplated the layers of divinity. In the *Zohar*, the Torah was compared to a beautiful maiden, secluded in a palace, who had a secret lover. She knew that he was forever walking up and down the street outside her chamber in the hope of seeing her, so she opened a door to show him her face – just for a second – and then withdrew. Only her lover understood the significance of her fleeting appearance. This was the way Torah revealed herself to a mystic. First she gave him a sign; next she spoke with him 'from behind the veil which she has hung before her words, so that they suit the manner of understanding in order that he may progress gradually'.[44] Very slowly, the kabbalist progressed from one level of scripture to another – through the moral reflections of *darash* and the riddles and allegories of *remez*. The veils became thinner and less opaque, until at last, as he reached the culminating insight of *sod*, the beloved 'stands disclosed, face to face with him, and holds converse with him concerning all of her secret mysteries, and all the secret ways which have been hidden in her heart from immemorial time'.[45] The mystic must strip away the surface meaning of the Bible – all the stories, laws and genealogies – as a lover unveils his beloved and learns to recognize not only her body but her soul.

> People without understanding see only the narratives, the
> garment; those somewhat more penetrating see also the
> body. But the truly wise, those who serve the most high King
> and stand on Mount Sinai, pierce all the way through to the
> soul, to the true Torah, which is the root principle of all.[46]

Anybody who simply read the Bible literally 'as a book presenting narratives and everyday matters', had missed the point. There was nothing special about the literal Torah: anybody could write a better book – even the gentiles had produced greater works.[47]

Kabbalists combined their mystical meditations on scripture with vigils, fasts and constant self-examination. They had to live together in fellowship, repressing selfishness and egotism because anger entered into the psyche like an evil spirit and shattered the divine harmony of his soul. It was impossible to experience the unity of the *sefiroth* in such a divided state.[48] The love of friends was fundamental to the *ekstasis* of Kabbalah. In the *Zohar*, one of the signs of a successful piece of exegesis is the cry of joy uttered by the interpreter's colleagues when they have heard what they experience as divine truth or when the exegetes kiss one another before they resume their mystical journey.

Kabbalists believed that the Torah was flawed, incomplete and presented relative rather than absolute truth. Some thought that two whole books were missing from our Torah or that our alphabet lacked one of its letters, so that language itself had been dislocated. Others developed a version of the myth of the Seven Ages of Man, each of which lasted seven thousand years and was ruled by one of the seven 'lower' *sefiroth*. The First Age had been governed by *Rekhamim/ Tifereth* (Grace and Compassion). All creatures had lived together in harmony and their Torah never spoke of the serpent, the Tree of Knowledge or death because these realities did not exist. But we were living in the Second Age of *Din*, the Stern Judgement that reflects the darker side of God, so our Torah spoke of constant conflict between good and evil, was full of laws, judgements and prohibitions, and its stories were often violent and cruel. But in the Third Cycle, under *Hesed* (Mercy), the Torah would be good and holy once more.

Kabbalah began as a tiny, esoteric movement, but it would

become a mass movement in Judaism and its mythology would influence even those who had no mystical talent. As their history became more tragic, Jews found the dynamic God of the mystics more sympathetic than the remote God of the philosophers, and felt increasingly that the plain sense of scripture was unsatisfactory and could shed no light without the interpretation of an inherited tradition (*kaballah*).

In Europe, however, Christians were coming to the opposite conclusion. The Franciscan scholar Nicholas of Lyre (1270–1340) combined the older methods of interpretation with the new insights of the scholastics. He defended the use of the three 'spiritual senses' of the Bible, but preferred the plain sense of historical exegesis. He had taught himself Hebrew, was familiar with the work of Rashi and proficient in Aristotelian philosophy. His *Postillae*, a literal exegesis of the whole of the Bible, became a standard textbook.

Other developments revealed a growing dissatisfaction with the traditional interpretation. Roger Bacon (1214–92), an English Franciscan, had no patience with scholastic theology and urged scholars to study the Bible in the original languages. Marsilio of Padua (1275–1342) was incensed by the growing power of the established Church and challenged papal claims to be the supreme guardian of the Bible. Henceforth all reformers would link their dislike of popes, cardinals and bishops with a rejection of their claim to be the arbiters of exegesis. John Wycliffe (1329–84), an Oxford academic, became enraged by the corruption of the Church and argued that the Bible should be translated into the vernacular, so that the common people did not have to rely on the priesthood but could read the Word of God for themselves. 'Crist seith that the gospel shold be prechid in al the world,' he insisted: 'Holi writ is the scripture of pupilis for it is maad that alle pupilis shulden knowe it.'[49] And William Tyndale (c. 1494–1536), who translated the Bible into English, raised the same issues: should the authority of the Church be greater than that of the gospel or should the gospel be elevated above the Church? By the sixteenth century this discontent would erupt in a biblical revolution that urged the faithful to rely on scripture alone.

CHAPTER 7

Sola Scriptura

By the sixteenth century, a complex process was under way in Europe that would irrevocably change the way Western people experienced the world. Inventions and innovations, none of which seemed momentous at the time, were occurring simultaneously in many different fields, but their cumulative effect would be decisive. The Iberian explorers had discovered a new world, astronomers were opening up the heavens, and a new technical efficiency was giving Europeans more control over their environment than ever before. A pragmatic, scientific spirit was very slowly beginning to undermine medieval sensibility. A series of catastrophes had left people feeling helpless and anxious. During the fourteenth and fifteenth centuries, the Black Death had killed a third of the population of Europe, the Ottoman Turks had conquered Christian Byzantium in 1453, and the papal scandals of the Avignon captivity and the Great Schism, when as many as three pontiffs had claimed the See of Peter, had alienated many from the established Church. People would soon find it impossible to be religious in the traditional way and this would affect their reading of the Bible.

The West was about to create a civilization that had no precedent in world history, but on the threshold of this new era, many wanted to return *ad fontes*, 'to the wellsprings' of their culture, to the classical world of Greece and Rome as well as to early Christianity. The philosophers and humanists of the Renaissance were highly critical of much medieval piety, especially of scholastic theology, which they found too dry and abstract, and wanted to go back to the Bible and the fathers of the Church.[1] Christianity, they believed, should be an experience rather than a body of doctrines. But the humanists had also imbibed the scientific spirit of the age and began to study the biblical text more objectively. The Renaissance is usually remembered for its rediscovery of classical paganism, but it also had a strong biblical character, which was in part inspired by a wholly new enthusiasm for the study of Greek. The humanists had started to read Paul as well as Homer in the original language and found the experience electrifying.

Very few Western people had been familiar with Greek in the Middle Ages, but Byzantine refugees from the Ottoman wars had fled to Europe in the fifteenth century and hired themselves out as tutors. In 1519, the Dutch humanist Desiderius Erasmus (1466–1536) published the Greek text of the New Testament, which he had translated into an elegant Ciceronian Latin that was very different from the Vulgate. The humanists valued style and rhetoric above all else. They were also concerned about the errors that had accumulated in the text over the centuries, and wanted to liberate the Bible from the accretions and baggage of the past.

The fact that the invention of the printing press made it possible for Erasmus to publish his translation was of immense importance. Anybody who knew Greek could now immediately read the gospels in the original. Other scholars could review the translation more quickly than ever before and suggest improvements. Erasmus profited from these suggestions and published several more editions of his New Testament before he died. He had been greatly influenced by the Italian humanist Lorenzo Valla (1405–57), who had produced an anthology of the main New Testament 'proof texts' used to support Church doctrine; but he had placed the Vulgate version alongside the original Greek, pointing out that these texts did not always 'prove' what they claimed because the Vulgate was so inaccurate. But Valla's *Collatio* had appeared only in manuscript; Erasmus had it printed and immediately it reached a far wider audience.

It would now be de rigueur to read the Bible in the original languages, and this scholarly requirement encouraged a more detached, historical attitude towards biblical antiquity. Hitherto, exegetes had viewed the Bible as a single work rather than a collection of diverse books. They may never have physically seen the scriptures in a single volume, but the practice of linking disparate texts together had encouraged them to downplay differences of vision and period. Now the humanists began to study the biblical authors as individuals, noting their special talents and idiosyncracies. They were especially drawn to Paul, whose style took on new immediacy in the original *koine* Greek. His passionate quest for salvation seemed a salutary antidote to scholastic rationalism. Unlike humanists today, they were not sceptical about religion, but had become ardent Pauline Christians.

They could particularly empathize with Paul's acute sense of sin. A period of wrenching social change is often characterized by anxiety. People feel lost and impotent; living *in medias res*, they cannot see the direction their society is taking but experience its subterranean transformation in incoherent, sporadic ways. Alongside the enthralling achievements of the early sixteenth century, there was widespread distress. The Protestant reformers Huldrych Zwingli (1484–1531) and John Calvin (1509–64) both felt a sense of acute failure and powerlessness before they found a new religious solution. The Catholic reformer Ignatius Loyola (1491–1556), founder of the Society of Jesus, wept so copiously during Mass that doctors warned him that he could easily lose his sight. And the Italian poet Francesco Petrarch (1304–74) was equally lacrymose: 'With what floods of tears I have sought to wash away my stains so that I can scarce speak of it without weeping, yet hitherto all is vain. God indeed is the best: and I am the worst.'[2]

Few experienced the angst of the age more painfully than a young monk in the Augustinian monastery of Erfurt in Germany:

> Although I lived a blameless life as a monk, I felt I was a
> sinner with an uneasy conscience before God. I also could
> not believe that I had pleased him with my works. Far from

loving that righteous God who punished sinners, I actually
loathed him . . . My conscience would not give me certainty,
but I always doubted and said, 'You did not do that right.
You weren't contrite enough. You left that out of your confession.'[3]

Martin Luther (1483–1546) had been educated in the scholastic philosophy of William of Ockham (c.1287–1347), who had
urged Christians to try to merit God's grace by their good
works.[4] But Luther fell prey to agonizing depression and none
of the traditional pieties could assuage his extreme terror of
death.[5] To escape his fears, he plunged into a frenzy of reform-
ing activity and was especially incensed by the papal policy of
selling indulgences to swell the coffers of the Church.

Luther was rescued from his existential distress by exegesis. The first time he saw a copy of the whole Bible he had
been astonished that it contained so many more writings
than he had realized.[6] He felt that he was seeing it for the
first time.[7] Luther became Professor of Scripture and
Philosophy at the University of Wittenberg and during the
lectures that he gave on the Psalms and Paul's epistles to the
Romans and Galatians (1513–18) he experienced a spiritual
breakthrough that enabled him to break free from his
Ockhamite prison.[8]

The lectures on the Psalms began conventionally enough –
Luther expounded the text verse by verse according to each
of the four senses in turn. But there were two significant
changes. First, Luther asked the university printer Johannes

Gutenberg to produce a custom-made Psalter for him with an ample margin and wide spaces for his own annotations. He had, as it were, wiped the sacred page clean, erasing the traditional gloss in order to start again. Second, he introduced an entirely novel definition of the literal sense. By 'literal' he did not mean the original intention of the author; he meant 'christological'. 'In the whole of scripture,' he claimed, 'there is nothing else but Christ, either in plain words or involved words.'[9] 'Take Christ from the scriptures,' he asked on another occasion, 'and what else will you find there?'[10]

The quick answer to that question is that you will find a great deal. As he grew more familiar with the whole of the Bible, Luther became aware that much of the Bible had very little to do with Christ. Even in the New Testament, there were books that were more Christ-centred than others. This compelled him over the years to invent a new hermeneutics. Luther's solution was to create a 'canon within the canon'. A man of his time, he was especially drawn to Paul, finding his letters describing the Christian experience of the risen Christ far more valuable than the synoptic gospels which were merely about Christ. For the same reason, he privileged John's gospel and the First Epistle of Peter but relegated Hebrews, the epistles of James and Jude, and Revelation to the periphery. He applied the same criteria to the 'Old Testament': he discarded the Apocrypha and had little time for the historical books and the legal sections of the Pentateuch. But he admitted Genesis to his personal canon because Paul quoted it, together with the prophets, who had foreseen the coming of Christ, and the Psalms, which had helped him to understand Paul.[11]

During his lectures on the Psalter, Luther began to ponder the meaning of the word 'righteousness' (Hebrew: *tseddeq*; Latin: *justitia*). Christians had traditionally read the psalms of the royal House of David as direct prophecies of Jesus. Thus, for example, the verse 'God, give your justice to the king, your own righteousness to the royal son'[12] referred to Christ. But Luther's emphasis was different. Understood *literally* – that is, for Luther, christologically – the plea 'In your righteousness, deliver me'[13] was a prayer uttered by Jesus to his Father. But according to the *moral* sense, the words referred to the deliverance of the individual, on whom Christ had bestowed his own righteousness.[14] Luther was gradually moving towards the idea that virtue was not a prerequisite for God's grace but a divine gift, relating the text directly to his own spiritual dilemma: God gave his own justice and righteousness to human beings.

Not long after these lectures on the Psalms, Luther achieved an exegetical breakthrough in his study in the monastery tower. He had been struggling to understand Paul's description of the gospel as a revelation of the righteousness of God: 'In[the gospel], the righteousness of God is revealed, as it is written, *The righteous man shall live through faith.*'[15] His Ockhamite teachers had taught him to understand 'the righteousness (*justitia*) of God' as the divine justice that condemns the sinner. How could this be 'good news'? And what did God's justice have to do with faith? Luther meditated on the text day and night until light dawned: the 'righteousness of God' in the gospel was the divine mercy which clothes the sinner in God's own goodness. All the sinner needed was faith. Immediately Luther's anxieties fell away. 'I felt as though I had been born again, and as though I had entered through open gates into paradise itself.'[16]

After this, the whole of scripture took on new meaning. During Luther's lectures on Romans, there was a marked change. His approach was more informal and less tied to medieval custom. He no longer bothered with the four senses but concentrated on his christological interpretation of the Bible and was openly critical of the scholastics. There was no need for fear. As long as he had 'faith', the sinner could say 'Christ has done enough for me. He is just. He is my defence. He has died for me. He has made his righteousness my righteousness.'[17] But by 'faith' Luther did not mean 'belief' but an attitude of trust and self-abandonment: 'Faith does not require information, knowledge and certainty, but a free surrender and a joyful bet on [God's] unfelt, untried and unknown goodness.'[18]

In his lectures on Galatians, Luther expanded on 'justification by faith'. In this epistle, Paul had attacked those Jewish-Christians who wanted gentile converts to observe the entire law of Moses, when, according to Paul, all that was necessary was trust (*pistis*) in Christ. Luther had begun to develop a dichotomy between Law and Gospel.[19] Law was the means God used to reveal his wrath and the sinfulness of human beings. We encountered the Law in the inflexible commands that we find in scripture, such as the Ten Commandments. The sinner quails before these demands, which he finds impossible to fulfil. But the Gospel revealed the divine mercy that saves us. 'Law' was not confined to the Mosaic law: there was 'Gospel' in the Old Testament (when the prophets looked forward to Christ) and plenty of daunting commandments in the New. Both Law and Gospel came from God, but only the Gospel could save us.

On 31 October 1517, Luther nailed ninety-five theses on the church door in Wittenberg, protesting against the sale of indulgences and the Pope's claim to forgive sins. The very first thesis pitted the authority of the Bible against sacramental tradition: 'When our Lord and Master Jesus Christ said "Repent," he willed the entire life of believers to be one of repentence.' Luther had learned from Erasmus that *metanoia*, which the Vulgate translated *poenitentiam agere* ('do penance'), meant a 'turning around' of the Christian's whole being. It did not mean going to confession. No practice or tradition of the Church could claim divine sanction unless it had the support of the Bible. In his public debate in Leipzig with Johann Eck, theology professor at Ingolstadt (1519), Luther made his controversial new doctrine *sola scriptura* ('scripture alone') explicit for the first time. How could Luther understand the Bible, Eck asked, without the popes, councils and universities? Luther replied: 'A simple layman armed with scripture is to be believed above a pope or a council without it.'[20]

This was an unprecedented claim.[21] Jews and Christians

had always upheld the sacred importance of inherited tradition. For Jews, the oral Torah was essential to the understanding of the written Torah. Before the New Testament had been
written, the gospel had been preached by word of mouth and
the Christians' scripture had been the Law and the prophets.
By the fourth century, when the canon of the New Testament
was finalized, the churches relied on their creeds, liturgies
and the pronouncements of the church councils as well as
upon scripture.[22] Nevertheless, the Protestant Reformation, a
deliberate attempt to return to the origins of the faith, made
sola scriptura one of its most important principles. In fact,
Luther himself did not reject tradition. He was happy to use
the liturgy and creeds, as long as they did not contradict scripture and he was well aware that the gospel had originally
been preached orally. It had only been written down, he
explained, because of the danger of heresy and it represented
a falling away from the ideal. The gospel must remain a 'loud
cry', a vocal summons. The Word of God could not be confined to a written text; it must be brought to life by the human
voice in preaching, lectures and the singing of hymns and
psalms.[23]

But despite his commitment to the spoken Word, Luther's
greatest achievement was probably his translation of the Bible
into German. He began with the New Testament, which he
translated from Erasmus's Greek text (1522), and then,
working at breakneck speed, he completed the Old Testament
in 1534. By the time of Luther's death, one German in seventy
owned a copy of the vernacular New Testament and Luther's

German Bible became a symbol of German integrity. During the sixteenth and seventeenth centuries, kings and princes throughout Europe started to declare independence of the papacy and form absolute monarchies. The centralized state was an essential part of the modernizing process, and the vernacular Bible became a symbol of the nascent national will. The translation of the Bible into English, which culminated in the King James Bible (1611), was endorsed and controlled at almost every step by the Tudor and Stuart monarchies.

Zwingli and Calvin also based their reforms on the principle of *sola scriptura* but they differed from Luther in several important respects. They were less interested in theology and more concerned with the social and political transformation of the Christian life. They both owed a great deal to the humanists, and insisted on the importance of reading the Bible in the original languages. But they did not approve of Luther's 'canon within the canon'. They both wanted their congregations to be acquainted with the entire Bible. Zwingli's theological seminary in Zurich published excellent biblical commentaries, which were distributed all over Europe, and the Zurich translation of the Bible was published before Luther's. Calvin was convinced that the Bible had been written for simple, unlettered people and had been stolen from them by the scholars. But he realized that they would need guidance. Preachers must be well read in rabbinical and patristic exegesis and acquainted with contemporary scholarship. They must always see a biblical passage in its original context but at the same time they must make the

Bible relevant to the daily needs of their congregations.

Zwingli's study of the Greek and Roman classics had taught him to appreciate other religious cultures:[24] the Bible did not have the monopoly of revealed truth; Socrates and Plato had also been inspired by the Spirit and Christians would meet them in heaven. Like Luther, Zwingli believed that the written Word must be spoken aloud. Because a preacher was guided by the Spirit in the same way as the biblical authors, Zwingli regarded his own sermons as prophetic. His task was to animate the written Word and make it a living force in the community.The Bible was not about what God had done in the past, but what he did here and now.[25]

Calvin, however, had no time for classical culture. He agreed with Luther that Christ was the focus of scripture and the ultimate manifestation of God. But Calvin had a far greater appreciation of the Hebrew Bible. God's revelation had been a gradual, evolutionary process; at each stage of their history, he had adapted his truth to the limited capacity of human beings. The teaching and guidance that God had given to Israel had changed and developed over time.[26] The religion entrusted to Abraham was tailored to the needs of a simpler society than the *torah* bestowed upon Moses or David. The revelation became progressively clearer and more focused on the *christos*, right up to the time of John the Baptizer, who had looked directly into the eyes of Jesus. But the Old Testament was not simply about Christ, as Luther had argued. The covenant with Israel had its own integrity; it came from the same God, and the study of the Torah would help Christians to understand the Gospel. Calvin would become the most influential of the Protestant reformers and make the Jewish scriptures more important to Christians – especially in the Anglo-Saxon world – than ever before.

Calvin never tired of pointing out that in the Bible God condescended to our limitations. The Word was conditioned by the historical circumstances in which it was uttered, so the less edifying stories of the Bible must be seen in context, as a phase in an ongoing process. There was no need to explain them away allegorically. The creation story in Genesis was an example of this divine *balbative* ('baby talk'), which adapted immensely complex processses to the mentality of unedu-cated people.[27] It was not surprising that the Genesis story dif-fered from the new theories of learned philosophers. Calvin had great respect for modern science. It should not be con-demned simply 'because some frantic persons are wont boldly to reject whatever is unknown to them. For astronomy is not only pleasant but also very useful to be known: it cannot be denied that this art unfolds the admirable wisdom of God.'[28] It was absurd to expect scripture to teach scientific fact; anybody who wanted to learn about astronomy should look elsewhere. The natural world was God's first revelation, and Christians should regard the new geographical, biological and physical sciences as religious activities.[29]

The great scientists shared this view. Nicolaus Copernicus (1473–1543) regarded science as 'more divine than human'.[30] His heliocentric hypothesis was so radical that few people could take it in: instead of being located in the centre of the universe, the earth and the other planets were rotating around the sun; the world appeared to be stable, but was in fact in rapid motion. Galileo Galilei (1564–1642) tested the Copernican theory empirically by observing the planets through his telescope. He was silenced by the Inquisition and forced to recant, but his somewhat aggressive and provocative temperament had also played a part in his condemnation. At first, Catholics and Protestants did not automatically reject the new science. The Pope approved of Copernicus's theory when he first presented it in the Vatican and the early Calvinists and Jesuits were both keen scientists. But some were disturbed by the new theories. How could you reconcile Copernicus's theory with a literal reading of Genesis? If, as Galileo suggested, there was life on the moon, how had these people descended from Adam? How could the revolutions of the earth be squared with Christ's ascension to heaven? Scripture said that the heavens and the earth had been created for man's benefit, but how could this be so if the earth was just another planet revolving round an undistinguished star?[31] The old allegorical exegesis would have made it much easier for Christians to cope with their changing world.[32] But the increasing emphasis on the literal meaning of scripture was the product of early modernity: the scientific bias of early modern thought required people to see truth as conforming to the laws of the external world. It would not be long before some Christians would conclude that unless a book was historically or scientifically demonstrable it could not be true at all.

*

The Jewish people had not yet succumbed to this enthusiasm for the literal: in 1492 they had suffered a disaster, which made many turn to the mystical consolations of Kabbalah. In 1492, Ferdinand and Isabella, the Catholic monarchs of Aragon and Castile, had conquered the kingdom of Granada, the last Muslim stronghold in Europe. Jews and Muslims were given the option of conversion to Christianity or deportation. Many Jews chose exile and took refuge in the new Ottoman empire where a significant number settled in Palestine, which was now an Ottoman province. In Safed in northern Galilee, the saintly mystic Isaac Luria (1534–72) developed a kabbalastic myth that bore no resemblance to the first chapter of Genesis, and yet by the mid-seventeenth century Lurianic Kabbalah had a mass following in Jewish communities from Poland to Iran.[33] Exile had been a central preoccupation for Jews since their deportation to Babylonia. For the Spanish Jews – the Sephardim – the loss of their homeland was the worst disaster to have befallen their people since the destruction of the temple. They felt that everything was in the wrong place and that their entire world had collapsed. Snatched forever from places that were saturated in memories essential to their identity, exiles can feel that their very existence is in jeopardy. When exile is also associated with human cruelty, it raises urgent problems about the nature of evil in a world supposedly created by a just and benevolent God.

In Luria's new myth, God began the creative process by

going voluntarily into exile. How could the world exist if God was everywhere? Luria's answer was the myth of *zimzum* ('withdrawal') : the infinite En Sof had, as it were, to evacuate a region within itself to make room for the cosmos. This cosmology was punctuated by accidents, primal explosions and false starts, quite different from the orderly, peaceful creation described in P. But to the Sephardim, Luria's myth seemed a more accurate appraisal of their unpredicatable, fragmented world. At an early stage in the creative process, En Sof had tried to fill the vacuum it had created by *zimzum* with divine light, but the 'vessels' or 'pipes' designed to channel it had broken. So sparks of the primal light fell into the abyss that was not-God. Some of these returned to the divine world, but others remained trapped in the Godless realm dominated by the evil potential of *Din*, which En Sof had – as it were – attempted to purge from itself. After this accident, everything was in the wrong place. Adam could have rectified the situation on the first Sabbath, but he sinned and henceforth the divine sparks remained trapped in matter. The Shekhinah, now in permanent exile, wandered through the world, yearning to be reunited with the rest of the *sefiroth*. Yet there was hope. Jews were not outcasts, but essential to the redemption of the world. Their careful observance of the commandments and the special rituals evolved in Safed could effect the 'restoration' (*tikkun*) of the Shekhinah to the Godhead, the Jews to the Promised Land, and the world to its rightful state.[34]

In Lurianic Kabbalah, the literal, surface meaning of the Bible was a symptom of the primal disaster. Originally the letters of the Torah had been numinous with divine light and had come together to form the *sefiroth*, the secret names of God. When he was first created, Adam had been a spiritual being, but when he sinned his 'great soul' was shattered and his nature became more material. After this catastrophe, humanity needed a different Torah: the divine letters now formed words that related to human beings and earthly events while the commandments required physical actions to separate profane from sacred matter. But when *tikkun* was complete, the Torah would be restored to its original spirituality. 'What pious men now enact in material performance of the commandments,' Luria explained, 'they will then, in the paradisical garment of the soul, so enact as God intended when he created man.'[35]

The restoration of *tikkun* would also redeem the Bible. Kabbalists had long been aware of the flaws in their scriptures. In Lurianic Kabbalah, the God of the Hebrew Bible was one of the 'faces' (*parzufim*) of Adam Kadmon, primordial man, which was composed of six of the 'lower' *sefiroth*: Judgement (*Din*), Mercy, Compassion, Patience, Majesty and Stability. Originally they had been in perfect balance, but after the breaking of the vessels the destructive tendency of *Din* was no longer held in check by the other *sefiroth*. Dominated by *Din*, they became collectively *Zeir Anpin*, 'the Impatient One', the deity revealed in the post-lapsarian Torah. This was why the biblical God often appeared so cruel and irascible.

Separated from the Shekhinah, his female counterpart, he was also irredeemably male.

But there was optimism in this tragic myth. Where Luther felt that he could contribute nothing towards his own salvation, the kabbalists believed that they could transform the world, restore God to his true nature, and reform their scriptures. They did not deny their pain: indeed, the rituals of Safed were designed to help them to face it. They made night vigils, weeping and rubbing their faces in the dust, to identify their own exile with that of the Shekhinah. But Luria was adamant that there must be no wallowing. Kabbalists must work through their sorrow in a purposeful way until they achieved a measure of joy. The vigil always ended with a meditation on the final reunion of the Shekhinah with *Zeir Anpin* in which they imagined that their bodies had become an earthly shrine for the divine presence. They saw visions, shook with wonder and awe, and experienced a rapturous transcendence that transformed the world that had seemed so cruel and alien.[36]

This sense of unity and joy had to be translated into practical action because the Shekhinah could not live in a place of sorrow and pain. Sadness sprang from the forces of evil in the world, so the cultivation of happiness was essential to *tikkun*. To counterbalance the prevalence of *Din*, there must be no anger or aggression in the kabbalists' heart, even for the *goyim* who had oppressed and dispossessed them. There were severe penances for faults that injured others: for sexual exploitation, malicious gossip, humiliating others and dishonouring parents.[37] Luria's mythical rewriting of the creation story helped Jews to develop a spirit of joy and kindness at a time when they could have been overcome by rage and despair.

The new discipline of *sola scriptura* was not able to do this for the Christians of Europe. Even after his great breakthrough, Luther remained terrified of death. He seemed constantly in a state of simmering rage: against the Pope, the Turks, Jews, women, rebellious peasants, scholastic philosophers and every single one of his theological opponents. He and Zwingli engaged in a furious controversy about the meaning of Christ's words when he had instituted the Eucharist at the last supper, saying 'This is my body'.[38] Calvin was appalled by the anger that had clouded the minds of the two reformers and caused an unholy rift that could and should have been avoided: 'Both parties failed altogether to have patience to listen to each other, in order to follow truth without passion, wherever it might be found,' he concluded. 'I deliberately venture to assert that, if their minds had not been partly exasperated by the extreme vehemence of the controversies, the disagreement was not so great that conciliation could easily have been achieved.'[39] It was impossible for interpreters to agree on every single passage of the Bible; disputes must be conducted humbly and with an open mind. Yet Calvin himself did not always live up to these high principles, and was prepared to execute dissenters in his own church.

The Protestant Reformation expressed many of the ideals

of the new culture that was emerging in the West. Instead of being based on a surplus of agricultural produce, like every previous civilization, its economy would be based on the scientific and technological replication of resources and the constant reinvestment of capital. This society had to be productive, and Calvin's theology would be used to support the work ethic. Individuals had to participate, even at a humble level, as printers, factory hands and office clerks, and had, therefore, to acquire a modicum of education and literacy. As a result, they would eventually demand a greater share in the decision-making process of government. There would be political upheaval, revolutions and civil war to establish more democratic regimes. Social, political, economic and intellectual change was part of an interlocking process; each element depended upon the others and religion was inevitably drawn into this spiral of development.

People now read scripture in a 'modern' way. Protestants stood alone before God, relying on the Bible alone. But this would have been impossible before the invention of printing made it feasible for all Christians to own individual copies and before they had the literacy skills to read it. Increasingly, as the pragmatic, scientific ethos of modernity took hold, scripture was read for the information that it imparted. Science depended upon rigorous analysis, and this made the symbolic system of the perennial philosophy incomprehensible. The eucharistic bread – the issue that had divided Luther and Zwingli – was now 'only' a symbol. The words of scripture, once seen as earthly replicas of the divine Logos, had also lost their numinous dimension. But the silent, solitary reading, which freed Christians from the supervision of religious experts, expressed the independence that would become essential to the modern spirit.

Sola scriptura had been a noble, if controversial ideal. But in practice it meant that everybody had a God-given right to interpret these extremely complex documents as they chose.[40] Protestant sects proliferated, each claiming that it alone understood the Bible. In 1534, a radical apocalyptic group in Munster set up an independent theocratic state based on a literal reading of scripture, which licensed polygamy, condemned all violence and outlawed private ownership. This short-lived experiment lasted only a year, but it alarmed the reformers. If there was no authoritative body to control biblical reading, how could anybody know who was right? 'Who will give our conscience sure information about which party is teaching us the pure Word of God, we or our opponents?' asked Luther. 'Is every fanatic to have the right to teach whatever he pleases?'[41] Calvin agreed: 'If everyone has a right to be judge and arbiter in this matter, nothing can be set down as certain and our whole religion will be full of uncertainty.'[42]

Religious liberty was becoming problematic in a political world that increasingly demanded conformity, and was prepared to achieve it by coercive means. In the seventeenth century, Europe was convulsed by wars, which may have been articulated in a religious imagery, but which were really caused by the need for a different kind of political organization in the new Europe. The old feudal kingdoms had to be transformed into efficient, centralized states, initially under absolute monarchs, who could impose unity by force. Ferdinand and Isabella were welding together the old Iberian kingdoms to form a united Spain, but they did not yet have the resources to allow their subjects untrammelled freedom. There was no room for autonomous, self-governing bodies, such as the Jewish communities. The Spanish Inquisition, which hounded these dissidents, was a modernizing institution, designed to create ideological conformity and national unity.[43] As modernization progressed, Protestant rulers in such countries as England were just as ruthless to their Catholic subjects, who were regarded as enemies of state. The so-called Wars of Religion (1618–48) were in fact a thirty-year struggle on the part of the kings of France and the German princes to become politically independent of the Holy Roman Empire and the papacy, even though it was complicated by the confrontation of militant Calvinism and a reinvigorated, reformed Catholicism.

Modernization was progressive and empowering, but it had an inbuilt intolerance: there would always be people who experienced this new Western society as cruel and invasive. Freedom for some meant enslavement for others. In 1620, a party of English settlers made the perilous journey across the Atlantic in the *Mayflower* and arrived in the harbour of Plymouth, Massachusetts. They were English Puritans, radical Calvinists who felt persecuted by the Anglican establishment and decided to migrate to the New World. They had inherited Calvin's interest in the Old Testament and were particularly drawn to the story of the Exodus, which seemed a literal forecast of their own project. England was their Egypt; the transatlantic voyage their sojourn in the wilderness, and they had now arrived in the Promised Land, which they christened New Canaan.[44]

The Puritans gave their colonies biblical names: Hebron, Salem, Bethlehem, Sion and Judaea. When John Winthrop, who would become their leader, arrived on the *Arbella* in 1630, he proclaimed to his fellow passengers that America was Israel; like the ancient Israelites, they were about to take possession of the land but he quoted Moses's words in Deuteronomy: the Puritans would succeed if they kept the Lord's commandments, but would perish if they were disobedient.[45] Appropriating the land brought the Puritans into collision with the native Americans. Here too, they found a mandate in scripture. Like later colonialists, some believed that the indigenous inhabitants deserved their fate: they 'are not industrious, neither have art, science, skill or faculty to cure either the land or the commodities of it,' wrote Robert Cushman, the colony's business agent. 'As the ancient patriarchs therefore removed from straiter places into more roomy, where the land lay waste and idle and none used it . . . so it is lawful now to take a land which none seek to make use of it.'[46] When the Pequots remained hostile, other Puritans compared them with the Amalekites and Philistines 'that did confederate against Israel' and had, therefore, to be destroyed.[47] But some of the settlers believed that the native Americans were the ten lost tribes of Israel, who had been deported by the Assyrians in 722 BCE. Because Paul had predicted that Jews would accept Christianity before the end, the conversion of the Pequot would hasten the Second Coming of Christ.

Many of the Puritans were convinced that their migration to America was a prelude to the last days. Their colony was the 'city on the hill' foreseen by Isaiah, the beginning of a new era of peace and beatitude.[48] In 1654, Edward Johnson published a history of New England:

> Know this is the place where the Lord will create a new
> heaven and new earth, and a new commonwealth together.
> . . . These are but the beginning of Christ's glorious reforma-
> tion and restoration of his churches to a more glorious splen-
> dour than ever. He hath therefore caused the dazzling
> brightness of his presence to be contracted in the burning
> glass of his people's zeal, from whence it begins to be felt in
> many parts of the world.[49]

Not all the American colonists shared the Puritan vision, but it left an indelible impression on the ethos of the United States. The Exodus would remain a crucial text. It was cited by the revolutionary leaders of the War of Independence against Britain. Benjamin Franklin wanted the great seal of the nation to depict the parting of the Sea of Reeds, but the eagle that became America's symbol was not only an ancient imperial emblem but was also linked with the Exodus.[50]

Other migrants drew on the Exodus story in the same way: the Mormons, the Afrikaaners of South Africa, and the Jews who fled persecution in Europe and found refuge in the United States. God had saved them from oppression and established them in a new land – sometimes at the expense of others. Many Americans still regard themselves as a chosen people with a manifest destiny, and see their nation as a beacon to the rest of the world. There has been a tradition of American reformers making an 'errand into the wilderness' in order to make a new start. As we shall see in the next chapter, a significant number of American Protestants continued to be preoccupied by the last days and felt a strong identity with Israel. Yet even though Americans were committed to liberation and freedom, for two hundred years there was an enslaved Israel in their midst.

In 1619, the year before the *Mayflower* arrrived in Plymouth, a Dutch frigate had cast anchor off the shore of Virginia, with twenty 'negars' who had been captured in West Africa and forcibly conveyed to America. By 1660, the status of such Africans had been defined. They were slaves, who could be bought and sold, flogged, fettered and separated from their tribes, wives and children.[51] They were introduced to Christianity as slaves, and the Exodus became their story. At first they probably retained their traditional religion: slave masters were wary of their conversion, lest they used the Bible to demand freedom and basic human rights. But Christianity would have seemed grossly hypocritical to the slaves, since preachers quoted scripture to justify their enslavement. They cited Noah's curse of his grandson Canaan, the son of Ham, ancestor of the African peoples: 'He shall be his brothers' meanest slave.'[52] They referred to Paul's instructions that slaves be obedient to their masters.[53] Yet by the 1780s, African American slaves had redefined the Bible on their own terms.

Central to their Christianity was the 'spiritual', a song based on a biblical theme, accompanied by the stamping, sobbing, clapping and shrieking that had characterized African worship. Only about 5 per cent of the slaves could read, so the spirituals focused on the essence of the biblical story instead of the literal sense of the words. Like Luther, they created their own 'canon within the canon', concentrating on stories that spoke directly to their own condition: Jacob wrestling with the angel, Joshua entering the Promised Land, Daniel in the Lion's Den, and the suffering and resurrection of Jesus. But the most important narrative was the Exodus: the slaves' Egypt was America, but one day God would liberate them:

> When Israel was in Egypt's land,
>   O let my people go!
> Oppressed so hard they could not stand,
>   O let my people go!
> *Chorus:* O go down, Moses
> Away to Egypt's land,
> And tell King Pharaoh
> To let my people go!

The slaves used the Exodus story to raise their consciousness, to help them endure the dehumanizing conditions in
which they lived, and to demand justice. The spirituals per-
sisted long after the abolition of slavery by Abraham Lincoln;
the Exodus story inspired Martin Luther King Jr during the
civil rights movement in the 1960s, and after the assassina-
tions of King (1968) and Malcolm X (1965), the black liberation
theologian James Hal Cone argued that Christian theology
must become black theology, wholly identified with the cause
of the oppressed and affirmative of the divine character of
their struggle for freedom.[54]

A single text could be interpreted to serve diametrically
opposed interests. The more people were encouraged to
make the Bible the focus of their spirituality, the more difficult it became to find a core message. At the same time as
African Americans drew on the Bible to develop their theology of liberation, the Ku Klux Klan used it to justify their
lynching of blacks. But the Exodus story did not mean liberation for everybody. Israelites who rebelled against Moses
in the wilderness were exterminated; the indigenous
Canaanites were massacred by Joshua's armies. Black femi-
nist theologians have pointed out that the Israelites owned
slaves; that God had permitted them to sell their daughters
into slavery; and that God actually ordered Abraham to
abandon the Egyptian slave girl Hagar in the wilderness.[55]
Sola scriptura could point people in the direction of the Bible,
but it could never provide an absolute mandate: people
could always find alternative texts to support an opposing

point of view. By the seventeenth century, religious people were becoming acutely aware that the Bible was a very confusing book, and this at a time when clarity and rationality were prized as never before.

CHAPTER 8

Modernity

By the late seventeenth century, Europeans had entered the age of reason. Instead of relying on sacred tradition, scientists, scholars and philosophers were becoming future-oriented, ready to jettison the past and start again. Truth, they were beginning to discover, was never absolute, since new discoveries habitually undermined old certainties. Increasingly, truth had to demonstrated empirically and objectively, assessed by its efficiency in and fidelity to the external world. Consequently, the more intuitive modes of thought became suspect. Instead of conserving what had been achieved, scholars were becoming pioneers and specialists. The 'renaissance man', with an encyclopaedic grasp of knowledge, belonged to the past. It would soon be almost impossible for an expert in one field to be truly competent in another. The rationality of the philosophical movement known as the Enlightenment encouraged an analytic mode of thought: instead of trying to see things whole, people were learning to dissect a complex reality and study its component parts. All this would have a profound effect on the way they read the Bible.

In his seminal treatise, the *Advancement of Learning* (1605),

Francis Bacon (1561–1626), counsellor to King James I of England, was one of the first to argue that even the most sacred doctrines must be subjected to the stringent methods of empirical science. If these beliefs contradicted the evidence of our senses, they had to go. Bacon was enthralled by science, convinced that it would save the world and inaugurate the millennial kingdom foretold by the prophets. Its progress must not, therefore, be impeded by timorous, simple-minded clergymen. But Bacon was convinced that there could be no conflict between science and religion, since all truth was one. Bacon's view of science was, however, different from our own. For Bacon, the scientific method consisted of assembling proven facts; he did not appreciate the importance of guess-work and hypothesis in scientific research. The only information upon which we could rely came from our five senses; anything that could not be demonstrated empirically – philosophy, metaphysics, theology, art, mysticism and mythology – was irrelevant. His definition of truth would become extremely influential, not least among the more conservative champions of the Bible.

The new humanism was increasingly antagonistic to religion. The French philosopher René Descartes (1596–1650) maintained that there was no need for revealed scripture, since reason provided us with ample information about God. The British mathematician Isaac Newton (1642–1727) scarcely mentioned the Bible in his copious writings, because he derived his knowledge of God from an intensive study of the universe. Science would soon clear up the irrational 'mysteries' of traditional faith. The new religion of Deism, espoused by John Locke (1632–1704), one of the founders of the Enlightenment, was rooted in reason alone. Immanuel Kant (1724–1804) was convinced that a divinely revealed Bible violated the autonomy and freedom of the human being. Some thinkers went further. The Scottish philosopher David Hume (1711–76) argued that there was no reason to believe that anything lay beyond the experience of our senses. Denis Diderot (1713–84), philosopher, critic and novelist, simply did not care whether God existed or not, while Paul Heinrich, Baron of Holbach (1723–89) argued that belief in a supernatural God was an act of cowardice and despair.

Yet many of the men of reason were in love with the classics of Graeco-Roman antiquity, which seemed to fulfil many of the functions of scripture.[1] When Diderot read the classics, he experienced 'transports of admiration ... thrills of joy ... divine enthusiasm'.[2] Jean-Jacques Rousseau (1712–72) declared that he would study the Greek and Roman authors again and again.'I took fire!' he cried on reading Plutarch.[3] When the English historian Edward Gibbon (1737–94) visited Rome for the first time, he found that he could not proceed with his reasearch because he was 'agitated' by such 'strong emotions' and experienced a quasi-religious 'intoxication' and 'enthusiasm'.[4] They all invested these ancient works with their deepest aspirations, allowed them to shape their minds, inform their interior world, and found that, in return, the texts gave them moments of transcendence.

*

Other scholars applied their sceptically critical skills to the Bible. Baruch Spinoza (1632–77), a Sephardic Jew of Spanish descent born in the liberal city of Amsterdam, had studied mathematics, astronomy and physics and found them incompatible with his religious beliefs.[5] In 1655 he started to voice doubts that unsettled his community: the manifest contradictions in the Bible proved that it could not be of divine origin; the idea of revelation was a delusion; and there was no supernatural deity – what we called 'God' was simply nature itself. On 27 July 1656 Spinoza was excommunicated from the synagogue and became the first person in Europe to live successfully beyond the reach of established religion. Spinoza dismissed conventional faith as 'a tissue of meaningless mysteries'; he preferred to get what he called 'beatitude' from the untrammelled exercise of his reason.[6] Spinoza studied the historical background and literary genres of the Bible with unprecedented objectivity. He agreed with Ibn Ezra that Moses could not have written the entire Pentateuch but went on to claim that the extant text was the work of several different authors. He had become the pioneer of the historical-critical method that would later be called the Higher Criticism of the Bible.

Moses Mendelssohn (1729–86), the brilliant son of a poor Torah scholar in Dessau, Germany, was less radical. He had fallen in love with modern secular learning, but, like Locke, had no difficulty in accepting the idea of a benevolent God, which seemed to him a matter of common sense. He created the *Haskalah,* a Jewish 'enlightenment' which presented

Judaism as a rational faith well suited to modernity. On Mount Sinai, God had revealed himself in a law code, not a set of doctrines, so Jewish religion was concerned only with ethics and left the mind entirely free. Before they accepted the authority of the Bible, Jews must convince themselves rationally of its claims. It is difficult to recognize this as Judaism. Mendelssohn had tried to force it into a rationalistic mould that was alien to spirituality. Nevertheless many Jews, who became known as the *maskilim* (the 'enlightened ones'), were ready to follow him. They were eager to escape the intellectual constraints of the ghetto, move in gentile society, study the new sciences, and keep their faith a private matter.

But this rationalism was countered by a mystical movement among the Jews of Poland, Galicia, Belorusssia and Lithuania that amounted to a rebellion against modernity.[7] In 1735, Israel ben Eliezer (1698–1760), a poor Jewish tavern-keeper in south-eastern Poland, announced that he had become a *baal shem*, a 'Master of the Name', one of the many faith-healers who wandered through the rural districts of Eastern Europe, preaching in the name of God. This was a dark time for Polish Jewry. During a peasant uprising against the nobility (1648–67), Jews had been massacred in large numbers and were still vulnerable and economically deprived. There was an ever-widening gap between rich and poor, and many of the rabbis had simply retreated into Torah study and neglected their congregations. Israel ben Eliezer initiated a reform movement and became known as the *Baal Shem Tov* – or the 'Besht' – a master of exceptional status. By the end of his life, there were about forty thousand of his *Hasidim* ('pious ones').

The Besht claimed that he had not been singled out by God because he had studied the Talmud, but because he recited the traditional prayers with such fervour and concentration that he achieved ecstatic union with God. Unlike the rabbis of the Talmudic age, who believed that Torah study took precendence over prayer,[8] the Besht insisted on the primacy of contemplation.[9] A rabbi must not bury himself in his books and neglect the poor. Hasidic spirituality was based on Isaac Luria's myth of the divine sparks trapped in the material world, but the Besht transformed this tragic vision into a positive appreciation of the ubiquitous presence of God. A spark of the divine could be found in any material object, however lowly, and no activity – eating, drinking, making love or conducting business – was profane. By the constant practice of *devekut* ('attachment'), a Hasid cultivated a perpetual awareness of God's presence. Hasidim expressed this enhanced consciousness in ecstatic, noisy and tumultuous prayer, accompanied by extravagant gestures – such as turning somersaults that symbolized a total reversal of vision – that helped them to throw their whole being into their worship.

Just as the Hasidim looked through the veil of matter to see the divine spark latent within the most commonplace object, so too they learned to penetrate the words of the Bible and glimpse the divinity hidden beneath the surface. The words and letters of the Torah were vessels that contained the light of En Sof, so a Hasid must not concentrate on the purely literal sense of the text but on the spiritual reality it enclosed.[10] He must cultivate a receptive attitude and allow the Bible to speak to him by reining in his mental powers. One day, the Besht was visited by Dov Ber (1716–72), a learned kabbalist who would eventually succeed him as leader of the Hasidic movement. The two men studied Torah together and became immersed in a text about the angels. Dov Ber approached the passage in a rather abstract way and the Besht asked him to show respect for the angels they were discussing by standing up. As soon as he rose to his feet, 'the whole house was suffused with light, a fire burned all around, and they [both] sensed the presence of the angels'. 'The simple reading is as you say,' the Besht told Dov Ber, 'but your manner of studying lacked soul.'[11] A commonsense reading, without the attitudes and gestures of prayer, would not yield a vision of the unseen.

Without such prayer, Torah study was useless. As one of Dov Ber's disciples explained, Hasidim must read scripture 'with burning enthusiasm of the heart, with a coercion of all man's psychological faculties in the direction of clear and pure thoughts on God constantly, and in separation from every pleasure'.[12] The Besht told them that if they approached the story of Mount Sinai in this way, they would 'always hear God speak to them, as he did during the revelation on Sinai, because it was Moses's intention that all Israel be worthy of attaining the same level as he did'.[13] The point was not to read *about* Sinai but to experience Sinai itself.

When Dov Ber became the Hasidic leader, his scholarly

reputation attracted many rabbis and scholars to the movement. But his exegesis was no longer dry and academic. One
of his disciples recalled that 'When he opened his mouth to
speak words of Truth, he looked as if he was not of this world
at all and the Divine Presence spoke out of his throat.'[14]
Sometimes, in the middle of a word, he would pause and wait
for a while in silence. The Hasidim were evolving their own
lectio divina, making a quiet place for scripture in their hearts.
Instead of analysing a text and pulling it apart, the Hasid had
to still his critical faculties. 'I will teach you the way Torah is
best taught,' Dov Ber used to say: 'not to feel [conscious of]
oneself at all, but to be like a listening ear that hears the world
of sound speaking but does not speak itself.'[15] The exegete had
to make himself a vessel for the divine presence. The Torah
must act upon him, as though he were its instrument.[16]

Hasidism aroused fierce opposition from orthodox Jews,
who were appalled by the Besht's apparent denigration of the
scholarly study of Torah. They became known as the *Misnagdim* ('opponents'). Their leader was Elijah ben Solomon
Zalman (1720–97), head (*gaon*) of the academy of Vilna in
Lithuania. Torah study was the Gaon's chief passion, but he
was also proficient in astronomy, anatomy, mathematics and
foreign languages. Even though he studied scripture more
aggressively than the Hasidim, the Gaon's method was in its
own way mystical. He relished what he called the 'effort' of
study, an intense mental activity that tipped him into a new
level of consciousness, and kept him at his books all night, his
feet immersed in icy water to prevent him from falling asleep.

When he did allow himself to doze off, the Torah penetrated his dreams and he experienced an ascent to the divine. 'He who studies Torah communes with God,' one of his disciples claimed, 'for God and the Torah are one.'[17]

In Western Europe, however, it was becoming increasingly difficult to find God in scripture. The ethos of the Enlightenment had inspired more scholars to study the Bible critically, but it was impossible to experience its transcendent dimension without the gestures and disposition of prayer. In England, some of the more radical deists used the new scholarly methods to undermine the Bible.[18] The mathematician William Whiston (1667–1752) believed that early Christianity had been a more rational faith. In 1745 he published a version of the New Testament from which he had erased every reference to the Incarnation and the Trinity, doctrines that, he claimed, had been foisted on the faithful by the fathers of the Church. The Irish deist John Toland (1670–1722) tried to replace the New Testament with a manuscript that purported to be the long-lost Jewish-Christian gospel of Barnabas, which denied the divinity of Christ. Other sceptics argued that the text of the New Testament was so corrupt that it was impossible to determine what the Bible actually said. But the distinguished classicist Richard Bentley (1662–1742) mounted a scholarly campaign in the Bible's defence. Using the critical techniques now applied to Graeco-Roman literature, he showed that it was possible to reconstruct the original manuscripts by collating and analysing the variants.

In Germany the Pietists, who wanted to get beyond the arid doctrinal polemics of the competing Protestant sects, also seized on these analytic methods to reinstate the Bible, convinced that the biblical critic should be above denominational loyalty.[19] The Pietists' aim was to liberate religion from theology and recover a more personal experience of the divine. In 1694, they founded a university at Halle to bring the new scholarship to the laity in a non-sectarian guise and Halle became the centre of a biblical revolution.[20] Between 1711 and 1719, its press printed 100,000 copies of the New Testament and 80,000 complete Bibles. Halle scholars also produced the *Biblia Pentapla* to encourage a trans-denominational reading of scripture: five different translations were printed side by side, so that Lutherans, Calvinists and Catholics could read the version of their choice but could consult the wording in another column if they encountered a difficulty. Others translated the Bible in a wholly literal way to show that even in the vernacular the Word of God was far from clear. Theologians should be more reticent in their use of 'proof texts' that could not bear the weight of theological interpretation imposed upon them. If the original could not be rendered into elegant German, the Bible sounded strange and unfamiliar and this was a salutary reminder that it was always difficult to understand God's Word.[21]

By the end of the eighteenth century, German scholars led the way in biblical studies and were taking Spinoza's historical-critical method to new lengths. They agreed that Moses had certainly not written the entire Pentateuch, which seemed to have a number of different authors who all wrote in a distinctive style. One favoured the divine title 'Elohim'; another preferred to call God 'Yahweh'. There were duplicate narratives, obviously by different hands, such as the two creation accounts in Genesis.[22] So Jean Astruc (1684–1766), a Paris physician, and Johann Gottfried Eichhorn (1752–1827), Professor of Oriental Languages at Jena University, argued that there were two main documents in Genesis: the 'Yahwist' and the 'Elohist'. But in 1798, Karl David Igen, Eichhorn's successor, claimed that the Elohist material derived from two separate sources. Other scholars, including Johann Severin Vater (1771–1826) and Wilhelm DeWette (1780–1849) believed that this was too simplistic: the Pentateuch consisted of numerous, separate fragments that had been put together by a redactor.

By the nineteenth century, it was generally agreed by the scholars of the Higher Criticism that the Pentateuch was a combination of four originally independent sources. In 1805, DeWette argued that Deuteronomy ('D') was the latest book of the Pentateuch and was probably the *sefer torah* discovered in the time of Josiah. Hermann Hupfeld (1796–1866), a professor at Halle, agreed with Igen that the 'Elohist' source consisted of two separate documents: E1 (a priestly work) and E2. E1, he believed, was the earliest source, followed by E2, J and D, in that order. But Karl Heinrich Graf (1815–69) made an important breakthrough when he argued that the priestly document (E1) was in fact the latest of the four sources.

Julius Wellhausen (1844–1918) seized upon Graf's theory because it solved a problem that had long troubled him. Why did the prophets never refer to the Mosaic law? And why was the Deuteronomist, who was clearly familiar with the work of the Yahwist and Elohist, ignorant of the priestly document? All this could be explained if the priestly source (E1) was indeed a late composition. Wellhausen also showed that the four-document theory was too simplistic; there had been additions to all four sources before they had been combined into a single narrative. His work was regarded by his contemporaries as the culmination of the critical method, but Wellhausen himself realized that research had only just begun – and, indeed, it continues to the present day.

How would these discoveries affect the religious lives of Jews and Christians? Some Christians embraced the insights of the Enlightenment. Friedrich Schleiermacher (1768–1834) was initially disturbed that the Bible seemed such a flawed document.[23] His response was to promote a spirituality based on an experience that was fundamental to all religion, but which Christianity had expressed in a distinctive way. He defined this experience as 'the feeling of absolute dependence'.[24] This was no abject servility but a sense of reverence and awe before the mystery of life, which made us aware that we were not the centre of the universe. The gospels showed that Jesus perfectly embodied this attitude of wonder and surrender, and the New Testament described the impact of his personality on the disciples who founded the early church.

Scripture was, therefore, essential to the Christian life

because it provided us with our only access to Jesus. But because its authors were conditioned by the historical circumstances in which they lived, it was legitimate to subject their testimony to critical scrutiny. The life of Jesus had been a divine revelation, but the writers who recorded it were ordinary human beings, subject to sin and error. It was quite possible that they had made mistakes. But the Holy Spirit had guided the Church in its selection of canonical books, so Christians could put their trust in the New Testament. The scholar's task was to peel away its cultural shell to reveal the timeless kernel within. Not every word of scripture was authoritative, so the exegete must distinguish marginal ideas from the gospel's main thrust.

The Law and the prophets had been the scripture of the New Testament authors. But Schleiermacher believed that the Old Testament was not as authoritative as the New for Christians. It had different views of God, sin and grace and relied on law rather than spirit. In time, the Old Testament might even be relegated to an appendix. Schleiermacher's biblical theology gave birth to a new Christian movement known as Liberalism, which looked for the universal religious message in the gospels, discarded what seemed peripheral, and tried to express these essential truths in a way that would engage a modern audience.

In 1859, Charles Darwin (1809–82) published *On the Origin of Species by Means of Natural Selection*, which marked a new phase in the history of science. Instead of merely collecting facts, Baconian-style, Darwin put forward an hypothesis:

animals, plants and human beings had not been created fully formed but had developed slowly in a long period of evolutionary adaptation to their environment. In *The Descent of Man*, a later work, he suggested that *Homo sapiens* had evolved from the same proto-ape as the gorilla and chimpanzee. The *Origin* was a sober, careful exposition of a scientific theory that attracted a large popular audience: 1,400 copies were sold on the day of publication.

Darwin did not intend to attack religion and at first the religious response was muted. There was far greater outcry when seven Anglican clergymen published *Essays and Reviews* (1861), which made the Higher Criticism accessible to the general reader.[25] The public were now informed that Moses had not written the Pentateuch nor David the Psalms. Biblical miracles were simply literary tropes and should not be understood literally, and most of the events described in the Bible were clearly not historical. The authors of *Essays and Reviews* argued that the Bible should not be given special treatment but must be approached with the same critical rigour as any other ancient text.

At the end of the nineteenth century, the Higher Criticism rather than Darwinism was the main bone of contention betwen liberal and conservative Christians. Liberals believed that in the long term the critical method would lead to a deeper understanding of the Bible. But for conservatives, the Higher Criticism symbolized everything that was wrong with the post-Enlightenment world that was sweeping old certainties away.[26] In 1888, the British novelist Mrs Humphry Ward published *Robert Elsmere,* the story of a young clergyman whose faith was destroyed by the Higher Criticism. It became a bestseller, indicating that many people sympathized with Robert's dilemma. As his wife said: 'If the Gospels are not true as fact, as history, I cannot see that they are true at all, or of any value.'[27] It is a sentiment that many would share today.

The rational bias of the modern world made it difficult – if not impossible – for an increasing number of Western Christians to appreciate the role and value of mythology. There was, therefore, a growing sense that the truths of religion must be factual and a deep fear that the Higher Criticism would leave a dangerous void. Discount one miracle and consistency demanded that you reject them all. If Jonah did not spend three days in the whale's belly, asked a Lutheran pastor, did Jesus really rise from the tomb?[28] Clergymen blamed the Higher Criticism for widespread drunkenness, infidelity, and the rising crime and divorce rates.[29] In 1886, the American revivalist preacher Dwight Moody (1837–99) founded the Moody Bible Institute in Chicago to combat the Higher Criticism. His aim was to create a cadre of true believers to fight the false ideas that, he was convinced, had brought the nation to the brink of destruction. The Bible Institute would become a crucial fundamentalist phenomenon, representing a safe and sacred haven in a Godless world.

Conservatives who felt outnumbered by the liberals in the denominations started to band together. In the last years of the nineteenth century, the Bible Conference, where conservatives could read scripture in a literal, no-nonsense manner and purge their minds of the Higher Criticism, became increasingly popular in the United States. There was a widespread hunger for certainty. People now expected something entirely new from the Bible – something it had never pretended to offer hitherto. In his book, tellingly entitled *Many Infallible Proofs* (1895), the American Protestant Arthur Pierson wanted the Bible discussed 'in a truly impartial and scientific spirit':

> I like Biblical theology that . . . does not begin with an
> hypothesis and then wraps the facts and the philosophy to
> fit the crook of our dogma, but a Baconian system, which
> first gathers the teachings of the word of God and then seeks
> to deduce some general law upon which the facts can be
> arranged.[30]

At a time when so many traditional beliefs were being eroded, this was an understandable desire but the myths of the Bible could not possibly provide the scientific certainty that Pierson expected.

The Presbyterian seminary at Princeton, New Jersey, became the bastion of this 'scientific' Protestantism. The term 'bastion' is appropriate, because this quest for a wholly rationalistic interpretation of the Bible seemed chronically defensive. 'Religion has to fight for its life against the large class of scientific men,' wrote Charles Hodge (1797–1878), Princeton professor of theology.[31] In 1871, Hodge published the first volume of his *Systematic Theology*. The title alone revealed its

Baconian bias. The theologian, Hodge argued, was not to look for a meaning beyond the words of scripture but should simply arrange the teachings of the Bible into a system of general truths – a project that would involve a good deal of misplaced effort, because this type of system was entirely alien to the Bible.

In 1881, Archibald A. Hodge, Charles's son, published a defence of the literal truth of the Bible with his younger colleague Benjamin Warfield. It became a classic: 'The scriptures not only contain but are the Word of God, and hence all their elements and all their affirmations are absolutely errorless and binding on the faith and obedience of men.' Every biblical statement – on any subject – was absolute 'truth to the facts'.[32] The nature of faith was changing. It was now no longer 'trust' but intellectual submission to a set of beliefs. But for Hodge and Warfield, this required no suspension of disbelief because Christianity was entirely rational. 'It is solely by reasoning that it has come thus far on its way,' Warfield argued in a later article, 'And it is solely by reasoning that it will put its enemies under its feet.'[33]

This was an entirely new departure. In the past, some interpreters had favoured the study of the literal sense of the Bible but they had never believed that every single word of scripture was factually true. Many had admitted that, if we confined our attention to the letter, the Bible was an impossible text. The belief in biblical inerrancy, pioneered by Warfield and Hodge, would, however, become crucial to Christian fundamentalism and would involve considerable denial. Hodge and Warfield were responding to the challenge of modernity but in their desperation were distorting the scriptural tradition they were trying to defend.

The same was true of the new apocalyptic vision that gripped conservative American Protestants in the late nineteenth century. This was the creation of an Englishman, John Nelson Darby (1800–82), who found few followers in Britain but toured the United States to great acclaim between 1859 and 1877.[34] He was convinced, on the basis of a literal reading of Revelation, that God would shortly bring this era of history to an end in an unprecedentedly terrible disaster. Antichrist, the fake redeemer whose coming before the end had been foretold by St Paul,[35] would initially be welcomed and would deceive the unwary. He would then inflict seven years of tribulation, war and massacre upon humanity, but eventually Jesus would descend to earth and defeat him on the plain of Armageddon outside Jerusalem. Christ would then rule on earth for a thousand years until the Last Judgement brought history to a close. The attraction of this theory was that true believers would be spared. On the basis of a chance remark of St Paul, who suggested that at the Second Coming Christians would be 'taken up in the clouds' to meet Jesus,[36] Darby maintained that shortly before Tribulation, there would a 'rapture', a 'snatching' of born-again Christians, who would be whisked up to heaven and would thus escape the sufferings of the end time.

Bizarre as it sounds, this Rapture theory was in line with aspects of nineteenth-century thought. Darby spoke of historical eras or 'dispensations', each of which had ended in destruction; this was not dissimilar to the successive epochs that geologists had found in the strata of fossils in rocks and cliffs – each one of which, some thought, had ended in catastrophe. In line with the modern spirit, Darby's theory was literal and democratic. There was no hidden truth, accessible only to a learned elite. The Bible meant exactly what it said. A millennium meant ten centuries; if the prophets spoke of 'Israel' they meant Jews not the Church; if Revelation prophesied a battle outside Jerusalem, that was exactly what would happen.[37] This reading of scripture would become even easier after the publication of *The Scofield Reference Bible* (1909), which became an instant bestseller. Cyrus I. Scofield explained the Rapture theory in detailed notes – a gloss, which for many Christian fundamentalists has become almost as authoritative as the Bible itself.

The Jewish world was also divided between those who wanted to embrace modernity and those determined to fight it. In Germany, the *maskilim* who had embraced the Enlightenment believed that they could be a bridge between the ghetto and the modern world. In the early years of the nineteenth century, some decided to reshape the religion itself. Reform Judaism, whose worship was conducted in German, with choral singing and mixed choirs, seemed more Protestant than Jewish. To the disgust of the orthodox rabbis, synagogues – now called 'temples' – were established in

Hamburg and Berlin. In America, the playwright Isaac Harby founded a reformed temple in Charleston, and by 1870 a substantial proportion of the two hundred synagogues in the United States had adopted at least some Reform practices.[38]

The Reformers belonged to the modern world. They had no time for the irrational, the mystical or the mysterious. By the 1840s, some Reform scholars who had embarked on a critical study of Jewish history founded a school aptly known as the Science of Judaism. They were influenced by the philosophies of Kant and Georg Wilhelm Friedrich Hegel (1770–1831), who had argued in *The Phenomenology of Mind* (1807) that God, which he called the universal Spirit, could achieve its full potential only if it came down to earth and was most fully realized in the human mind. Both Hegel and Kant had seen Judaism as the epitome of bad religion: the Jewish God, Hegel argued, was a tyrant, who required unquestioning submission to his intolerable laws. Jesus had tried to liberate humans from this base servitude, but Christians had reverted to the old tyranny.

The scholars of the Science of Judaism all rewrote the biblical story in Hegelian terms to correct this prejudice. In their work, the Bible recorded the spiritualizing process whereby Judaism attained self-consciousness.[39] In *The Religion of the Spirit* (1841), Solomon Formstecher (1808–89) argued that Jews had been the first to arrive at a Hegelian notion of God. The Hebrew prophets had initially imagined that their inspiration had come from an external force, but eventually understood that it was due to their own Spirit-nature. The exile had weaned Jews away from external props and controls so that they were now able to approach God in freedom. Samuel Hirsch (1815–89) argued that Abraham had been the first human being to abandon pagan fatalism and dependence to stand alone in God's presence in total control of himself, whereas Christianity had reverted to the superstition and irrationality of heathenism. Nachman Krochmal (1785–1840) and Zachariah Frankel (1801–75) agreed that the whole of the written Torah had been revealed to Moses on Sinai, but denied the divine inspiration of Oral Law, which was entirely man-made and could be altered to meet the demands of the present. Abraham Geiger (1810–74), an out-and-out rationalist, believed that the naive, creative and spontaneous period of Jewish history, which had begun in biblical times, had come to an end. With the Enlightenment, a higher stage of reflective contemplation was under way.

But some of these historians could see the value of ancient rituals, such as the wearing of phylacteries or the dietary laws, that the Reformers wanted to abolish. Frankel and Leopold Zunz (1794–1886) both believed that there was great danger in wholesale abolition of tradition. Those practices had become an essential part of the Jewish experience and without them, Judaism could degenerate into a system of abstract, lifeless doctrines. Zunz in particular feared that the Reform was losing touch with the emotions: reason alone could not produce the delight and joy that characterized Judaism at its best. It was an important point. In the past, the reading of the Bible had always been accompanied by rituals

– by liturgy, exercises in concentration, silence, fasting, chanting and ceremonial gestures – which had brought the sacred page to life. Without this ritual context, the Bible could be reduced to a document that provided information but no spiritual experience. Eventually Reform Judaism would recognize the truth of Zunz's critique and restore some of the rites that it had discarded.

As they watched their fellow Jews assimilating, many Jews were deeply concerned for the loss of tradition and the more orthodox felt increasingly embattled. In 1803, R. Hayyim Volozhiner, a disciple of the Gaon of Vilna, took a decisive step when he founded the Etz Hayyim yeshiva in Volozhin, Lithuania. Similar yeshivoth were founded in other parts of Eastern Europe during the nineteenth century and became the Jewish equivalents of the American Bible colleges. In the past, a yeshivah had simply consisted of a few rooms for the study of Torah and Talmud behind the synagogue. Etz Hayyim, where hundreds of gifted students from all over Europe gathered to study with experts, was quite different. R. Hayyim taught Torah and Talmud in the method he had learned from the Gaon, analysing the text logically but in a way that produced a spiritual experience. Students were not there to learn *about* Torah; the process of rote-learning, preparation, and lively, heated discussion were rituals that were just as important as any conclusion reached in class. This method was a form of prayer, and its intensity reflected the spirituality of the Gaon. The curriculum was demanding, the hours long, and the young men were separated from family and friends. Some were allowed to spend a little time on secular subjects, but these were secondary, regarded as stealing time from Torah.[40]

The original purpose of Etz Hayyim had been to counter Hasidism and reinstate rigorous study of Torah. But as the nineteenth century progressed the threat of the Jewish Enlightenment became a more pressing danger, and Hasidim and *misnagdim* joined forces against the *maskilim*, whom they saw as a sort of Trojan horse, smuggling the evils of secular culture into the Jewish world. Gradually the new yeshivoth became bastions of orthodoxy to ward off this encroaching peril. Jews were developing their own type of fundamentalism, which rarely begins as a battle with an external foe, but rather as an internal struggle in which traditionalists fight their co-religionists. Fundamentalist institutions respond to modernity by creating an enclave of pure faith – the yeshiva or the Bible college – where the faithful can reshape their lives. It is a defensive move, which has the potential for a future counter-offensive. The students of a yeshiva, madrasah or Bible college are likely to become a cadre, with a shared training and ideology, in their local communities.

By the end of the nineteenth century the world could indeed seem a Godless place. Instead of being a shunned minority, as in the past, atheists were beginning to take the high moral ground. Hegel's pupil Ludwig Feuerbach (1804–72) argued that the idea of God diminished and devalued our humanity.

For Karl Marx (1818–83), religion was the symptom of a sick society, an opiate that made the diseased social system bearable and removed the will to find a cure. And radical Darwinists fired the first shots in a war between scripture and science that continues to the present day. In England, Thomas H. Huxley (1825–95) and on the Continent, Karl Vogt (1817–95), Ludwig Buchner (1824–99), Jakob Moleschott (1822–93) and Ernst Haeckel (1834–1919) popularized evolutionary theory to prove that religion and science were utterly incompatible. For Huxley, there could be no compromise between science and traditional religion: 'one or the other must go after a struggle of unknown duration'.[41]

If religious people felt embattled by the twentieth century, that is because they were indeed under attack. Jews were imperilled by a new 'scientific' racism, which defined the essential biological and genetic characteristics of the peoples of Europe so narrowly that the Jew became 'other'.[42] In Eastern Europe, a new wave of pogroms at the turn of the twentieth century led some non-religious Jews to create Zionism, a political movement to establish a Jewish homeland in Palestine. Even though it used the biblical symbol of the Land of Israel, the Zionists were not motivated by religion but by secular modern thought: nationalism, colonialism and socialism.

Secular modernity was in many ways benign, but it was also violent and tended to romanticize armed struggle. Between 1914 and 1945, seventy million people in Europe and the Soviet Union died as the result of war and conflict.[43] There were two world wars, brutally efficient ethnic cleansing and acts of genocide. Some of the worst atrocities had been perpetrated by the Germans, who had created one of the most cultivated societies in Europe. It was no longer possible to assume that a rational education would eliminate barbarism. The sheer scale of the Nazi Holocaust and the Soviet Gulag reveals their modern origins. No previous society had the technology to implement such grandiose schemes of extermination. The horrors of the Second World War (1939–45) ended with the explosion of the first atomic bombs over the Japanese cities of Hiroshima and Nagasaki. For centuries, men and women had dreamed of a final apocalypse wrought by God. Now they had used their prodigious learning to find the means of doing this very efficiently for themselves. The death camp, the mushroom cloud, and – today – the wanton destruction of the environment reveal a nihilistic ruthlessness at the heart of modern culture. The interpretation of the Bible had always been affected by historical conditions, and during the twentieth century Jews and Christians, as well as Muslims, began to develop scripturally based ideologies that had absorbed the violence of modernity.

During the First World War, an element of terror entered conservative Protestantism in the United States: the unprecedented slaughter was on such a scale that, they reasoned, these must be the battles foretold in Revelation. Because conservatives now believed that every word of the Bible was literally true, they began to view current events as the fulfilment of precise biblical predictions. Hebrew prophets had declared that the Jews would return to their land before the end, so when the British government issued the Balfour Declaration (1917), pledging support for a Jewish homeland in Palestine, Christian fundamentalists felt a mixture of awe and exultation. Cyrus Scofield had suggested that Russia was 'the power from the North'[44] that would attack Israel before Armaggedon: the Bolshevik Revolution (1917), which made atheistic communism the state ideology, seemed to confirm this. The creation of the League of Nations after the war obviously fulfilled the prophecy of Revelation 16:14. This was the revived Roman empire that would shortly be led by the Antichrist. What had once been a purely doctrinal dispute with the liberals was becoming a struggle for the future of civilization. When they read the Bible, Christian fundamentalists saw – and still see – themselves on the frontline against satanic forces that will shortly destroy the world. The wild tales of German atrocities circulating during and after the war seemed to prove the corrosive effects of the Higher Criticism on the nation that had spawned it.[45]

It was a vision inspired by deep fear. Christian fundamentalists were now ambivalent about democracy, which could lead to the 'most devilish rule this world has ever seen'.[46] Peace-keeping institutions such as the League of Nations – and, today, the United Nations – would always be associated with absolute evil: the Bible said that there would be war, not peace at the end, so the League was dangerously on the wrong track. Indeed, Antichrist himself, whom Paul had described as a plausible liar, would probably be a peacemaker.[47] Jesus was no longer a loving saviour, but the warlike

Christ of Revelation, who, said Isaac Haldemann, one of the leading Rapture ideologues, 'comes forth as one who no longer seeks either friendship or love . . . His garments are dipped in blood, the blood of others. He descends that he may shed the blood of men.'[48] In the past, exegetes had tried to see the Bible as a whole. Now the selection of one text at the expense of others – the fundamentalist 'canon within the canon' – led to a shocking distortion of the gospel.

In 1920, the Democratic politician William Jennings Bryan (1860–1925) launched a crusade against the teaching of evolution in the public schools. In his view, although the two were linked, it was not the Higher Criticism but Darwinism that had been responsible for the atrocities of the Great War.[49] Bryan's research had convinced him that the Darwinian conviction that only the strong should survive had 'laid the foundation for the bloodiest war in history'. It was no accident that 'the same science that manufactured poisoned gases to suffocate soldiers is preaching that man has a brutal ancestry and eliminating the miraculous and supernatural from the Bible'.[50] For Bryan, evolution was surrounded by a nimbus of evil, which symbolized the ruthless potential of modernity.

Bryan's conclusions were naive and incorrect but people were ready to listen to him. The war had ended the honeymoon period with science and they wanted it kept within due bounds. Those who espoused plain-speaking Baconian religion found it in Bryan, who singlehandedly pushed the topic of evolution to the top of the fundamentalist agenda, where it has remained. But it might never have replaced the Higher

Criticism had it not been for a dramatic development in Tennessee.

The southern states had hitherto taken little part in the fundamentalist movement but they were worried about the teaching of evolution. Bills were introduced into the state legislatures of Florida, Mississippi, Louisiana and Arkansas to ban the teaching of Darwinian theory. The anti-evolutionary laws in Tennessee were particularly strict and John Scopes, a young teacher in the small town of Dayton, decided to strike a blow for freedom of speech and confessed that he had broken the law when he had taken a biology class in place of his principal. In July 1925 he was brought to trial. The new American Civil Liberties Union (ACLU) sent a team of lawyers to defend him, headed by the rationalist campaigner Clarence Darrow. Bryan agreed to support the law. Immediately the trial became a contest between the Bible and science.

Bryan was a disaster on the stand and Darrow emerged from the trial as the champion of rational thought. The press gleefully denounced the fundamentalists as hopeless anachronisms, who could take no part in the modern world. This had an effect that is instructive to us today. When fundamentalist movements are attacked they usually become more extreme. Before Dayton, the conservatives were wary of evolution, but very few had espoused 'creation science', which maintained that the first chapter of Genesis was factually true in every detail. After Scopes, however, they became more vehemently literal in their interpretation of scripture, and creation science became the flagship of their movement. Before

Scopes, fundamentalists had been willing to work for social reform with people on the left; after Scopes, they swung to the far right of the political spectrum, where they have remained.

After the Holocaust, orthodox Jews felt impelled to rebuild the Hasidic courts and *misnagdic* yeshivoth in the new Jewish state of Israel and the United States as an act of piety to the six million.[51] Torah study was now a lifelong, full-time pursuit. Men would continue at the yeshivah after they married and, supported financially by their wives, had minimal contact with the outside world.[52] These ultra-orthodox Jews, known as the Haredim (the 'trembling ones'),[53] observed the commandments more rigorously than ever before,[54] finding new ways of being punctilious about diet and purification.[55] Before the Holocaust, excessive stringency had been discouraged as divisive. But now the Haredim were creating a Bible-based counter-culture in diametrical opposition to the rationalized efficiency that had helped to slaughter six million Jews. Yeshivah study had nothing in common with the pragmatism of modernity: many of the laws studied, such as the laws of temple service, could no longer be implemented. The repetition of the Hebrew words that God had spoken on Sinai was a form of communion with the divine. Exploring the minutiae of the law was a way of symbolically entering the mind of God. Becoming familiar with the *halakha* of the great rabbis was a way of appropriating the tradition that had so nearly been destroyed.

Zionism had originally been a secular ideology, a rebellion against religious Judaism that was reviled by the Orthodox for profaning the land of Israel, one of the most sacred symbols of Judaism. But during the 1950s and 1960s, a group of young religious Israelis began to develop a religious Zionism based on a literal interpretation of the Bible. God had promised the land to the descendants of Abraham, and this gave Jews a legal title to Palestine. The secular Zionists had never made this claim: they had tried to make the land their own by pragmatic diplomacy, working the land, or by fighting for it. But the religious Zionists saw life in Israel as a spiritual opportunity. In the late 1950s, they found a leader in R. Zvi Yehuda Kook (1891–1982), who was by then almost seventy years old. According to Kook, the secular state of Israel was the kingdom of God *tout court*; every clod of its earth was holy. Like the Christian fundamentalists, he interpreted literally the Hebrew prophecies about the Jews' return to their land: to settle territory now inhabited by the Arabs would hasten the final Redemption and political involvement in the affairs of Israel was an ascent to the pinnacles of holiness.[56] Unless Jews occupied the whole land of Israel, exactly as this was defined in the Bible, there could be no Redemption. The annexation of territory belonging to the Arabs was now a supreme religious duty.[57]

When the Israeli army occupied the West Bank, the Sinai peninsula, the Gaza Strip and the Golan Heights during the June War of 1967, Zionists saw this literal fulfilment of a scriptural imperative as proof positive that the end time had begun. There could be no question of returning the new territories to the Arabs in exchange for peace. Radical Kookists began to squat in Hebron and built a city at nearby Kiryat Arba, even though this contravened Geneva Conventions that forbade settlement in territories occupied during hostilities. This settlement initiative intensified after the October War of 1973. Religious Zionists joined forces with the secular right in opposition to any peace deal. True peace meant territorial integrity and the preservation of the whole land of Israel. As the Kookist rabbi Eleazar Waldman explained, Israel was engaged in a battle against evil, on which hung the prospects of peace for the entire world.[58]

This intransigence sounds perverse, but it was not unlike that of secularist politicians, who also habitually spoke of wars to end all wars and of the grim necessity of going to war to preserve world peace. In another vein, a small group of Jewish fundamentalists formulated a biblical version of the genocidal ethos of the twentieth century, comparing the Palestinians to the Amalekites, a people so cruel that God commanded the Israelites to kill them without mercy.[59] The same tendency was also evident in the movement founded by R. Meir Kahane, whose reading of scripture was so reductionist that it became a deadly caricature of Judaism, giving a biblical rationale to ethnic cleansing. The promise to Abraham was still valid, so the Arabs were usurpers and must go.[60] 'There are not several messages in Judaism,' he insisted. 'There is only one . . . God wanted us to live in a country on our own, isolated, so that we have the least possible contact with what is foreign.'[61]

In the early 1980s, a small group of Kookists plotted to

destroy the Muslim shrines on the Haram al-Sharif, which had been built on the site of Solomon's temple and was the third holiest place in the Islamic world. How could the Messiah return when this holy place was polluted? In a literal interpretation of the kabbalistic principle that events on earth could influence the divine, the extremists calculated that by risking all-out war with the entire Muslim world, they would 'force' God to send the messiah to save Israel.[62] Not only could the plot, had it been implemented, have had fatal consequences for the Jewish state, but Washington strategists believed that in the context of the Cold War, when the Soviets supported the Arabs and the United States Israel, it could even have sparked a third world war.[63] Yet this nihilistic project was not out of place in a world where the great powers were prepared to expose their own people to nuclear annihilation in order to defeat the enemy.

Occasionally these pernicious interpretations of scripture have resulted in atrocity. Kahane's ideology inspired Baruch Goldstein, a settler in Kiryat Arba, to shoot twenty-nine Palestinian worshippers in the Cave of the Patriarchs in Hebron on the festival of Purim, 25 February 1994. On 4 November 1995, Yigal Amir, a former student of a Zionist yeshiva, assassinated Prime Minister Yitzhak Rabin during a peace rally in Tel Aviv. His study of Jewish law, he said later, had convinced him that in signing away the sacred land in the Oslo Accords, Rabin was a *rodef* ('pursuer') who endangered Jewish life and was therefore worthy of punishment.

*

In the United States, Protestant fundamentalists had evolved a Christian Zionism that was paradoxically anti-Semitic. The Jewish people had been central to the 'Rapture' vision of John Darby.[64] Jesus could not return unless the Jews were living in the Holy Land.[65] The creation of the State of Israel in 1948 was seen by fundamentalist ideologue Jerry Falwell as the 'greatest single sign indicating the imminent return of Jesus Christ'.[66] Support for Israel was mandatory. But Darby had taught that the Antichrist would slaughter two-thirds of the Jews living in Palestine in the end time, so fundamentalist writers looked forward to a massacre in which Jews would die in ghastly numbers.[67]

Like the Kookists, the Christian fundamentalists were not interested in peace. During the Cold War they were adamantly opposed to any detente with the Soviet Union, the 'enemy from the north'. Peace, said televangelist James Robison was 'against the Word of God'.[68] They were not perturbed by nuclear catastrophe, which had been predicted by St Peter[69] and would not, in any case, affect true believers, who would be raptured before Tribulation. Rapture is still a potent force in the politics of the United States. The Bush administration, which relied on the support of the Christian right, occasionally reverted to Rapture-speak. For a time, after the demise of the Soviet Union, Saddam Hussein filled the role of the 'enemy of the north', and his place was soon taken by Syria or Iran. There is still unqualified support for Israel, which can become pernicious. In January 2006, after Prime Minister Ariel Sharon suffered a massive stroke, fundamentalist leader Pat Robertson claimed that this was God's punishment for withdrawing Israeli troops from Gaza.

Pat Robertson is associated with a form of Christian fundamentalism that is more extreme than Jerry Falwell's Moral Majority. The Reconstruction movement, founded by the Texan economist Gary North and his father-in-law Rousas John Rushdoony, is convinced that the secular administration in Washington is doomed.[70] God will soon replace it with a Christian government run along strictly biblical lines. Reconstructionists are thus planning the Christian commonwealth in which the modern heresy of democracy will be abolished and every single law of the Bible implemented literally: slavery will be re-established, contraception prohibited, adulterers, homosexuals, blasphemers and astrologers will be executed, and persistently disobedient children stoned to death. God is not on the side of the poor: indeed, North explains, there is a 'tight relationship between wickedness and poverty'.[71] Taxes must not be used for welfare, since 'subsidizing sluggards is the same as subsidizing evil'.[72] The Bible forbids all foreign aid to the developing world: its addiction to paganism, immorality and demon worship is the cause of its economic problems.[73] In the past, exegetes tried to bypass these less than humane portions of the Bible or had given them an allegorical interpretation. The Reconstructionists seem to seek these passages out deliberately and interpret them ahistorically and literally. Where other fundamentalists have absorbed the violence of modernity, the Reconstruc-

tionists have produced a religious version of militant capitalism.[74]

Fundamentalists grab the headlines but other biblical
scholars have tried to revive traditional biblical spirituality
in a more eirenic spirit. Writing in the 1940s, the Jewish
philosopher Martin Buber (1878–1965) believed that the
Bible witnessed to God's presence at a time when he
seemed absent. Exegesis could never stand still, since the
Bible represented an ongoing dialogue between God and
humanity. The study of the Bible must lead to a transformed lifestyle. When we open the Bible, we must be ready
to be fundamentally changed by what we hear. Buber was
much struck by the fact that the rabbis called scripture a
miqra, a 'calling out'. It was a summons that did not allow
readers to abstract themselves from the problems of the
world but trained them to stand fast and listen to the under-
current of events.

His friend Franz Rosenzweig (1886–1929) agreed that the
Bible compelled us to face the crises of the hour. Readers must
respond to its *miqra* in the same way as the prophets, crying:
'*Hinneni*: "Here I am" – all ready, all soul . . . to the reality at
hand.'[75] The Bible was not a preordained script. Our daily
lives should illuminate the Bible, and in turn the Bible will
help us to discover the sacred dimension of our day-to-day
experience. Reading scripture was an introspective process.
Rosenzweig knew that modern human beings could not
respond to the Bible in the same way as earlier generations.
We needed the new covenant described to Jeremiah, when the

law would be written within our hearts.[76] The text must be appropriated and interiorized in patient, disciplined study and translated into action in the world.

Michael Fishbane, currently Professor of Jewish Studies at the University of Chicago, believes that exegesis could help us to retrieve the idea of a sacred text.[77] Historical criticism of the Bible makes it impossible for us to read the scriptures synchronistically any longer, linking passages widely separated in time. But modern literary criticism acknowledges that our inner world is created by fragments of many different texts, which live together in our minds, one qualifying another. Our moral universe is shaped by *King Lear*, *Moby Dick* and *Madame Bovary* as well as by the Bible. We rarely absorb texts whole: isolated images, phrases and gobbets live in our minds in myriad, fluid groupings, acting and reacting on one another. Similarly, the Bible does not exist in our minds whole and entire but in fragmentary form. We create our own 'canon within a canon' and should deliberately ensure that our selection is a collection of benign texts. The historical study of the Bible shows that there were many contesting visions in ancient Israel, each claiming – often aggressively – to be the official version of Yahwism. We can read the Bible today as a prophetic commentary on our own world of raging orthodoxies; it can provide us with the compassionate distance to realize the dangers of this strident dogmatism and replace it with a chastened pluralism.

The main thrust of Fishbane's work has been to show how the Bible constantly interpreted and corrected itself. Isaiah had envisaged all the nations making their way to Mount Zion, the city of peace, saying, 'Come, let us go up to the mounain of Yahweh . . . that he may teach us his ways . . . since the Law will go out from Zion, and the oracle of Yahweh from Jerusalem.'[78] When Micah quoted these words, he also looked forward to a universal peace when the nations would speak gently to one another. But he added an astonishingly daring coda. Each nation, including Israel, 'will go forward, each in the name of its own god'. It is almost as though Micah foresaw our own time of multiple visions converging on a common truth, which for Israel had been expressed by the idea of their god.[79]

Christian exegetes have continued to see Christ at the heart of the Bible. In his biblical theology, the Swiss Jesuit Hans Urs von Balthasar (1905–88) drew on the notion of incarnation. Jesus, like scripture, was God's Word in human form. God is knowable and can express himself in terms that we can understand. But we have constantly to wrestle with these difficult but indispensable texts. The Bible presented archetypal stories of encounters between God and human beings, which helped readers to see the divine as an ideal dimension of their own lives. They can seize the imagination, in the same way as *King Lear* or Michelangelo's *David*. But it was impossible to extract definitive 'essentials' or 'fundamentals' of God's revelation in the Bible. Theology could 'never be more than a reflection in words and concepts, never capable of being brought to a close . . . never be completely pinned down'.[80] But scripture was still authoritative, and everybody, including the Pope and the hierarchy, was subject to its summons and critique. Catholics had a duty to challenge the Church if they saw it departing from the spirit of the gospel.

Hans Frei (1922–88), a convert from Judaism who became an episcopal priest and a professor at Yale, noted that in the pre-critical world, most readers assumed that the biblical stories were historical, even if they were chiefly concerned with figurative types of exegesis.[81] But this consensus broke down during the eighteenth century: after the Enlightenment, some saw the biblical narratives as purely factual, forgetting that they were written as stories. The author's use of syntax and vocabulary were supposed to affect the way we understood these tales. Jesus was certainly a historical figure, but when we examine the gospel narratives of the resurrection, for example, it becomes impossible to decide what actually happened. Like the Jewish exegetes, Frei believed that the Bible must be read in conjunction with a sustained reflection on our own times. The juxtaposition of the gospel and current events should not lead to facile interpretations, but enable us to enter more deeply into the complexity of each. The Bible was subversive. These stories must not be used simply to back up the ideology of the establishment, but we should expose the hopes, claims and expectations of our time to the gospel story and examine, deconstruct and refashion them accordingly.

More recently, Wilfred Cantwell Smith (1916–2000), formerly Professor of Comparative Religion at Harvard, stressed the importance of understanding the Bible historically.[82] It was impossible to say what the Bible 'really' meant when any one of its verses was likely to have been interpreted in several different ways. Religious people have all worked out their salvation within the confines of a particular place and time. The Bible has meant different things to Jews and Christians at different stages of their history, and their exegesis was inevitably coloured by their particular circumstances. If an interpretation concentrated only on what the biblical author said, and ignored the way generations of Jews and Christians had understood it, it distorted the significance of the Bible.

EPILOGUE

What is the way forward? This short biography makes it clear that many modern assumptions about the Bible are incorrect. The Bible did not encourage slavish conformity. In the Jewish tradition especially, as we saw with the story of R. Eliezer, not even the voice of God could force an exegete to accept another person's interpretation. From the first, the biblical authors contradicted each other and their conflicting visions were all included by the editors in the final text. The Talmud was an interactive text that, properly taught, compelled a student to find his own answers. Hans Frei was right: the Bible has been a subversive document, suspicious of orthodoxy since the time of Amos and Hosea.

The modern habit of quoting proof-texts to legitimize policies and rulings is out of key with interpretive tradition. As Wilfred Cantwell Smith explained, scripture was not really a text but an activity, a spiritual process that introduced thousands of people to transcendence. The Bible may have been used to back up doctrines and beliefs but that was not its chief function. The fundamentalist emphasis on the literal reflects the modern ethos but is a breach with tradition, which usually preferred some kind of figurative or innovative interpretation. There is, for example, no single doctrine of creation in the Bible and the first chapter of Genesis was rarely read as a factual description of the origins of the cosmos. Many of the Christians who oppose Darwinism today are Calvinists, but Calvin insisted that the Bible was not a scientific document and that those who wanted to learn about astronomy or cosmology should look elsewhere.

We have seen that different texts have been used to support entirely opposed programmes. Athanasius and Arius could both produce quotations to prove their personal beliefs about the divinity of Christ. Because they could find no definitive warrant in scripture to decide this matter, the fathers found theological solutions that owed little to the Bible. Slaveowners interpreted the Bible one way, the slaves in quite another. The same applies today in the Christian debate about ordaining women to the priesthood. Like nearly all premodern documents, the Bible is a patriarchal text. Opponents of feminism and women priests can find a host of biblical texts to prove their case, but some of the New Testament authors had very different views and can be cited to show that in Christ there was neither male nor female and that women worked as 'co-workers' and 'co-apostles' in the early Church. Hurling texts around polemically is a sterile pursuit. Scripture is not able to provide certainty on this type of question.

This is also the case with the question of scriptural violence. There is indeed a great deal of violence in the Bible –

far more than there is in the Qur'an. And it is unquestionably true that throughout history people have used the Bible to justify atrocious acts. As Cantwell Smith observed, the Bible and its interpretation must be seen in historical context. The world has always been a violent place and scripture and its exegesis has often fallen prey to contemporary aggression. Joshua was presented by the Deuteronomists fighting with all the ruthlessness of an Assyrian general. The Crusaders ignored the pacifist teachings of Jesus and signed up for an expedition to the Holy Land because they were soldiers, wanted a militant religion and applied their distinctively feudal ethos to the Bible. The same is true in our own time. The modern period has seen violence and slaughter on an unprecedented scale and it is not surprising that this has affected the way some people have read the Bible.

But because scripture has been so flagrantly abused in this way, Jews, Christians and Muslims have a duty to establish a counter-narrative that emphasizes the benign features of their exegetical traditions. Interfaith understanding and coopera-tion are now essential to our survival: perhaps members of the three monotheistic faiths should work together to estab-lish a common hermeneutics. This would consist of a sus-tained critical, moral and spiritual examination of the problematic texts themselves, the way they have been inter-preted throughout history, and an in-depth examination of the exegesis of the people who exploit them today. Their sig-nificance in the tradition as a whole should be defined clearly.

Michael Fishbane's suggestion that we construct a 'canon

within the canon' to moderate the religiously articulated hatred of our time is extremely apposite. The Bible is indeed a witness to the danger of raging orthodoxies – and in our own day, not all these orthodoxies are religious. There is a form of 'secular fundamentalism' that is as bigoted, biased and inaccurate about religion as any Bible-based fundamentalism about secularism. There are good things and bad things in the Bible. The kabbalists were acutely aware of the flaws of their Torah and found inventive ways to qualify the harsh predominance of *Din*. There was a similar debate in the Bible itself. In the Pentateuch, P's message of reconciliation opposed the stridency of Deuteronomy. In the New Testament, the battles of Revelation are juxtaposed with the pacifism of the Sermon on the Mount. In the early fifth century, Jerome railed savagely against his theological opponents, while Augustine pleaded for kindness and humility in biblical debate, just as, later, Calvin was horrified by the polemical diatribes of Luther and Zwingli. The canon that is selected to counter the prevailing enthusiasm for biblical aggression should, as Fishbane suggested, make this alternative Word more audible in our divided world. Buber, Rosenzweig and Frei all argued that the study of the Bible should not be confined to the ivory tower of academe but should be applied rigorously to the contemporary scene. Midrash and exegesis were always supposed to relate directly to the burning issues of the day, and the fundamentalists should not be the only people who attempt this.

Buber and Rosenzweig both stressed the importance of

listening to the Bible. Throughout this biography, we have considered the ways in which Jews and Christians have tried to cultivate a receptive, intuitive approach to scripture. This is difficult for us today. We are a talkative and opinionated society and not always good at listening. The discourse of politics, media and academe is essentially adversarial. While this is undoubtedly important in a democracy, it can mean that people are not really receptive to an opposing viewpoint. It is often apparent during a parliamentary debate or a panel discussion on television that while their opponents are speaking, participants are simply thinking up the next clever thing that *they* are going to say. Biblical discourse is often conducted in the same confrontational spirit, very different from the 'listening ear' proposed by the Hasidic leader, Dov Ber. We also expect immediate answers to complex questions. The soundbite is all. In biblical times, some people feared that a written scripture encouraged a slick, superficial 'knowing'. This is surely an even greater danger in the electronic age, when people are used to finding truth at the click of a mouse.

This makes a truly spiritual reading of the Bible difficult. The achievements of the historical-critical method have been magnificent; it has given us unprecedented knowledge *about* the Bible but has not yet provided us with a spirituality. Fishbane is right: the *horoz* and *pesher* exegesis of the past are no longer an option. Nor are the elaborate allegories of Origen, who was able to find a gospel *miqra* in every word of the Hebrew scriptures. This type of figurative exegesis offends modern academic sensibilities, because it violates the integrity of the original text. But there was a generosity in *allegoria* that is often lacking in modern discourse. Philo and Origen did not dismiss the biblical texts with disdain but gave them the benefit of the doubt. Modern philosophers of language have argued that 'the principle of charity' is essential for any form of communication. If we truly want to understand the other, we have to assume that he or she is speaking the truth. *Allegoria* was an attempt to find truth in texts that seemed barbarous and opaque and then 'translate' them into a more congenial idiom.[1] The logician N. L. Wilson has argued that a critic who confronts an alien body of texts must apply the 'principle of charity'. He or she must seek interpretation, which 'in light of what it knows of the facts, will maximize truth among the sentences of the corpus'.[2] The linguist Donald Davidson maintains that 'Making sense of the utterance and behaviour of others, even their most aberrant behaviour, requires you to find a great deal of truth and reason in them.'[3] Even though their beliefs may be very different from your own, 'you have to assume that the alien is very much the same as you are,' otherwise you are in danger of denying their humanity. 'Charity is forced upon us,' Davidson concludes. 'Whether we like it or not, if we want to understand others, we must regard them as right in most matters.'[4] In the public arena, however, people are often presumed to be wrong before they are proved right, and this has inevitably affected our understanding of the Bible.

The 'principle of charity' accords with the religious ideal of compassion, the duty to 'feel with' the other. Some of the greatest exegetes of the past – Hillel, Jesus, Paul, Johanan ben Zakkai, Akiba and Augustine – insisted that charity and loving kindness were essential to biblical interpretation. In our dangerously polarized world, a common hermeneutics among the religions should surely emphasize this tradition. Jews, Christians and Muslims must first examine the flaws of their own scriptures and only then listen, with humility, generosity and charity to the exegesis of others.

What would it mean to interpret the whole of the Bible as a 'commentary' on the Golden Rule? It would first demand an appreciation of other people's scriptures. R. Meir said that any interpretation that spread hatred or denigrated other sages was illegitimate. Today these 'other sages' must include Muhammad, Buddha and the *rishis* of the Rig Veda. In the spirit of Michael Fishbane's reading of Micah's coda, Christians must cease regarding the Tanakh as a mere prelude to Christiantiy and learn to value the insights of the rabbis; Jews should acknowledge the Jewishness of Jesus and Paul and learn to appreciate the fathers of the Church.

Augustine claimed that scripture teaches nothing but charity. How then do we interpret the massacres of Joshua, the gospel abuse of the Pharisees and the battles of Revelation? As Augustine advised, these episodes should first be placed in their historical context and studied in the way we have already considered. How have they been interpreted in the past? And do they throw light on the lack of charity in contemporary discourse and the modern political scene?

Today we see too much strident certainty in both the religious and the secular spheres. Instead of quoting the Bible in order to denigrate homosexuals, liberals or women priests, we could recall Augustine's rule of faith: an exegete must always seek the most charitable interpretation of a text. Instead of using a biblical passage to back up a bygone orthodoxy, modern hermeneutics could bear in mind the original meaning of midrash: 'to go in search of'. Exegesis is a quest for something new. Buber said that each reader should stand before the Bible as Moses stood before the burning bush, listening intently and preparing for a revelation that will force him or her to lay aside former preconceptions. If this offends the religious establishment, we might remind them, with Balthasar, that the authorities are also accountable to the *miqra* of scripture.

The major religions all insist that the practice of daily, hourly compassion will introduce us to God, Nirvana and the Dao. An exegesis based on the 'principle of charity' would be a spiritual discipline that is deeply needed in our torn and fragmented world. The Bible is in danger of becoming a dead or an irrelevant letter; it is being distorted by claims for its literal infallibility; it is derided – often unfairly – by secular fundamentalists; it is also becoming a toxic arsenal that fuels hatred and sterile polemic. The development of a more compassionate hermeneutics could provide an important counter-narrative in our discordant world.

GLOSSARY OF KEY TERMS

Allegory (Greek, *allegoria*) A discourse that describes one thing under the guise of another.

Anagogy; anagogical (Greek) The mystical or eschatological meaning of a biblical text.

Apatheia (Greek) Indifference to earthly conditions, impassibility, serenity, selflessness and invulnerability.

Apocalypse (Greek, *apokalypsis*) Literally, 'unveiling' or revelation. Often used to refer to a revelation about the last days or the end time.

Apologia (Latin) A rational explanation. Christian apologists tried to give a reasonable account of their faith to convince their pagan neighbours.

Apophatic (Greek) Silent; an experience beyond the reach of speech. Greek Christians came to believe that all theology should have an element of stillness, paradox and restraint in order to emphasize the ineffability and mystery of God.

Bavli The Babylonian Talmud (q.v.)

Binah (Hebrew) Intelligence; the third *sefirah* (q.v.) in the kabbalistic myth of creation and redemption. Binah is also known as 'the Supernal Mother', the womb which, once penetrated by *Hokhmah* (q.v.), gave birth to seven 'lower' *sefiroth* and thence to all that is.

Breaking of the Vessels A term in Lurianic Kabbalah (q.v.) describing the primal catastrophe, when sparks of divine light fell to earth and were trapped in matter.

Canon Literally, a rule or decree; the list of officially accepted books in the Hebrew and Christian Bible.

Christ (Greek, *christos*) A Greek translation of the Hebrew *meshiah* ('anointed one') (q.v.); a title applied by the early Christians to Jesus of Nazareth.

Coincidentia Oppositorum (Latin) 'An agreement of opposites'; the term applied to an ecstatic experience, when divisions and contradictions fade in an apprehension of the unity of all things; a numinous intimation of harmony and wholeness.

Darash (Hebrew) 'To study', 'to investigate', 'to go in search of'. The term was also used by kabbalists to describe the moral or homiletic sense of scripture in *Pardes* exegesis (q.v.).

Demiourgos (Greek) 'Craftsman'. In Plato's *Timaeus*, the demiourgos was the divine craftsman, the subordinate of the Supreme God, who gave shape and coherence to the material world, making it conform to the eternal forms. The Gnostics used the term *demiourgos* to describe the God of the Jewish Bible, who was responsible for the creation of the evil world of matter.

Deuteronomy; Deuteronomist (Greek, *deuteronomion*: 'second law') Originally the term implied to Moses's final discourse before his death on Mount Nebo, which is described in the fifth book of the Pentateuch. The term is also used of the reformers who composed the book of Deuteronomy and the historical books of Samuel and Kings in the seventh century BCE.

Devekut (Hebrew) 'Attachment' to God; the perpetual

consciousness of the divine to which the Hasidim aspired.

Din (Hebrew) Stern Judgement; the fifth *sefirah* (q.v.) in the kabbalistic myth of creation and revelation. In Lurianic Kabbalah (q.v.), *Din* represented the evil potential within the divine, which became predominant after the primal catastrophe of the 'breaking of the vessels' (q.v.).

Dogma (Greek) Term used by Greek-speaking Christians to describe the hidden, ineffable traditions of the Church, which could only be understood mystically and expressed symbolically. In the West, 'dogma' has come to mean a body of opinion, categorically and authoritatively stated.

Dynameis (Greek) The 'powers' of God, a term used by the Greeks to denote God's activity in the natural world and as described in the Bible; it was to be regarded as quite distinct from God's inaccessible *ousia* (q.v.), 'essence'.

Economy The divine government of the world; the divine dispensation; the system that underlies the whole of reality.

Ekstasis (Greek, 'stepping outside') An ecstasy that takes the worshipper beyond the self and outside mundane experience.

Ekklesia (Greek) Congregation, Church.

Emanation A process whereby the various grades of reality were imagined to flow from a single, primal source, which Jews, Christians and Muslims identified with God; some preferred to use the metaphor of emanation to describe the origins of life rather than creation *ex nihilo* (q.v.), the instantaneous creation of all things at a given moment in time.

En Sof (Hebrew, 'without end') The inscrutable, inaccessible and unknowable essence of God in the mystical philosophy of Kabbalah; the Godhead, the hidden source or root of the divine.

Energeiaei (Greek, 'energies') God's 'activities' in the world, which

enable us to catch a glimpse of him. Like *dynameis* (q.v.), the
term is used to distinguish the human conception of God from
the ineffable and incomprehensible reality itself.

Epithalamium: (Latin derivation) A marriage song, describing the
union of bride and groom.

Eschatology Derived from the Greek, *eskaton:* 'the end'. The study
of the last days and the end time.

Ex nihilo (Latin, 'out of nothing') The phrase used to describe
God's creation of the universe from nothing in a free,
spontaneous and unique act in time. Some philosophers found
this an impossible notion, because in Greek rational theology
the universe is eternal and God is impassible and not subject
to sudden actions and change.

Exegesis (Greek) To 'lead or guide out'; the art of interpreting and
explaining the biblical text.

Father: The title Jesus seems to have used when he spoke to God;
later identified with Christians as the first of the *dynameis*
(q.v.) of the Trinity.

Gaon (Hebrew) The 'head' or principal of a rabbinical academy.

Gemara (Hebrew) Exegesis. In the Talmud (q.v.) it refers to the
commentary on the Mishnah (q.v.)

Gentile A non-Jew; derived from the Latin *gentes,* a translation of
the Hebrew *goyim* (q.v.), the 'foreign nations'.

Gnostic (Greek) A form of Christianity that emphasized the
importance of *gnosis*, a redeeming 'knowledge', and
distinguished between the wholly spiritual Supreme God,
who had sent Jesus as his envoy, and the *demiourgos* (q.v.),
revealed in the Jewish Bible, who had created the evil world of
matter.

Godfearer A gentile pagan sympathizer, who was an honorary

member of the synagogue, with varying degrees of
commitment.

Godhead The source of divinity; the hidden root of the divine; *En
Sof* (q.v.)

Gospel Literally 'good news' (from the Anglo-Saxon *god spel)*. The
proclamation (Greek, *evangelion*) of the early Church. The term
is also applied to the various biographies of Jesus.

Goyim (Hebrew) The foreign nations; the gentiles.

Halakah; halakoth (Hebrew) A rabbinical legal ruling.

Haredim (Hebrew, 'the trembling ones') A term derived from
Isaiah 66:5, which refers to devout Israelites who 'tremble' at
God's word and which was applied to ultra-orthodox Jews.

Hasid (Hebrew, 'pious one'); **Hasidim** The Jewish mystical reform
movement founded in the eighteenth century by the Baal
Shem Tov.

Haskalah (Hebrew) The Jewish enlightenment founded by Moses
Mendelssohn.

Hermeneutics (Greek) The art of interpretation, especially of
scripture.

Hesed (Hebrew) Originally tribal or cultic 'loyalty'; later 'love' or
'mercy'. The sixth *sefirah* (q.v.) in the kabbalistic myth of
creation and revelation, paired with *Din* (q.v.); *hesed* must
always moderate the Stern Judgement of God.

Hod (Hebrew, 'Majesty') The eighth *sefirah* (q.v.) in the kabbalistic
myth of creation and revelation.

Holy Spirit Term used by rabbis in the Talmudic age, often
interchangeably with *Shekhinah* (q.v.) to denote God's presence
on earth; a way of distinguishing the God we experience from
the utterly transcendent divinity which forever eluded us. In
Christianity, this divine presence became one of the three
dynameis (q.v) recounted in scripture, which – along with

Father and Logos – constituted the revelation of God as Trinity.

Hokhmah (Hebrew, 'Wisdom') In the Bible, Wisdom is the blueprint of creation, the divine plan that governs the universe, which was eventually identified with the Torah (q.v.). *Hokhmah* is also the second *sefirah* (q.v.) of the kabbalistic myth of creation and revelation, which merges with the first *sefirah* as a 'point' that penetrates the womb of *Binah* (q.v.).

Horoz (Hebrew, 'enchaining') The rabbinic practice of 'linking' separate biblical quotations together in a 'chain' that yielded the ecstatic experience of *coincidentia oppositorum* (q.v.).

Hypothesis (Greek, 'underlying argument') Originally a subtext, the message that lies hidden beneath the surface meaning of the Bible. Later, a scientific theory put forward as a conjecture for empirical demonstration.

Incarnation (Latin derivation) The 'embodiment' of a spiritual reality in an earthly form; in Christianity it refers specifically to the descent of the Logos (q.v.), which was 'made flesh' in the human body of Jesus.

Kabbalah (Hebrew, 'inherited tradition') The mystical tradition of Judaism.

Kerygma (Greek) A term used by Greek Christians to denote the public teaching of the Church, based on scripture, which can be expressed adequately in words, as opposed to dogma (q.v.), which could not.

Kether Elyon (Hebrew, 'Supreme Crown') The first *sefirah* (q.v.) in the kabbalistic myth of creation and revelation, which emerges from the unfathomable depths of *En Sof* (q.v.) as a 'dark flame'. It is also known as 'Nothing', because it does not correspond to any category intelligible to human beings.

Kethuvim (Hebrew) The Writings, the third category of the Hebrew Bible; the canon of the Writings included Chronicles, Ezra, Nehemiah, Esther, Job, and the Wisdom books attributed to Solomon: Proverbs, Ecclesiastes and the Song of Songs.

Lectio Divina (Latin) 'Sacred Study': the monastic practice of reading the Bible slowly and meditatively, identifying with the action and experiencing moments of *ekstasis* (q.v.)

Logos (Greek) 'Reason', 'definition', 'word'. God's Logos was identified with the Wisdom (q.v.) and Word of God which brought everything into being, and had communicated with human beings throughout history. The prologue of John's gospel claimed that the Word had become incarnate in Jesus of Nazareth.

Lurianic Kabbalah The form of Kabbalah (q.v.) initiated by Isaac Luria in the sixteenth century, based on the myth of *Zimzum* (q.v.).

Malkuth (Hebrew, 'kingdom') The last of the *sefiroth* (q.v.) in the kabbalistic myth of creation and revelation; it is also called *Shekhinah* (q.v.), the divine presence on earth.

Maskilim (Hebrew, 'the enlightened ones') Followers of the Jewish Enlightenment, who wanted to privatize their religion, make it a rational faith, and participate in gentile (q.v.) culture.

Messiah (Hebrew *meshiah*, 'anointed one') Originally the term applied to anybody who was given a special task by God – notably the king, who was anointed at his coronation and became a 'son of God'. But the term was also used of prophets and priests, and also of Cyrus, king of Persia, who permitted the Jews to return to Judah and rebuild their temple after their long exile in Babylon. Later some Jews in the first century CE expected a *meshiah* to redeem Israel, assist Yahweh during the last days, and establish his reign on earth. The Christians believed that Jesus was this messiah.

Midrash (Hebrew) Derived from *darash* (q.v.); exegesis; interpretation, with connotations of investigation, quest.

Mishnah (Hebrew, 'learning by repetition') A Jewish scripture composed between 135 and 200 CE that consisted of a collection of oral traditions and rabbinic legal rulings.

Misnagdim (Hebrew) The 'opponents' of the Hasidim (q.v.).

Mythos (Greek, 'myth') A story that was not meant to be historical or factual, but which expressed the meaning of an event or narrative and encapsulated its timeless, eternal dimension. A myth can be described as an occurrence that in some sense happened once, but which also happens all the time. Myth has also been described as an early form of psychology, which described the labyrinthine and mysterious world of the psyche.

Netsakh (Hebrew, 'patience') The seventh *sefirah* (q.v.) in the kabbalistic myth of creation and revelation.

Neviim (Hebrew) The 'Prophets', the second category of the Hebrew Bible.

Ousia (Greek) The 'essence' of God, which is beyond our comprehension, remains utterly unknowable by human beings, and is not mentioned in the Bible. It is not dissimilar to *En Sof* (q.v.). Nevertheless, in the scriptures, God revealed itself in the three *dynameis* (q.v.): Father (q.v.), Logos (q.v.) and Holy Spirit (q.v.).

Pardes Originally a Persian word denoting 'orchard' but which indicated a high mystical state associated with 'paradise'. Later *Pardes* became a method of kabbalistic exegesis of scripture, which interpreted scripture according to the *Peshat* (literal), *Remez* (allegorical), *Darash* (moral) and *Sod* (mystical) senses (q.v.) and achieved a spiritual ascent to the divine.

Pentateuch The first five books of the Bible, also called the Torah: Genesis, Exodus, Leviticus, Numbers and Deuteronomy.

Peshat (Hebrew) The literal sense of scripture in the kabbalistic exegesis of *Pardes*.

Pesher (Hebrew, 'deciphering') A form of exegesis used by the Qumran sect and the early Christians, which saw the whole of scripture as a code, referring to their own community in the last days.

Pistis (Greek) The virtue of 'trust', often translated 'faith'.

Polis (Greek) A city state.

Rachamin (Hebrew, 'compassion') The fourth *sefirah* (q.v.) in the kabbalistic myth of creation and revelation. It is sometimes called *Tifereth* ('grace') (q.v.).

Remez (Hebrew, 'allegory') The second sense of scripture in kabbalistic *Pardes* exegesis.

Sefer Torah (Hebrew) The 'scroll of the law' discovered by the seventh-century reformers in the time of Josiah, which purported to be the document given to Moses on Mount Sinai.

Sephardim (Hebrew) The Jews of Spain (*Sepharad*).

Sefirah; Sefiroth (Hebrew, 'numerations') The inner dimensions of the divine psyche; the attributes of God which were not remote abstractions but dynamic potencies. In kabbalistic myth, the ten *sefiroth* were the ten emanations (q.v) or stages of God's revelation of himself. The ten sefiroth consisted of

- the 'higher' sefiroth: Kether Elyon (q.v.); Hokhmah (q.v.) and Binah (q.v)
- the seven 'lower' sefiroth: Rachamin/Tifereth (q.v.), Din (q.v), Hesed (q.v.), Netsakh (q.v.) Hod (q.v.), Yesod (q.v.) and Malkuth/Shekhinah (q.v.).

Shalom (Hebrew) Often translated 'peace' but more accurately 'wholeness, completeness'.

Shekhinah (Hebrew) Deriving from the verb *shakan:* to pitch one's tent; to live as a tent-dweller. The divine presence on earth, a term used by the rabbis to distinguish a Jew's experience of God from the ineffable reality itself. The kabbalists saw the *Shekhinah* as the tenth *sefirah*, and a female personality, who had been exiled from the rest of the *sefiroth* and wandered perpetually on earth.

Sola Scriptura (Latin) 'Scripture alone!', the watchword of the Protestant reformation.

Synoptics (Greek, 'seeing together') The three gospels of Mark, Matthew and Luke, who shared more or less the same theology and vision of Jesus.

Sod (Hebrew) The 'mystical' sense of scripture in the kabbalistic *Pardes* exegesis.

Tanna; Tannaim (Hebrew, 'reciters, repeaters') The rabbinic scholars who collated the Mishnah (q.v.)

Talmud (Hebrew, 'teaching study') The term refers to two scriptures, the Yerushalmi, the Jerusalem Talmud, completed in the early fifth century CE, and the Bavli, the Babylonian Talmud, completed in the sixth century. Both took the form of a *gemara* ('commentary') (q.v.) on the Mishnah (q.v.).

Tanakh (Hebrew acronym) The Hebrew Bible, which consisted of the Torah (q.v), the Neviim (q.v.) and the Kethuvim (q.v.) – the Law, the Prophets and the Writings.

Text (Latin, *textus*) A piece of writing 'woven' of myriad intertwining strands, meanings and realities.

Theophany (Greek) A revelation of God.

Theoria (Greek) Contemplation, meditation.

Tifereth (Hebrew, 'grace', beauty) The fourth *sefirah* (q.v.) in the kabbalistic myth of creation and revelation; often called *Rachamin* (q.v.).

Tikkun (Hebrew) The 'restoration' of the *Shekhinah* (q.v.) to the rest of the *sefiroth* (q.v.), the Jews to their homeland, the world to its rightful state, and scripture to its original spirituality and grace. *Tikkun* could be effected by Jews by means of the dedicated observance of Torah, *Pardes* exegesis (q.v.) and kabbalistic rituals.

Torah (Hebrew) Often simply translated 'law', it derives from a verb meaning to instruct, teach or guide. In the Bible, Torah included the fact of God's guidance in the world and the words he used to formulate it. Thus the Torah often refers to the Pentateuch, which consists of narratives that reveal God's care and tutelage as well as legislation. Later, Torah was linked with God's Wisdom (*Hokhmah*) (q.v.) and the Word that brought the world into being: it thus became synonymous with the highest knowledge and with transcendent goodness.

Wisdom see *Hokhmah*.

Yerushalmi The Jerusalem Talmud (q.v.).

Yeshivah; Yeshivoth (Hebrew) Derives from the verb *shivah* 'to sit'. A house of studies; a series of rooms attached to a synagogue, where Jews could study Torah (q.v.) and Talmud (q.v.).

Yesod (Hebrew, 'stability') The ninth *sefirah* (q.v.) in the kabbalistic myth of creation and revelation.

Zeir Anpin (Hebrew, 'the Impatient One') In Lurianic Kabbalah (q.v.), the God revealed in the Hebrew Bible, which consisted of six of the lower *sefiroth* (q.v.). Because *Din* (q.v.) had become predominant after the 'breaking of the vessels' (q.v.) and was no longer moderated and balanced by *hesed* (q.v.), God often seemed irascible and even violent in scripture. Separated from the *Shekhinah*, Zeir Anpin was also now unmistakably masculine.

Zimzum (Hebrew, 'withdrawal') The process in Lurianic Kabbalah (q.v.), whereby *En Sof* (q.v.) shrank into itself at the beginning of the creative process in order to make room for the cosmos.

Introduction

1 Margaret Barker, *The Gate of Heaven: The History and Symbolism of the Temple in Jerusalem*, London, 1991, pp. 26–9; R. E. Clements, *God and Temple*, Oxford, 1965, p. 65.

Chapter 1

1 Ezekiel 1.

2 Ezekiel 3: 1–3.

3 Ezekiel 40–8; Psalm 137.

4 Geo Widengren, *The Ascension of the Apostle and the Heavenly Book*, Uppsala and Leipzig, 1950, *passim*; Wilfred Cantwell Smith, *What Is Scripture? A Comparative Approach*, London, 1993, pp. 59–61.

5 Deuteronomy 26: 5–9. This very early text was probably recited at one of the covenant festivals.

6 Joshua 3; 24.

7 For example, Psalms 2, 48, 87 and 110.

8 Frank Moore Cross, *Canaanite Myth and Hebrew Epic: Essays in the History of the Religion of Israel*, Cambridge, Mass., and London, 1973, pp. 148–50, 162–3.

9 William M. Schniedewind, *How the Bible Became a Book: The*

Textualization of Ancient Israel, Cambridge, 2004, pp. 35–47.

10 Frank Moore Cross, *From Epic to Canon: History and Literature in Ancient Israel*, Baltimore and London, 1998, pp. 41–2.

11 Judges 5:4–5; Habakkuk 3:4–8. These are very ancient texts, dating back to the tenth century BCE.

12 George W. Mendenhall, *The Tenth Generation: The Origins of Biblical Tradition*, Baltimore and London, 1973; N. P. Lemche, *Early Israel: Anthropological and Historical Studies on the Israelite Society Before the Monarchy*, Leiden, 1985; D. C. Hopkins, *The Highlands of Canaan*, Sheffield, 1985; James D. Martin, 'Israel as a Tribal Society' in R. E. Clements (ed.), *The World of Ancient Israel: Sociological, Anthropological and Political Perspectives*, Cambridge, 1989, pp. 94–114; H. G. M. Williamson, 'The Concept of Israel in Transition' in Clements, *The World of Ancient Israel*, pp. 141–63.

13 Deuteronomy 32: 8–9.

14 Psalm 82.

15 Psalms 47–48, 96, 148–51.

16 Psalm 89: 5–8; Mark S. Smith, *The Origins of Biblical Monotheism: Israel's Polytheistic Background and the Ugaritic Texts*, New York and London, 2001, p. 9.

17 Mark S. Smith, *The Early History of God: Yahweh and the Other Deities in Ancient Israel*, New York and London, 1990, pp. 44–9.

18 R. E. Clements, *Abraham and David*, London, 1967.

19 David S. Sperling, *The Original Torah: The Political Intent of the Bible's Writers*, New York and London, 1998, pp. 89–90.

20 Exodus 24: 9–31; 18. Schniedewind, *How the Bible Became a Book*, pp. 121–34.

21 Exodus 24 : 9, 11. Smith, *The Origins of Biblical Monotheism*, p. 86.

22 Hosea 6 : 6.

23 Hosea 11: 5–6.

24 Amos 1: 3–5; 6: 13; 2: 4–16.

25 Amos 5: 24.

26 Isaiah 6: 1–9.

27 Isaiah 6: 11–13.

28 Isaiah 6: 3.

29 Isaiah 2: 10–13; 10: 5–7. cf. Psalm 46: 5–6.

30 William G. Dever, *What Did the Biblical Writers Know and When Did They Know It? What Archaeology Can Tell Us About the Reality of Ancient Israel*, Grand Rapids, Mich., and Cambridge, UK, 2001, p. 280.

31 Isaiah 7: 14. This is a literal translation of the verse, and does not follow the traditional version of the Jerusalem Bible.

32 Isaiah 9: 1.

33 Isaiah 9: 5–7.

34 2 Kings 21: 2–7; 23: 11; 23: 10; Ezekiel 20: 25–6; 22: 30.

35 Cf. Psalms 68: 18; 84: 12. Gosta W. Ahlstrom, *The History of Ancient Palestine*, Minneapolis, 1993, p. 734.

36 2 Kings 22.

37 Exodus 24: 3.

38 Exodus 24: 4–8. This is the only other place in the Bible where the phrase *sefer torah* is found. Schniedewind, *How the Bible Became a Book*, pp. 124–6.

39 2 Kings 23: 4–20.

40 Deuteronomy 12–26.

41 Deuteronomy 11: 21.

42 R. E. Clements, *God and Temple*, Oxford, 1965, pp. 89–95; Sperling, *The Original Torah*, pp. 146–7.

43 1 Kings 8: 27.

44 Judges 2: 7.

45 1 Kings 13: 1–2; 2 Kings 23: 15–18; 2 Kings 23: 25.

46 Jeremiah 8: 8–9; Schniedewind, *How the Bible Became a Book*, pp. 114–17.

47 Haym Soloveitchik, 'Rupture and Reconstruction: The Transformation of Contemporary Orthodoxy', *Tradition*, 28, 1994.

48 Deuteronomy 12: 2–3.

49 Joshua 8: 24–5.

50 2 Kings 21: 10–15.

51 Cross, *Canaanite Myth and Hebrew Epic*, pp. 321–5.

52 Leviticus 17–26.

53 Leviticus 25–7; 35–8; 40.

54 Exodus 29: 45–6.

55 Cross, *Canaanite Myth and Hebrew Epic*, p. 321.

56 Exodus 40: 34, 36–8.

57 Cross, *Canaanite Myth and Hebrew Epic*, p. 421.

58 Peter Ackroyd, *Exile and Restoration: A Study of Hebrew Thought in the Sixth Century BC*, London, 1968, pp. 254–5.

59 Leviticus 19: 2; *qaddosh* (holy) means 'separate; other'.

60 Leviticus 26: 12; trans. Cross, *Canaanite Myth and Hebrew Epic*, p. 298.

61 Leviticus 25.

62 Leviticus 19: 33–4.

63 Genesis 2: 5–17.

64 Smith, *Origins of Biblical Monotheism*, pp. 167–71.

65 Psalms 89: 10–13; 93: 1–4; Isaiah 27: 1; Job 7: 12; 9: 8; 26: 12; 38: 7–11.

66 Genesis 1: 31.

67 Isaiah 44: 28.

68 Isaiah 41: 24.

69 Isaiah 45 : 5.

70 Isaiah 51: 9–10.

71 Isaiah 42: 1–4; 49: 1–6; 50: 4–9; 52 : 13; 53 : 12.

72 Isaiah 49 : 6.

Chapter 2

1 Malachi 1: 6–14; 2: 8–9.

2 It is very difficult to date this period accurately. See Gosta W. Ahlstrom, *The History of Ancient Palestine*, Minneapolis, 1993, pp. 880–83; Elias J. Bickerman, *The Jews in the Greek Age*, Cambridge, Mass., 1988, pp. 29–32; W. D. Davies and Louis Finkelstein (eds), *The Cambridge History of Judaism*, 2 vols, Cambridge, UK, 1984, vol. I, pp. 144–53.

3 The tribe of Levi had originally been singled out to serve Yahweh in the desert tabernacle (Numbers 1 : 48–53; 3: 5–40). But after the exile, they had become second-class priests, subject to those priests who were direct descendants of Aaron, Moses's brother.

4 Nehemiah 8: 7–8.

5 Nehemiah 8 : 12–16.

6 Michael Fishbane, *The Garments of Torah, Essays in Biblical Hermeneutics*, Bloomington and Indianapolis, 1989, pp. 64–5; Gerald L. Bruns, 'Midrash and Allegory; The Beginnings of Scriptural Interpretation', in Robert Alter and Frank Kermode (eds), *The Literary Guide to the Bible*, London, 1978, pp. 626–7.

7 Ezra 1 : 6. Fishbane translation in *Garments of Torah*, p. 65.

8 Ezra 1 : 10. Fishbane translation, ibid., p. 66.

9 Ezra 1 : 6, 9; cf. Ezekiel 1 : 3.

10 1 Samuel 9: 9; 1 Kings 22 : 8, 13, 19; cf. Nehemiah 7 : 65.

11 Wilfred Cantwell Smith, *What Is Scripture? A Comparative Approach*, London, 1993, p. 290.

12 Ezra 10.

13 Fishbane, *Garments of Torah*, p. 64.

14 Bruns, 'Midrash and Allegory', pp. 626–7.

15 Proverbs 29: 4–5.

16 I Kings 5: 9–14.

17 Job 42: 3.

18 Ben Sirah 24: 1–22. (This book is also called Ecclesiasticus.)

19 Ben Sirah 24: 23.

20 Proverbs 8: 22, 30–31.

21 Ben Sirah 24: 20.

22 Ben Sirah 24: 21.

23 Ben Sirah 24: 28–9.

24 Ben Sirah 35: 1–6.

25 Ben Sirah 35: 7–11.

26 Ben Sirah 24: 33.

27 Fishbane, *Garments of Torah*, pp. 67–9; Donald Harman Akenson, *Surpassing Wonder, The Invention of the Bible and the Talmuds*, New York, San Diego and London, 1998, pp. 89–90.

28 Ezekiel 14: 14; 28: 15.

29 Daniel 1: 4.

30 Daniel 1: 18.

31 Daniel 7: 25.

32 Daniel 11: 31.

33 Daniel 7: 13–14.

34 Jeremiah 25: 11–12; Daniel 9: 3.

35 Daniel 9: 3.

36 Daniel 10: 3.

37 Daniel 9: 21; 10: 16 cf. Isaiah 6: 6–7; Daniel 10: 4–6 cf. Ezekiel
   1: 1, 24, 26–8.
38 Daniel 11: 35; 12: 9–10.
39 Akenson, *Surpassing Wonder*, pp. 160–67.
40 Jacob Neusner, 'Judaism and Christianity in the First Century',
   in Philip R. Davies and Richard T. White (eds), *A Tribute to
   Geza Vermes; Essays in Jewish and Christian Literature and
   History*, Sheffield, 1990, pp. 256–7.
41 Fishbane, *Garments of Torah*, pp. 73–6.
42 Bruns, 'Midrash and Allegory', p. 634.
43 Flavius Josephus, *The Jewish Antiquities*, 18.21. Scholars give
   different estimates of the population of Palestine at this time;
   some put it at 2.5 million; others at 1 million; some at a mere
   500,000.
44 Jacob Neusner, 'Varieties of Judaism in the Formative Age', in
   Arthur Green (ed.), *Jewish Spirituality*, 2 vols, London, 1986,
   1988, p. 185; E. P. Sanders, *Judaism: Practice and Belief, 63 BCE to
   66 CE*, London and Philadelphia, 1992, pp. 342–7.
45 Josephus, *Jewish Antiquities*, 17.42.
46 Akenson, *Surpassing Wonder*, pp. 144–70.
47 Ibid., pp. 171–89.
48 Psalms of Solomon, 17: 3. Akenson translation.
49 Florentino Garcia Martinez (ed.), *The Dead Sea Scrolls
   Translated*, Leiden, 1994, p. 138.
50 Josephus, *The Jewish War*, translated by G. A. Williamson,
   Harmondsworth, 1959, 2: 258–60; Josephus, *Jewish Antiquities*,
   20: 97–9, cf. Acts of the Apostles 5: 36.
51 Matthew 3: 1–2.
52 Luke 3: 3–14; Josephus, *Jewish Antiquities*, 18: 116–19.
53 Mark 1: 14–15. The terms 'Kingdom of God' and 'Kingdom of

Heaven' were used interchangeably. Some Jews felt it more respectful to avoid the word 'God' and preferred 'Heaven' instead.

54 Jaroslav Pelikan, *Whose Bible Is It? A History of the Scriptures Through the Ages*, New York, 2005, pp. 36–44; Akenson, *Surpassing Wonder*, pp. 124–5; Cantwell Smith, *What Is Scripture?*, p. 58; Bruns, 'Midrash and Allegory', pp. 636–7.

55 Moses Hadas (ed. and trans.), *Aristeas to Philcrates*, New York, 1951, pp. 21–3.

56 Philo, *The Life of Moses* in *Philo*, translated by F. H. Colson, Cambridge, Mass., 1950, 6: 476.

57 Beryl Smalley, *The Study of the Bible in the Middle Ages*, Oxford, 1941, pp. 3–4; Bruns, 'Midrash and Allegory', pp. 637–42; Burton L. Mack, *Who Wrote the New Testament? The Making of the Christian Myth*, San Francisco, 1995, pp. 254–6; Akenson, *Surpassing Wonder*, pp. 128–32; Pelikan, *Whose Bible Is It?*, pp. 46–7.

58 Philo, *The Migration of Abraham*, l.16, in *Philo in Ten Volumes*, translated by F. H. Colson and G. H. Whitaker, Cambridge, Mass, and London, 1958, vol. II.

59 Bruns, 'Midrash and Allegory', pp. 638–9.

60 Philo, *On the Birth of Abel and the Sacrifices Offered by Him and His Brother Cain*, vol. II, ll. 95–7. Colson and Whitaker translation.

61 Philo, *Special Laws*, 1: 43. Colson and Whitaker translation.

62 Philo, *On the Confusion of Tongues*, ll. 146–7.

63 Philo, *Abraham*, l. 121. Colson and Whitaker translation.

64 Philo, *On the Confusion of Tongues*, l. 147. Colson and Whitaker translation.

65 Philo, *The Migration of Abraham*, ll. 34–5. Colvin and Whitaker translation.

66 Dio Cassius, *History*, 66: 6; Josephus, *Jewish War*, 6: 98.

Chapter 3

1 Donald Harman Akenson, *Surpassing Wonder, The Invention of the Bible and the Talmuds*, New York, San Diego and London, 1998, pp. 212–13.

2 Josephus, *The Jewish War*, translated by G. A. Williamson, Harmondsworth, 1959, 6: 312–13; Tacitus, *Histories*, 5: 13; Suetonius, *Vespasian*, 4. Paula Fredricksen, *Jesus of Nazareth, King of the Jews. A Jewish Life and the Emergence of Christianity*, London, 2000, p. 246.

3 Mark 8: 27–33.

4 Mark 5: 12; Matthew 27: 17, 22; cf. Josephus, *Jewish Antiquities* 18: 63–4.

5 1 Corinthians 15: 20.

6 Akenson, *Surpassing Wonder*, p. 94; Fredricksen, *Jesus*, pp. 262–3.

7 Matthew 19: 28.

8 Luke 24: 53; Acts 2: 46.

9 Matthew 26: 29; Mark 14: 25.

10 Acts 4: 32–5.

11 Matthew 5: 3–12; Luke 6: 20–23; Matthew 5: 38–48; Luke 6: 27–38; Romans 12: 9–13, 14; 1 Corinthians 6: 7; Akenson, *Surpassing Wonder*, p. 102; Fredricksen, *Jesus*, p. 243.

12 Matthew 12: 17; Romans 13: 6–7.

13 Matthew 5: 17–19; Luke 16: 17.

14 Luke 23: 56.

15 Galatians 2: 11–12.

16 Matthew 7: 12; Luke 6: 31; cf Romans 13: 10 and Shabbat 31a.

17 Mark 13: 1–2.

18 1 Corinthians 1: 22.

19 Matthew 21: 31.

20 Acts 8: 1, 18; 9:2; 11: 19.

21 Fredricksen, *Jesus*, pp. 60–61.

22 Galatians 2: 1–10; 5: 3; Acts 15.

23 Acts 10–11.

24 Acts 11: 26.

25 Thus Romans 1: 20–32.

26 In the ancient world, people did not usually eat red meat that had not been sacrificed and consecrated in a temple.

27 Isaiah 2: 2–3; Zephaniah 3: 9; Tobit 14: 6; Zechariah 8: 23.

28 Galatians 1: 1–16.

29 The authorship of the first epistle to the Thessalonians is disputed; it may not have been written by Paul.

30 1 Thessalonians 1:9; 1 Corinthians 5: 1–13; 8: 4–13; 10: 4.

31 Joel 3: 1–5; Acts 2: 14–21.

32 Romans 8: 9; Galatians 4: 16; Fredricksen, *Jesus*, pp. 133–5.

33 Romans 9: 1–33.

34 Julia Galambush, *The Reluctant Paring. How the New Testament's Jewish Writers Created a Christian Book*, San Francisco, 2005, p. 148.

35 Psalm 69: 9; Romans 15: 3.

36 Romans 15: 4. Jaroslav Pelikan, *Whose Bible Is It? A History of the Scriptures Through the Ages*, New York, 2005, p. 72. My italics.

37 2 Corinthians 3: 9–18. Galambush, *Reluctant Parting*, pp. 145–6.

38 Romans 5: 12–20; cf. 1 Corinthians 15: 45.

39 Genesis 15: 6.

40 Romans 4: 22–4. My italics.

41 Galatians 3: 8; Genesis 12: 3.

42 Galatians 4: 22–31.

43 Hebrews 3: 1–6.

44 Hebrews 4: 12–9: 28.

45 Hebrews 11: 1.

46 Hebrews 11: 32.

47 Hebrews 11: 40.

48 Akenson, *Surpassing Wonder*, p. 213.

49 2 Peter 3: 15; Ignatius of Antioch, *Letter to the Ephesians* 2: 12.

50 A collection of these Gnostic gospels was discovered at Nag Hammadi in Egypt in 1945.

51 Akenson, *Surpassing Wonder*, pp. 229–43.

52 See, for example, Mark 14: 61–4.

53 Philippians 2: 6–11.

54 Daniel 7: 13; Matthew 24: 30; 26: 65; Mark 13: 26; 14: 62; Luke 17: 22; 21: 25; 22: 69.

55 John 1: 1–14; Hebrews 1: 2–4.

56 Luke 2: 25; Matthew 12: 14–21; 26: 67; Acts 8: 32–4; 1 Peter 2: 23–4.

57 Psalms 69: 21; 31:6; 22:18; Matthew 33–6.

58 Isaiah 7: 14; Matthew 1: 22–3.

59 David Flusser, *Jesus*, New York, 1969, p. 72.

60 Fredricksen, *Jesus*, p. 19.

61 There is a widespread belief that Luke was a gentile, but there is no hard evidence for this.

62 Mark 13: 9–19, 13.

63 Mark 4: 3–9; 8: 17–18.

64 Mark 2: 21–2.

65 Mark 13: 33–7.

66 Mark 14: 58–61; 15: 29.

67 Mark 13: 5–27.

68 Mark 13: 14; Daniel 9: 27.

69 Mark 11: 15–19; Isaiah 56: 7; Jeremiah 7: 11.

70 Mark 14: 21, 27.

71 Psalm 41: 8.

72 Zechariah 13: 7.

73 Mark 16: 8. In the earliest manuscripts Mark's gospel ends here. The next twelve verses describing Jesus's resurrection appearances were almost certainly added later.

74 Mark 1: 15. This is a literal translation of the Greek and does not follow the Jerusalem Bible.

75 Matthew 13: 31–50.

76 Matthew 5: 17.

77 Matthew 5: 11; 10: 17–23.

78 Matthew 24: 9–12.

79 Genesis 16: 11; Judges 13: 3–5; Genesis 17: 15–21.

80 Matthew 8: 17; Isaiah 53: 4.

81 Matthew 5: 1.

82 Matthew 5: 19.

83 Matthew 5: 21–39.

84 Matthew 5: 38–48.

85 Matthew 9: 13; Hosea 6: 6; cf. Aboth de Rabbi Nathan 1.4.11a.

86 Matthew 7: 12; cf. B. Shabbat, 31a.

87 Matthew 12: 16, 41, 42.

88 M. Pirke Avoth, 3: 3, in C. C. Montefiore and H. Loewe (eds), *A Rebbinic Anthology*, New York, 1974, p. 23.

89 Matthew 18: 20; Galambush, *Reluctant Parting*, pp. 67–8.

90 Luke 24: 13–35; Galambush, *Reluctant Parting*, pp. 91–2; Gabriel Josipovici, 'The Epistle to the Hebrews and the Catholic Epistles', in Robert Alter and Frank Kermode (eds),

The Literary Guide to the Bible, London, 1987, pp. 506–7.

91 John 1: 1–5.

92 John 1: 30.

93 1 John 4: 7–12; John 15: 12–13.

94 John 15: 18–27; 1 John 3: 12–13.

95 John 6: 60–66.

96 1 John 2: 18–19.

97 1 John 4: 5–6.

98 John 7: 34; 8: 19–21.

99 John 2: 19–21.

100 John 8: 57.

101 M. Sukkah 4: 9; 5: 2–4; John 7: 37–39; 8: 12.

102 John 6: 32–6.

103 John 8: 58. The phrase *Ani Waho*: I Am, was used in the Sukkoth rituals and was probably a term for the *Shekhinah*; W. D. Davies, *The Gospel and the Land: Early Chrisitainity and Jewish Territorial Doctrine*, Berkeley, 1974, pp. 294–5.

104 Galambush, *Reluctant Parting*, pp. 291–2.

105 Revelation 21: 22–4.

106 Luke 18: 9–14.

107 Matthew 27: 25.

108 Matthew 23: 1–33.

109 John 11: 47–53; 18: 2–3. The one honourable exception is the Pharisee Nicodemus, who comes secretly to Jesus for private instruction (John 3: 1–21).

Chapter 4

1 Donald Harman Akenson, *Surpassing Wonder, The Invention of the Bible and the Talmuds*, New York, San Diego and London, 1998), pp. 319–25.

2 B. Berakhot 8b; 63b; B. Avodah Zarah 3b.

3 Pesikta Rabbati 14: 9 in William Braude (trans.), *Pesikta Rabbati: Discourses for Feasts, Fasts and Special Sabbaths*, 2 vols, New Haven, 1988; Gerald L. Bruns, 'Midrash and Allegory: The Beginnings of Scriptural Interpretation', in Robert Alter and Frank Kermode (eds), *The Literary Guide to the Bible*, London, 1987, p. 630.

4 Bruns, 'Midrash and Allegory', p. 629.

5 B. Shabbat, 31a in A. Cohen (ed.), *Everyman's Talmud*, New York, 1975, p. 65.

6 Sifra on Leviticus 19: 11.

7 Genesis 5: 1; C. G. Montefiore, 'Preface' in C. G. Montefiore and H. Loewe (eds), *A Rabbinic Anthology*, New York, 1974, p. xl.

8 Aboth de Rabbi Nathan, 1.4.11a in Montefiore and Loewe (eds), *A Rabbinic Anthology*, pp. 430–1. Hosea 6: 6.

9 Michael Fishbane, *The Garments of Torah, Essays in Biblical Hermeneutics*, Bloomington and Indianapolis, 1989, p. 37.

10 Ben Sirah, 50.

11 M. Pirke Avoth, 1: 2.

12 Psalm 89: 2; Aboth de Rabbi Nathan, 1.4.11a in Montefiore and Loewe (eds), *A Rabbinic Anthology*, p. 430.

13 B. Menahoth, 29b.

14 M. Rabbah, Numbers 19: 6.

15 M. Avoth, 5: 25; Fishbane, *Garments of Torah*, p. 38.

16 Eliyahu Zatta, 2.

17 Sifra on Leviticus 13.47 in Fishbane, *Garments of Torah*, p. 115.

18 John Bowker, *The Targums and Rabbinic Literature, An Introduction to Jewish Interpretations of Scripture*, Cambridge, 1969, pp. 54–5.

19 Bruns, 'Midrash and Allegory', p. 629.

20 Fishbane, *Garments of Torah*, pp. 22–32.

21 Deuteronomy 21 : 23.

22 M. Sanhedrin, 6: 4–5.

23 Fishbane, *Garments of Torah*, p. 30.

24 Sifre Benidbar, Pisqa 84; Zechariah 2 : 12; Fishbane translation, *Garments of Torah*, pp. 30–31.

25 Deuteronomy 30 : 12.

26 Exodus 33 : 2, as interpreted in the midrash.

27 Baba Metziah, 59b in Montefiore and Loewe (eds), *A Rabbinic Anthology*, pp. 340–41.

28 Genesis Rabbah 1 : 14.

29 B. Sanhedrin, 99b.

30 Ibid.

31 Jeremiah 23 : 29.

32 M. Song of Songs Rabbah 1.10.2; Bruns, 'Midrash and Allegory', p. 627; Fishbane, 'Midrash and the Nature of Scripture', p. 19.

33 B. Hagigah 14b; T. Hagigah 2: 3–4; J. Hagigah 2: 1, 77a.

34 M. Tohorot; Yadayim 3: 5, translated by Wilfred Cantwell Smith, *What is Scripture? A Comparative Approach*, London, 1993, p. 253.

35 Leviticus Rabbah 8: 2; Sotah 9b.

36 J. Hagigah 2: 1.

37 T. Sanhedrin 11: 5; T. Zabiim 1: 5; T. Maaser Sheni 2: 1; Bowker, *The Targums*, pp. 49–53.

38 Dio Cassius, *History*, 69: 2.

39 Traditionally this is believed to have happened at Yavneh, but there are good arguments for assigning this development to the Usha period, which was more committed to written scripture.

40 Akenson, *Surpassing Wonder*, pp. 324–5.

41 In M. Yadayim 4: 3; M. Edayyoth 8: 7; M. Peah 2: 6; M. Rosh Hashanah 2: 9 the Mishnah gives a Mosaic reference to its *halakoth*, but does not claim to derive them from Moses or Sinai; Akenson, *Surpassing Wonder*, pp. 302–303.

42 Cantwell Smith, *What Is Scripture?*, pp. 116–17.

43 Jacob Neusner, *Medium and Message in Judaism*, Atlanta, 1989, p. 3; 'The Mishnah in Philosophical Context and Out of Canonical Bounds', *Journal of Biblical Literature*, 11, Summer 1993; Akenson, *Surpassing Wonder*, pp. 305–20.

44 Jacob Neusner, *Judaism. The Evidence of the Mishnah*, Chicago, 1981, pp. 87–91, 97–101, 132–1–37, 150–53.

45 B. Menahoth, 110a.

46 Akenson, *Surpassing Wonder*, pp. 329–39.

47 This is a body of doubtful historicity, not mentioned in the Mishnah.

48 Joshua 24: 51.

49 Gershom Scholem, *On the Kabbalah and Its Symbolism*, New York, 1995, p. 46.

50 Pirke Avoth, 1: 1; 3: 13 in Jacob Neusner (trans.), *The Mishnah, A New Translation*, New Haven, 1988.

51 Akenson, *Surpassing Wonder*, pp. 361–2.

52 Ibid., pp. 366–95.

53 Jaroslav Pelikan, *Whose Bible Is It? A History of the Scriptures Through the Ages*, New York, 2005, pp. 67–8.

54 B. Yoma, 81a.

55 Davod Kraemer, *The Mind of the Talmud. An Intellectual History of the Bavli*, New York and Oxford, 1990, p.151.

56 B. Zebatim, 99a.

57 B. Baba Batara, 12a.

58 Cantwell Smith, *What Is Scripture?*, pp. 102–4; Pelikan, *Whose Bible Is It?*, p. 66.

59 Louis Jacobs, *The Talmudic Argument. A Study in Talmudic Reasoning and Methodology*, Cambridge, 1984, pp. 20–23; 203–13.

60 Akenson, *Surpassing Wonder*, p. 379.

61 Mekhilta de R. Ishmael, Beshalah, 7; Fishbane, *Garments of Torah*, p. 124.

62 B. Qedoshim, 49b; Cantwell Smith, *What Is Scripture?*, pp. 116–17.

63 William G. Braude (ed. and trans.), *Pesikta Rabbati Discourses for Feasts, Fasts and Special Sabbaths*, 2 vols, New Haven, 1968, *Piska* 3 : 2.

Chapter 5

1 Burton L. Mack, *Who Wrote the New Testament? The Making of the Christian Myth*, San Francisco, 1995, pp. 266–73.

2 Justin, *Apology*, 1.36; Mack, *Who Wrote the New Testament?*, p. 269.

3 Apologia 1 : 63.

4 Irenaeus, *Against Heresies*, 4 : 23.

5 R. R. Reno, 'Origen', in Justin S. Holcomb (ed.), *Christian Theologies of Scripture: A Comparative Introduction*, New York and London, 2006, pp. 23–4; R. M. Grant, *Irenaeus of Lyon*, London, 1997, pp. 47–51.

6 Ephesians 1 : 10, Revised Standard Version. Ephesians was probably not written by Paul himself.

7 David S. Pacini, 'Excursus: Reading Holy Writ: the Locus of Modern Spirituality', in Louis Dupre and Don E. Saliers, *Christian Spirituality: Post Reformation and Modern*, London and New York, 1989, p. 177.

8 Irenaeus, *Against Heresies*, 1: 8–9.

9 Mack, *Who Wrote the New Testament?* pp. 285–6.

10 Matthew 13: 38–44.

11 Irenaeus, *Against Heresies*, 4.26.1; Reno, 'Origen', p. 24.

12 Eusebius, *Demonstratio* Evangelium, 4: 15 in J. P. Migne (ed.), *Patrologia Graeca*, Paris, 1857–66, vol. 22, p. 296. My italics.

13 Ibid.

14 Reno, 'Origen'; David W. Kling, *The Bible in History: How the Texts Have Shaped the Times*, Oxford and New York, 1994, pp. 89–91; Jaroslav Pelikan, *Whose Bible Is It? A History of the Scriptures Through the Ages*, New York, 2005, pp. 61–2.

15 R. B. Tollington (trans.), *Selections from the Commentaries and Homilies of Origen*, London, 1929, p. 54. Gerald L. Bruns, 'Midrash and Allegory: The Beginnings of Scriptural Interpretation', in Robert Alter and Frank Kermode (eds), *A Literary Guide to the Bible*, London, 1987, p. 365.

16 Matthew 5: 29.

17 Origen, *On First Principles*, 4.3.1. He is commenting on a verse as translated in the Septuagint.

18 Exodus 25–31; 35–40.

19 Genesis 3: 8.

20 Matthew 10: 9.

21 *On First Principles*, 4.3.1 in G. W. Butterworth (trans.), *Origen; On First Principles*, Gloucester, Mass., 1973.

22 Homilies on Ezekiel 1: 2 quoted in Jaroslav Pelikan, *Whose Bible Is It? A History of the Scriptures Through the Ages*, New York, 2005, p. 60.

23 Genesis 20.

24 Exodus 12: 37.

25 Matthew 6: 20.

26 Exodus 13 : 21.

27 1 Corinthians 10: 1–4.

28 Ibid., cf. John 6 : 51.

29 Matthew 6 : 20.

30 Matthew 19 : 21.

31 Ronald E. Haine (trans.), *Origen: Homilies on Genesis and Exodus*, Washington DC, 1982, p. 277; Reno, 'Origen', pp. 25–6.

32 Reno, 'Origen', p. 29.

33 Mircea Eliade, *The Myth of the Eternal Return, or, Cosmos and History*, translated by Willard R. Trask, New York, 1959.

34 Origen, *On First Principles*, Preface, para. 8. Butterworth translation.

35 Ibid., 4.2.3.

36 Ibid., 2.3.1.

37 Ibid., 4.2.9.

38 Ibid.

39 Ibid., 4.2.3.

40 Ibid., 4.2.7.

41 Ibid., 4.1.6.

42 R. P. Lawson (trans.), *Origen, The Song of Songs: Commentary and Homilies*, New York, 1956, p. 44.

43 Song of Songs 1 : 2.

44 Ephesians 5 : 23–32.

45 Lawson, *Song of Songs*, p. 60.

46 Ibid., p. 61.

47 Origen, *Commentary on John*, 6 : 1 in Reno, 'Origen', p. 28.

48 Matthew 19 : 21.

49 Douglas Burton Christie, *The Word in the Desert: Scripture and the Quest for Holiness in Early Christian Monasticism*, New York and Oxford, 1993, pp. 297–8; Kling, *Bible in History*, pp. 23–40.

50 Beldon C. Lane, *The Solace of Fierce Landscapes: Exploring Desert and Monastic Spirituality*, New York and Oxford, 1998, p. 175.

51 Jaroslav Pelikan, *The Christian Tradition, A History of the Development of Doctrine.1. The Emergence of Catholic Tradition (100–600)*, Chicago and London, 1971, pp. 191–200.

52 Matthew 26: 39; 24: 36; 17: 5.

53 Basil, *On the Holy Spirit*, 28: 66.

54 Basil, *Epistle*, 234: 1.

55 Denys the Areopagite was the name of St Paul's first convert in Athens.

56 Denys, *Mystical Theology*, 3 in Paul Rosea, 'The Uplifting Spirituality of Pseudo-Dionysius' in Bernard McGinn and John Meyendorff (eds), *Christian Spirituality: Origins to the Twelfth Century*, London, 1985, p. 142.

57 Maximus, *Ambigua*, in Migne, *Patrologia Graeca*, vol. 91, p. 1085.

58 Romans 13: 13–14.

59 Augustine, *Confessions*, 8.12.29, in Philip Burton (trans.), *Augustine, The Confessions*, London, 2001.

60 Ibid., *Confessions*, 7.18.24.

61 Ibid., *Confessions*, 13.15.18. Pamela Bright, 'Augustine', in Holcomb (ed.), *Christian Theologies of Scripture*, pp. 39–50.

62 Exodus 33: 23. Augustine, *The Trinity*, 2.16.27; G. R. Evans, *The Language and Logic of the Bible: The Earlier Middle Ages*, Cambridge, 1984, pp. 3–6.

63 Augustine, *Confessions*, 12.25.35.

64 Ibid., Burton translation.

65 Deuteronomy 6: 5; Matthew 22: 37–9; Mark 23: 30–31; Luke 10: 17.

66 John 5: 10. Augustine, *Confessions*, 12.25.35.

67 Augustine, *Confessions*, 12.25.34–5, in Philip Burton (trans.) *Augustine, The Confessions*, London, 1907.

68 Deuteronomy 6: 5; Matthew 22:37–9; Mark 12: 30–31; Luke 10: 17; Augustine, *Confessions*, 12.25.35, Burton translation.

69 Beryl Smalley, *The Study of the Bible in the Middle Ages*, Oxford, 1941, p. 11.

70 D. W. Robertson (trans.), *Augustine: On Christian Doctrine*, Indianapolis, 1958, p. 30.

71 Ibid.

72 Augustine, On Psalm 98: 1 in Michael Cameron. 'Enerrationes in Pslamos', in Allen D. Fitzgerald (ed.), *Augustine Through the Ages*, Grand Rapids, 1999, p. 292.

73 1 Corinthians 12: 27–30; Colossians 1: 15–20. Charles Kannengiesser, 'Augustine of Hippo', in Donald Mc.Kim (ed.), *Major Biblical Interpreters*, Downers Grove, Ill., 1998, p. 22.

Chapter 6

1 John Cassian, *Collationes*, 1.17.2.

2 Ewart Cousins, 'The Humanity and Passion of Christ', in Jill Raitt (ed.), with Bernard McGinn and John Meyendorff, *Christian Spirituality: High Middle Ages and Reformation*, London, 1988, pp. 377–83.

3 Gregory, *Homilies on Ezekiel*, 2.2.1.

4 Gregory, *Morals on Job*, 4.1.1. G. R. Evans, *The Language and Logic of the Bible: The Earlier Middle Ages*, Cambridge, 1984, pp. 56, 143, 164.

5 Gregory, *On the First Book of Kings*, 1.

6 James F. McCrae, 'Liturgy and Eucharist: West', in Raitt, *Christian Spirituality*, pp. 428–9.

7 Luke 14: 27.

8 Jonathan Riley-Smith, 'Crusading as an Act of Love', *History*, 65, 1980.

9 Evans, *Language and Logic*, pp. 37–47; Beryl Smalley, *The Study of the Bible in the Middle Ages*, Oxford, 1941, pp. 31–57.

10 Ibid., pp. 121–7. Jaroslav Pelikan, *Whose Bible Is It? A History of the Scriptures Through the Ages*, New York, 2005, p. 106.

11 Smalley, *Study of the Bible*, p. 123.

12 Joseph Bekhor Shor, *Commentary on Exodus*, 9: 8.

13 Hugh of St Victor, *Didascalion*, 8–11; Smalley, *Study of the Bible*, pp. 69–70.

14 Smalley, *Study of the Bible*, pp. 86–154.

15 Ibid., p. 139.

16 Evans, *Language and Logic*, pp. 17–23.

17 Anselm, *Cur Deus Homo*, 1: 11–12; 1: 25; 2: 4; 2: 17.

18 Evans, *Language and Logic*, pp. 70–71; 134–41.

19 Bernard, *Epistle*, 191.1 in J. P. Migne (ed) *Patrologia Latina*, Paris, 1878–90, vol. 182, p. 357.

20 Cf. 1 Corinthians 13: 12. Quoted in Henry Adams, *Mont St Michel and Chartres*, London, 1986, p. 296.

21 Wilfred Cantwell Smith, *What Is Scripture? A Comparative Approach*, London, 1993, pp. 29–37; David W. Kling, *The Bible in History: How the Texts Have Shaped the Times*, Oxford and New York, 2004, pp. 96–112.

22 Irene M. Edmonds and Killian Walsh (trans.), *The Works of Bernard of Clairvaux: On the Song of Songs*, 4 vols, vol. 1, Spencer, Mass.; vols 2–4, Kalamazoo, Michigan, 1971–1980, vol. 1, p. 54.

23 Ibid., vol. 2, p. 28.

24 Ibid., vol. 2, pp. 30–32.

25 Ibid., vol. 1, p. 2.

26 Ibid., vol. 4, p. 86.

27 Ibid., p. 4.

28 Kling, *The Bible in History*, p. 103.

29 Edmonds and Walsh, *On the Song of Songs*, vol. 1, p. 16.

30 Evans, *Language and Logic*, pp. 44–7.

31 Henry Malter, *Saadia Gaon, His Life and Works*, Philadelphia, 1942.

32 Abraham Cohen, *The Teachings of Maimonides*, London, 1927; David Yellin and Israel Abrahams, *Maimonides*, London, 1903.

33 Moses Friedlander, *Essays on the Writings of Abraham Ibn Ezra*, London, 1877; Louis Jacobs, *Jewish Biblical Exegesis*, New York, 1973, pp. 8–21.

34 Deuteronomy 1: 1; my italics. This does not follow the Jerusalem Bible but is a literal translation of the Hebrew, as read by Ibn Ezra.

35 Hyam Maccoby, *Judaism on Trial: Jewish–Christian Disputation in the Middle Ages*, London and Toronto, 1982, pp. 95–150; Solomon Schechter, *Studies on Judaism*, Philadelphia, 1945, pp. 99–141.

36 Moshe Idel, 'PaRDeS: Some Reflections on Kabbalistic Hermeneutics', in John J. Collins and Michael Fishbane (eds), *Death, Ecstasy and Other-Worldly Journeys*, Albany, 1995, pp. 251, 255–6.

37 See Chapter 4, p. 90.

38 Collins and Fishbane, *Death, Ecstasy and Other-Worldly Journeys*, p. 249–57; Michael Fishbane, *The Garments of Torah, Essays in Biblical Hermeneutics*, Bloomington and Indianapolis, 1989, pp. 113–20.

39 Cantwell Smith, *What Is Scripture?*, p. 112.

40 Gershom Scholem, 'The Meaning of Torah in Jewish Mysticism', in *On the Kabbalah and Its Symbolism*, translated by Ralph Manheim, New York, 1965, p. 33.

41 Ibid., pp. 11–158; Gershom Scholem, *Major Trends in Jewish Mysticism*, New York, 1995 edn, pp. 1–79, 119–243; Michael Fishbane, *The Exegetical Imagination: On Jewish Thought and Theology*, Cambridge, Mass., and London, 1998, pp. 99–126; Fishbane, *Garments of Torah*, pp. 34–63.

42 Zohar, 1.15.a in Gershom Scholem (trans. and ed.), *Zohar, The Book of Splendor; Basic Readings from the Kabbalah*, New York, 1949, pp. 27–8.

43 Fishbane, *The Exegetical Imagination*, pp. 100–1.

44 Zohar, II.94b in Scholem, *Zohar, The Book of Splendor*, p. 90.

45 Ibid.

46 Ibid., p. 122.

47 Zohar, III. 152a in Scholem, *Zohar, The Book of Splendor*, p. 121.

48 Zohar, II. 182a

49 A. Hudson, *Selections from English Wycliffite Writings*, Cambridge, 1978, pp. 67–8.

Chapter 7

1 Jerry S. Bentley, *The Humanists and Holy Writ; New Testament Scholarship in the Renaissance*, Princeton, 1983; Debora Kuller Shuger, *The Renaissance Bible, Scholarship, Sacrifice, Subjectivity*, Berkeley, Los Angeles and London, 2004); Jaroslav Pelikan, *Whose Bible Is It? A History of Scripture Through the Ages*, New York, 2005, pp. 112–28; William J. Bouwsma, 'The Spirituality of Renaissance Humanism', in Jill Raitt (ed.) with Bernard McGinn and John Meyendorff, *Christian Spirituality: High Middle Ages and Reformation*,

London, 1988; James D. Tracy, 'Ad Fontes, The Humanist Understanding of Scripture', in Raitt (ed.), *Christian Spirituality*.

2 Charles Trinkaus, *The Poet as Philosopher, Petrarch and the Formation of Renaissance Consciousness*, New Haven, 1977, p. 87.

3 Quoted in Alastair McGrath, *Reformation Thought, An Introduction*, Oxford and New York, 1988, p. 73.

4 Marc Leinhard, 'Luther and the Beginnings of the Reformation', in Raitt (ed.), *Christian Spirituality*, p. 269.

5 Richard Marius, *Martin Luther: The Christian between God and Death*, Cambridge, Mass., and London, 1999, pp. 73–4, 213–15, 486–7.

6 G. R. Evans, *The Language and Logic of the Bible: the Road to Reformation*, Cambridge, 1985, p. 8.

7 Ibid., p. 100.

8 David W. Kling, *The Bible in History: How the Texts Have Shaped the Times*, Oxford and New York, 2004, pp. 120–49.

9 Philip S. Watson, *Let God Be God! An Interpretation of the Theology of Martin Luther*, Philadelphia, 1947, p. 149.

10 Martin Luther, *Luther's Works* (LW), 55 vols, edited by Jaroslav Pelikan and Helmut Lehmann, Philadelphia and St Louis, 1955–86, vol. 33, p. 26.

11 Emil G. Kraeling, *The Old Testament Since the Reformation*, London, 1955, pp. 145–6.

12 Psalm 72 : 1

13 Psalm 71 : 2.

14 Leinhard, 'Luther and the Beginnings of the Reformation', p. 22.

15 Romans 1 : 17, quoting Habakkuk 2 : 4.

16 McGrath, *Reformation Thought*, p. 74.

17 *LW*, vol. 25, pp. 188–9.

18 Martin Luther, *Sermons*, 25 : 7; *LW*, vol. 10, p. 239.

19 Mickey L. Mattox, 'Martin Luther', in Justin S. Holcomb (ed.), *Christian Theologies of Scripture*, New York and London, 2006, p. 101; Jaroslav Pelikan, *The Christian Tradition: Volume 4: Reformation of Church and Dogma*, Chicago and London, 1984, pp. 168–71; Leinhard, 'Luther and the Beginnings of the Reformation', p. 274–6.

20 Scott H. Hendrix, *Luther and the Papacy: Stages in a Reformation Conflict*, Philadelphia, 1981, p. 83; Roland H. Bainton, *Here I Stand: A Life of Martin Luther*, New York, 1950, p. 90.

21 Bernard Lohse, *Martin Luther: An Introduction to His Life and Work*, translated by Robert C. Schultz, Philadelphia, 1988, p. 154.

22 Wilfred Cantwell Smith, *What Is Scripture? A Comparative Approach*, London, 1993, pp. 204–5; Pelikan, *Whose Bible Is It?*, p. 145.

23 Leinhard, 'Luther and the Beginnings of the Reformation', pp. 276–86; Pelikan, *The Christian Tradition*, pp. 180–81.

24 He found biblical support for his belief in John 3 : 8.

25 Fritz Buster, 'The Spirituality of Zwingli and Bullinger in the Reformation of Zurich', in Raitt (ed.), *Christian Spirituality*; Kraeling, *The Old Testament*, pp. 21–2.

26 Kraeling, *The Old Testament*, pp. 30–32; Randall C. Zachman, 'John Calvin', in Holcomb (ed.), *Christian Theologies*, pp. 117–29.

27 Alastair McGrath, *A Life of John Calvin, A Study in the Shaping of Western Culture*, Oxford, 1990, p. 131; Zachmann, 'John Calvin', p. 129.

28 Commentary on Genesis 1 : 6 in *The Commentaries of John Calvin on the Old Testament*, 30 vols, Calvin Translation Society, 1643–48, vol. 1, p. 86.

29 Bernard Lohse, *Martin Luther: An Introduction to His Life and Work*, translated by Robert C. Schultz, Philadelphia, 1988, p. 154.

30 Quoted in Richard Tarnas, *The Passion of the Western Mind; Understanding the Ideas that have Shaped Our World View*, New York and London, 1990, p. 300.

31 William R. Shea, 'Galileo and the Church', in David C. Lindberg and Ronald E. Numbers (eds), *God and Nature; Historical Essays on the Encounter Between Christianity and Science*, Berkeley, Los Angeles and London, 1986, pp. 124–5.

32 Pelikan, *Whose Bible Is It?*, p. 128.

33 Gershom Scholem, *Sabbetai Sevi, The Mystical Messiah*, London and Princeton, pp. 30–45; Gershom Scholem, *Major Trends in Jewish Mysticism*, New York, 1995 edn, pp. 245–80; 'The Messianic Idea in Kabbalism' in Scholem, *The Messianic Idea in Judaism and Other Essays in Jewish Spirituality*, New York, 1971, pp. 43–8; 'The Meaning of the Torah in Jewish Mysticism' in Scholem, *On the Kabbalah and Its Symbolism*, translated by Ralph Manheim, New York, 1965; 'Kabbalah and Myth' in Scholem, *On the Kabbalah*, pp. 90–117.

34 Scholem, *Sabbetai Sevi*, pp. 37–42.

35 As reported in Hyam Vital, *Sh'ar Ma'amar Razal* 16c, in Scholem, 'The Meaning of the Torah in Jewish Mysticism', pp. 72–5.

36 R. J. Wenlowsky, 'The Safed Revival and Its Aftermath' in Arthur Green (ed.), *Jewish Spirituality*, 2 vols, London, 1986, 1989, vol. 2, pp. 15–17; Louis Jacobs, 'The Uplifting of the Sparks', in ibid., pp. 108–11.

37 Laurence Fine, 'The Contemplative Practice of Yehudim in Lurianic Kabbalah' in Green (ed.), *Jewish Spirituality*, vol. 2, pp. 73–8.

38 Matthew 26: 26.

39 John W. Fraser (trans.), *John Calvin: Concerning Scandals*, Grand Rapids, MI, 1978, p. 81.

40 Pelikan, *Whose Bible Is It?*, p. 132.

41 *LW*, vol. 36, p. 67.

42 Calvin, *Commentaries*, translated and edited by J. Harontinian and L. P. Smith, London, 1958, p. 104.

43 Yirmanyahu Yovel, *Spinoza and Other Heretics*, 2 vols, Princeton, 1989, vol. 1, p. 17.

44 Kling, *Bible in History*, pp. 205–7; Alan Heimert and Andrew Delbanco (eds), *The Puritans in America: A Native Anthology*, Cambridge, Mass., 1988.

45 Deuteronomy 30: 15–17; John Winthrop, 'A Model of Christian Charity', in Perry Miller, *The American Puritans: Their Prose and Poetry*, Garden City, NY, 1956, p. 83.

46 Robert Cushman, 'Reasons and Considerations' in Heimert and Delbanco (eds), *The Puritans in America*, p. 44.

47 Regina Sharif, *Non-Jewish Zionism: Its Roots in Western History*, London, 1983, p. 90.

48 Isaiah 2: 1–6.

49 Edward Johnson, 'Wonder-Working Providence of Sion's Savior in New England', in Heimert and Delbanco (eds), *The Puritans in America*, p. 115–16.

50 Exodus 19:4; Kling, *Bible in History*, pp. 206–7.

51 Kling, *Bible in History*, pp. 207–29; Theophilus H. Smith, 'The Spirituality of Afro-American Traditions', in Louis Dupre and Don E. Saliers, *Christian Spirituality: Post Reformation and Modern*, New York and London, 1989; Lewis V. Baldwin and Stephen W. Murphy, 'Scripture in the African-American Christian Tradition', in Holcomb (ed.), *Christian Theologies;*

Sterling Stuckey, *Slave Culture: Nationalist Theory and the Foundations of Black America*, New York and Oxford, 1987.

52 Genesis 9 : 25.

53 Ephesians 6 : 5.

54 James Hal Cone, *A Black Theology of Liberation*, Philadelphia, 1970, pp. 18–19, 26.

55 Exodus 21: 7–11; Genesis 16; 21: 8–21. Delores S. Williams, *Sisters in the Wilderness: The Challenge of Womanist God-Talk*, Maryknoll, NY, 2003, pp. 144–9.

Chapter 8

1 Wilfred Cantwell Smith, *What Is Scripture? A Comparative Approach*, London, 1993, pp. 184–94.

2 Diderot, Letter to Falconet, 1766, in Diderot, *Correspondence*, edited by Georges Roth, 16 vols, Paris, 1955–70, vol. VI, p. 261.

3 Rousseau, *Confessions*, Part I; Book I, in G. Petain (ed.), *Oeuvres complete de J. J. Rousseau*, 8 vols, Paris, 1839, vol. I. p. 19.

4 Edward Gibbon, *Memoirs of My* Life, edited by Georges A. Bonnard, London, 1966, p. 134.

5 Julius Guttman, *Philosophies of Judaism*, London and New York, 1964, pp. 265–85; R. M. Silverman, *Baruch Spinoza: Outcast Jew, Universal Sage*, Northwood, UK, 1995; Leo Strauss, *Spinoza's Critique of Religion*, New York, 1982; Yovel Yirmanyahu, *Spinoza and Other Heretics*, 2 vols, Princeton, 1989.

6 Spinoza, *A Theologico-Political Treatise*, translated by R. H. M. Elwes, New York, 1951, p. 7.

7 Gershom Scholem, *Major Trends in Jewish Mysticism*, New York, 1995 edn, pp. 327–429; Gershom Scholem, *The Messianic Idea in Judaism and Other Essays on Jewish Spirituality*, New York, 1971,

pp. 189–227; Gerschon David Hundert (ed.), *Essential Papers on Hasidism: Origins to Present*, New York and London, 1991.

8 B. Shabbat, 10a; 11a.

9 Louis Jacobs, 'Hasidic Prayer', in Hundert (ed.), *Essential Papers*, p. 330.

10 Scholem, *Messianic Idea in Judaism*, p. 211.

11 Quoted in Simon Dubnow, 'The Maggid of Miedzyryrecz, His Associates and the Center in Volhynia', in Hundert (ed.), *Essential Papers*, p. 61.

12 R. Meshullam Phoebus of Zbaraz, *Devekh emet*, n.p., n.d. in Jacobs, 'Hasidic Prayer', p. 333.

13 Benzion Dinur, 'The Messianic-Prophetic Role of the Baal Shem Tov', in Marc Saperstein (ed.), *Essential Papers on Messianic Movements and Personalities in Jewish History*, New York and London, 1992, p. 381.

14 Dubnow, 'The Maggid', p. 65.

15 Ibid.

16 Ibid.

17 Louis Jacobs (ed. and trans.), *The Jewish Mystics*, London, 1990; New York, 1991, pp. 208–15.

18 Jonathan Sheehan, *The Enlightenment Bible; Translation, Scholarship, Culture*, Princeton and Oxford, 2005, pp. 28–44.

19 Ibid., pp. 95–136.

20 Ibid., pp. 54–84.

21 Ibid., p. 68.

22 Ernest Nicholson, *The Pentateuch in the Twentieth Century: The Legacy of Julius Wellhausen*, Oxford, 1998, pp. 3–61.

23 John R. Franke, 'Theologies of Scripture in the Nineteenth and Twentieth Centuries', in Holcomb (ed.), *Christian Theologies of Scripture A Comparative Introduction*, New York and London,

2006; Jeffrey Hensley, 'Friedrich Schleiermacher' in Holcomb (ed.), ibid.

24 Friedrich Schleiermacher, *The Christian Faith*, translated by H. R. Mackintosh and J. S. Steward, Edinburgh, 1928, p. 12.

25 James R. Moore, 'Geologists and Interpreters of Genesis in the Nineteenth Century', in David C. Lindberg and Ronald E. Numbers (eds), *God and Nature; Historical Essays on the Encounter Between Christianity and Science*, Berkeley, Los Angeles and London, 1986, pp. 341–3.

26 Ferenc Morton Szasz, *The Divided Mind of Protestant America, 1880–1930*, University, Alabama, 1982, pp. 16–34, 37–41; Nancy Ammerman, 'North American Protestant Fundamentalism', in Martin E. Marty and R. Scott Appleby (eds), *Fundamentalisms Observed*, Chicago and London, 1991, pp. 11–12.

27 Mrs Humphry Ward, *Robert Elsmere*, Lincoln, Neb., 1969, p. 414.

28 *New York Times*, 1 February 1897.

29 Ibid., 18 April 1899.

30 George M. Marsden, *Fundamentalism and American Culture: The Shaping of Twentieth-Century Evangelicalism, 1870–1925*, New York and Oxford, 1980, p. 55.

31 Charles Hodge, *What is Darwinism?*, Princeton, 1874, p. 142.

32 A. A. Hodge and B. B. Warfield, 'Inspiration', *Presbyterian Review*, 2, 1881.

33 B. B. Warfield, *Selected Shorter Writings of B. B. Warfield*, 2 vols, edited by John B. Meeber, Nutley, NJ, 1902, pp. 99–100.

34 Paul Boyer, *When Time Shall Be No More: Prophecy Belief in Modern American Culture*, Cambridge, Mass., and London, 1992, pp. 87–90; Marsden, *Fundamentalism*, pp. 50–58.

35 2 Thessalonians 2: 3–8.

36 1 Thessalonians 4 : 16.

37 Marsden, *Fundamentalism*, pp. 57–63.

38 David Rudavsky, *Modern Jewish Religious Movements: A History
of Emancipation and Adjustment*, rev. edn, New York, 1967,
pp. 157–64, 286–90.

39 Guttman, *Philosophies of Judaism*, pp. 308–51; A. M. Eisen,
'Strategies of Jewish Faith', in Arthur Green (ed.), *Jewish
Spirituality*, 2 vols, London, 1986, 1989, vol. II, pp. 291–87.

40 Samuel C. Heilman and Menachem Friedman, 'Religious
Fundamentalism and Religious Jews', in Marty and Appleby
(eds), *Fundamentalisms Observed*, pp. 211–15; Charles Selengut, 'By
Torah Alone: Yashiva Fundamentalism in Jewish Life', in Martin
E. Marty and R. Scott Appleby (eds), *Accounting for
Fundamentalisms*, Chicago and London, 1994; Menachem
Friedman, 'Habad as Messianic Fundamentalism' in ibid., p. 201.

41 Quoted in Peter Gay, *A Godless Jew: Freud, Atheism, and the
Making of Psychoanalysis*, New Haven and London, 1987,
pp. 6–7.

42 Zygmunt Bauman, *Modernity and the Holocaust*, Ithaca, NY,
1989, pp. 40–77.

43 George Steiner, *In Bluebeard's Castle: Some Notes Towards the
Re-definition of Culture*, London and New Haven, 1971, p. 33.

44 Daniel 11 : 15; Jeremiah 1 : 14.

45 Robert C. Fuller, *Naming the Antichrist: The History of an
American Obsession*, Oxford and New York, 1995, pp. 115–17;
Paul Boyer, *When Time Shall Be No More*, pp. 101–5; Marsden,
Fundamentalism, pp. 141–4; 150; 157; 207–10.

46 Boyer, *When Time Shall Be No More*, p. 119; Marsden,
Fundamentalism, pp. 90–92.

47 Boyer, *When Time Shall Be No More*, p. 192; Marsden,

Fundamentalism, pp. 154–5.

48 Szasz, *The Divided Mind*, p. 85.

49 Ammerman, 'North American Protestant Fundamentalism',
   p. 26; Marsden, *Fundamentalism*, pp. 69–83; Ronald L.
   Numbers, *The Creationists: The Evolution of Scientific
   Creationism*, Berkeley, Los Angeles and London, 1992, pp.
   41–4; Szasz, *The Divided Mind*, pp. 107–18.

50 To J. Baldon, Mark 27, 1923, in Numbers, *The Creationists*, p. 41.

51 Heilman and Friedman, 'Religious Fundamentalism and
   Religious Jews', p. 220.

52 Michael Rosenek, 'Jewish Fundamentalism in Israeli Education',
   in Martin E. Marty and R. Scott Appleby (eds), *Fundamentalisms
   and Society*, Chicago and London, 1993, pp. 383–4.

53 The name is derived from Isaiah 66 : 5: 'Listen to the word of
   Yahweh, you who tremble at his word.'

54 Menachem Friedman, 'The Market Model and Religious
   Radicalism', in Laurence J. Silberstein (ed.), *Jewish
   Fundamentalism in Comparative Perspective: Religion, Ideology and
   the Crisis of Modernity*, New York and London, 1993, p. 194.

55 Heilman and Friedman, 'Religious Fundamentalism and
   Religious Jews', pp. 229–31.

56 Gideon Aran, 'The Roots of Gush Emunim', *Studies in
   Contemporary Judaism*, 2, 1986; Gideon Aran, 'Jewish Religious
   Zionist Fundamentalism' in Marty and Appleby (eds),
   Fundamentalisms Observed, pp. 270–71; 'The Father, the Son and
   the Holy Land', in R. Scott Appleby (ed.), *Spokesmen for the
   Despised, Fundamentalist Leaders in the Middle East*, Chicago,
   1997, pp. 318–20; Samuel C. Heilman, 'Guides of the Faithful,
   Contemporary Religious Zionist Rabbis', in ibid., pp. 329–38.

57 Ian S. Lustick, *For the Land and the Lord: Jewish Fundamentalism*

in Israel, New York, 1988, p. 84.

58 Eleazar Waldman, *Artzai*, 3, 1983, in Lustick, *For the Land and the Lord*, pp. 82–3.

59 1 Samuel 15: 3; R. Israel Hess, 'Genocide: A Commandment of the Torah', in *Bat Kol*, 26 February 1980; Haim Tzuria, 'The Right to Hate', *Nekudah*, 15; Ehud Sprinzak, 'The Politics, Institutions and Culture of Gush Eminim', in Silberstein (ed.), *Jewish Fundamentalism*, p. 127.

60 Ehud Sprinzak, *The Ascendance of Israel's Far Right*, Oxford and New York, 1991, pp. 233–5.

61 Raphael Mergui and Philippe Simonnot, *Israel's Ayatollahs: Meir Kahane and the Far Right in Israel*, London, 1987, p. 45.

62 Aviezer Ravitsky, *Messianism, Zionism and Jewish Religious Radicalism*, translated by Michael Swirsky and Jonathan Chipman, Chicago and London, 1983, pp. 133–4; Sprinzak, *Ascendance of Israel's Radical Right*, pp. 94–8.

63 Aran, 'Jewish Religious Zionist Fundamentalism', pp. 267–8.

64 John N. Darby, *The Hopes of the Church of God in Connexion with the Destiny of the Jews and the nations as Revealed in Prophecy*, 2nd edn, London, 1842.

65 Boyer, *When Time Shall Be No More*, pp. 187–8.

66 Jerry Falwell, *Fundamentalist Journal*, May 1968.

67 John Walvoord, *Israel and Prophecy*, Grand Rapids, Mich., 1962.

68 Boyer, *When Time Shall Be No More*, p. 145.

69 2 Peter 3: 10.

70 Ammerman, 'North American Protestant Fundamentalism', pp. 49–53; Michael Liensesch, *Redeeming America: Piety and Politics in the New Christian Right*, Chapel Hill, NC, and London, 1995, p. 226.

71 Gary North, *In the Shelter of Plenty: The Biblical Blueprint for*

Welfare, Fort Worth, Tex., 1986, p. xiii.

72 Ibid., p. 55.

73 Gary North, *The Sinai Strategy: Economics and the Ten Commandments*, Tyler Tex., 1986, pp. 213–14.

74 Ammerman, 'North American Protestant Fundamentalism', pp. 49–53; Liensesch, *Redeeming America*, p. 226.

75 Franz Rosenzweig, *The Star of Redemption*, translated by William W. Hallo, New York, 1970, p. 176.

76 Jeremiah 31 : 31–3.

77 Fishbane, 'The Notion of a Sacred Text', in *The Garments of Torah, Essays in Biblical Hermeneutics*, Bloomington and Indianapolis, 1989, pp. 122–32.

78 Isaiah 2: 1–4.

79 Fishbane, 'The Notion of a Sacred Text', p. 131.

80 Hans Urs von Balthasar, *The Glory of the Lord: A Theological Aesthetic*, vol VII, *Theology: the New Covenant*, edited by John Riches, translated by Brian McNeill C.R.V., San Francisco, 1989, p. 202.

81 Hans Frei, *The Eclipse of Biblical Narative*, New Haven, 1974.

82 Smith, *What Is Scripture?*

Epilogue

1 Gerald L. Bruns, 'Midrash and Allegory: The Beginnings of Scriptural Interpretation', in Robert Alter and Frank Kermode (eds), *The Literary Guide to the Bible*, London, 1987, pp. 641–2.

2 Quoted by Ian Hacking, *Why Does Language Matter to Philosophy?*, Cambridge, 1975, p. 148.

3 Donald Davidson, *Inquiries into Truth and Interpretation*, Oxford, 1984, p. 153.

4 Ibid.

INDEX

Note: Page references in italics
indicate Glossary definitions.

Abelard, Peter 137–8
Abraham 2, 13–14, 17, 63, 203,
   213
 and Jesus 75
Abraham ben Ezra 143
abuse of scripture 224
Akiba, R. 80, 83, 85–6, 89–92, 93,
   125, 144, 228
Alexandria
 and allegorical exegesis
   107–9, 121
 and Judaism 48–53
allegory 226–7, *231*
 in Christian exegesis 3, 63,
   106–9, 114, 121, 135,
   138–40, 168, 216
 in Jewish exegesis 3, 49–50,
   141–2, 144–5

see also remez
American colonies
 Puritan settlers 176–8
 and slavery 179–81
Amir, Yigal 214
Amos (prophet) 18, 19
anagogy 127, *231*
Andrew of St Victor 135–6
Anselm of Bec 136–7
Anselm of Laon 132
anti-Semitism 76–7, 215
Antioch, and tradition of
   exegesis 107
Antiochus Epiphanes 39–40
Antony of Egypt 116–17, 121
apatheia 116–17, *231*
apocalypse (*apokalypsis*) 65,
   69–70, 75–6, 200, *231*
apocalyptic
 fundamentalist 207–9
 Jewish 43, 45–6

Apocrypha 121, 160
apologia 102–5, 108, *231*
apophaticism 119–20, *231*
Aquinas, Thomas 140–1
Aristotle 49, 131, 133, 135, 140–2
Arius 117–18, 223
asceticism, Christian 115–17
Assyrian empire 18–21, 24, 178
Astruc, Jean 193
Athanasius of Alexandria
    117–18, 223
atheism 108, 205–6
Augustine of Hippo 121–5, 126,
    132, 225
   and principle of charity
      122–5, 228–9
authority, and interpretation
    175, 187, 195, 219

Baal cult 13, 17–18, 20
Baal Shem Tov (Israel ben
    Eliezer; Besht) 187–90, 235
Babylon
   conquest of Assyria 25
   conquest by Persia 29–30
   and exile 9–11, 25–8, 41, 169
   Jews in 65, 97–8
   and return from exile 30–1, 32
Bacon, Francis 184
Bacon, Roger 153
Balthasar, Hans Urs von
    219–20, 229

Bar Koseba, Simeon, revolt 92,
    96
Basil of Caesarea 118–19
Bavli (Babylonian Talmud)
    97–100, *231*, 240
Ben Sirah 37–9, 52, 92
Benedict of Nursia 127–8
Bentley, Richard 191–2
Bernard of Clairvaux 138–40
Besht *see* Baal Shem Tov
Binah (intelligence) 147–8, *231*,
    239
Breaking of the Vessels 170–1,
    232, 233
Bryan, William Jennings 209
Buber, Martin 217, 225–6, 229
Buchner, Ludwig 206
Buddhism, scriptures 2

Calvin, John 158, 165, 166–7,
    173–5, 225
Calvinism 176–7, 223
canon 4–5, 218, *232*
   and fundamentalism 209
   of Hebrew Bible 25, 43,
    92
   of New Testament 65–7, 76,
    164, 195
   within the canon 160, 165,
    180, 209, 224–5
Cantwell Smith, Wilfred 220–1,
    222, 224

capitalism 174, 217

cathedral schools, and exegesis
133, 135

charity 227–8
Christian 116–17, 122–5,
139
and Pharisees 84, 123

Christ (*christos*), as title 56, 62,
67–8, 73, 232

Christianity
and evolution 2
and gentiles 58–63
and Judaism 55–66, 71, 74–8,
103
and literary creativity 65–6,
68–9
and persecution 102
and Torah 61–4, 166–7, 228
see also Jesus movement

Chronicles (books) 35–6

Church, and the Bible 153–4,
155–6, 163–4, 219–20

Cluniac monks 129–30

coincidentia oppositorum 6, 85,
232, 236

compassion
and *midrash* 82–4, 86–8
in teaching of Jesus 71
see also charity

Cone, James Hal 181

conservatism, Christian
197–200, 207–8

contemplation *see theoria*

Copernicus, Nicolaus 167–8

creation
creationism 210, 223
ex nihilo 142, 149, 234
in Kabbalah 146–9, 169–70,
173
and literalism 27–8, 52, 167
in P strand 27–9

Crusades 130–1, 224

Cushman, Robert 177

Cyrus (king of Persia) 29–30, 40,
237

Daniel (book) 39–42, 70

darash (study) 34, 81, 144–5, 151,
232

Darby, John Nelson 200–1, 215

Darrow, Clarence 210

Darwin, Charles 195–6, 209

David (king of Israel), and
covenant 13, 17

Davidic monarchy 19–20, 23, 46,
56

Davidson, Donald 227

De Wette, Wilhelm 193

Deism 185, 191

demiourgos (craftsman) 52, 66,
232, 234

Denis the Areopagite 119–20

Descartes, René 184

Deuteronomist tradition 21–5,

35–6, 194, 224, 232
Deuteronomy (book) 21, 193, 225, 232
devekut (attachment) 188, 232
diaspora, Jewish 47–8, 53
and Christianity 58–61
Diderot, Denis 185
Din (stern judgement) 150, 152, 170–2, 225, 233
dogma 118, 120, 233
Dominicans 140
Dov Ber 189–90, 226
dynameis (powers) 52, 233, 235

'E' strand of Pentateuch 14, 15–17, 19, 21, 23, 193
Ecclesiastes (book) 36–7, 92, 113–14
Eck, Johann 163
economy, divine 104–6, 233
Egypt
and Assyria 20–1
and Judah 25
Eichhorn, Johann Gottfried 193
ekklesia (congregation) 59, 69–70, 73, 75, 233
ekstasis (stepping outside) 5–7, 90, 111, 152, 233, 237
Eliezer, R. 80, 87–8, 91, 222
emanations 142, 145, 233
En Sof (without end) 146–50, 170, 188, 233, 236, 238, 242

energeiai (divine energies) 52, 119, 233–4
Enlightenment 183–5, 191–5, 220
Jewish 186–91, 201–5, 235
epithalamium 114, 234
Erasmus, Desiderius 156–7, 163, 164
eschatology 234
Christian 60–1, 67, 127
Jewish 43
Essays and Reviews 196
Essene movement 44, 46, 47, 57
Eusebius of Caesarea 106
evolution
and the Bible 2, 195–6, 206, 223
in education 209–10
ex nihilo 234
exegesis
and charity 84, 116–17, 122–5, 227–9
Christological 160–2, 166
figurative *see* allegory
meaning 234
Pardes 144–5, 149–51, 232, 238, 238
as prophetic 41–2, 63–4
and sacred text 218
spiritual 5–7, 73, 90, 107–14, 123, 128–9, 140, 153, 189, 226

see also allegory; *lectio divina;*
    literal (plain) sense;
    literalism; *midrash;* moral
    sense; mystical sense;
    pesher
exile in Babylon 9–11, 25, 41,
    169
    and Exodus 26–7
    and literary creativity 25–8,
    65
    return *see* Golah
Exodus story 14–15, 23, 26, 177,
    178–9
    and American settlers 177,
    178
    and American slaves 180–1
    and black theology 181
Ezekiel (prophet) 10–11, 42
Ezra (Judean leader) 32–5

Falwell, Jerry 215–16
Father 234
fathers of the church 104–22,
    137, 140, 156, 191, 223
Ferdinand and Isabella of Spain
    169, 176
Feuerbach, Ludwig 205
First Book of Enoch 45
Fishbane, Michael 218–19,
    224–6, 228
Formstecher, Solomon 202–3
Frankel, Zachariah 203

Franklin, Benjamin 178
Frei, Hans 220, 222, 225
fundamentalism
    Jewish 204–5, 213–14
    Protestant 197, 199–201,
        207–11, 215–17, 222–3
    secular 225, 229

Galileo Galilei 168
gaon (head of academy) 190, 234
Garden of Eden 6–7, 27, 90, 108
Gelger, Abraham 203
Gemara (exegesis) 98–100, 234,
    240
Genesis (book)
    creation stories 27–8, 52,
        167–8, 193, 223
    and Luther 160
gentiles 58–63, 72–3, 77, 96, 234
Germany, and biblical criticism
    192–4
Gibbon, Edward 185
Gilbert of Poitiers 132
Glossa Ordinaria 132
Gnosticism/Gnostic 65–6, 145,
    234
Godfearers 234
    and Christianity 58–9
    and Judaism 47
Godhead 235
Golah (returned exiles) 30–1,
    32–5

Golden Rule 57, 71, 82–3, 87–8,
 228
Goldstein, Baruch 214
Gospel 55–78
 and Law 162–3
 meaning 235
 as *mysterium* 130
 as scripture 65
Gospel of Barnabas 191
Gospel of Thomas 65
gospels
 authorship 68–9
 gnostic 65–6
 Jewish-Christian 65, 68–9,
 191
 synoptic 67–73, 77, 240
goyim (Gentiles) 29–30, 33, 46,
 57–60, 172, 235
Graf, Karl Heinrich 193–4
Greek, and biblical text 155–7
Gregory the Great 128–9, 132
Gregory of Nazianzus 119
Gregory of Nyssa 119
Gutenberg, Johannes 159–60

Haeckel, Ernst 206
halakah/halakoth (legal ruling)
 87–8, 211, 235, 258 n.41
Haldemann, Isaac 209
Harby, Isaac 202
Haredim (trembling ones) 211,
 235

Hasid/Hasidim (pious ones) 188,
 235
Hasidism 187–90, 205, 211, 232
Haskalah (Jewish enlightenment)
 186–7, 235
Hasmonean dynasty 40, 42–3
Hebrew Bible 32–54
 canon 25, 43, 92
 and Christianity 57, 61–4, 66,
 67–8, 76, 93, 103–6, 166–7,
 195
Hebrews (letter to) 63–4, 66, 160
Hegel, Georg Wilhelm Friedrich
 202
Hellenism 39–41, 47–8, 69
hermeneutics 235
hesed (mercy) 18, 83–4, 148, 150,
 152, 171, 235
Hillel, R. 49, 95, 123, 125, 228
 and Golden Rule 57, 71, 82–3,
 123
 and *midrash* 82–4
Hirsch, Samuel 203
historical criticism 135–6, 143,
 186, 192–4, 196–8, 208–10,
 218, 226
history of Israel 13–31
 and Christianity 64–5, 103
 E strand 14, 15–17, 19, 21, 23
 J strand 14, 15–17, 21, 23, 25
 monarchy 13–14, 22
 P strand 25–9, 33, 36

tribes 12–13, 14–15, 26, 177–8
see also Deuteronomist
   tradition
Hod (majesty) 148, *235*
Hodge, Archibald A. 199–200
Hodge, Charles 198–9
Hokhmah (Wisdom) 36–7,
   235–6, 241
   Jesus as 67
   in Kabbalah 147, 231, 236, 239
Holbach, Paul Heinrich von 185
holiness
   and Mishnah 94
   in Torah 27, 33
Holiness Code 25
Holocaust 207, 211
Holy Spirit 235
horoz (enchaining) 84–5, 89, 91,
   106, 226, *236*
Hosea (prophet) 17–18, 19
Hugh of St Victor 135
humanism 156–8, 165, 184
Hume, David 185
Hupfeld, Hermann 193
Huxley, Thomas H. 206
hyponoia (higher thought) 50–1
hypostasis (manifestation) 119
hypothesis (underlying
   argument) 104, 184, *236*

Igen, Karl David 193
incarnation *236*

inerrancy, biblical 199–200
inspiration
   of biblical writers 99, 119
   of exegetes 40–41
   of preachers 166
   of prophets 34, 104, 202
   of Torah 203
   of translators 48–9
interpretation
   and revelation 4–5
   see also allegory; exegesis;
      pesher
Irenaeus of Lyons 66, 104–6, 124
Isaiah of Jerusalem 18–20, 42,
   143, 219
Ishmael, R. 86, 100
Islam
   mystical movements 145
   in Spain 131
   and violence 2, 131
Israel ben Eliezer *see* Baal Shem
   Tov
Israel (modern state), and
   Zionism 212–14, 215–16
Israel (northern kingdom)
   17–19, 21, 23, 36, 177–8

'J' strand of Pentateuch 14,
   15–17, 21, 23, 52, 193
James (brother of Jesus) 47, 59
Jeremiah (prophet) 23–4, 25,
   41–2, 217

Jerome 120–1, 129, 132, 225
Jerusalem
  Babylonian conquest 9–10,
    20, 25
  Christians in 59
  and return from exile 32–3
  Roman conquest 53–4, 64–5,
    79, 91
Jesus movement 47–8, 54, 55–8
  and destruction of Jerusalem
    64–5
  and gentiles 58–9
  and Torah 57, 61–4
Jesus of Nazareth
  and charity 228
  divinity 117–18, 120, 191,
    223
  historical 55–6, 125
  as Logos 73–4, 103–6
  as Messiah 56, 58–60, 62,
    67–8, 69
  resurrection 47, 56, 220
  as son of man and son of
    God 67, 117, 136
  and Torah 71–2
Jewish Christians 60, 62, 63–5,
    68–9, 75, 96, 162, 191
Job (book) 37, 92
Johanan ben Zakkai, R. 79–80,
    83–4, 91, 95, 228
John the Baptizer 46–7, 166
John Cassian 127

John Chrysostom 107
John (gospel) 67, 73–5, 77, 160
Johnson, Edward 178
Josephus, Flavius 56
Joshua, R. 80, 83–4, 88
Josiah (king of Judah) 20–3, 25,
    193
Jubilees (book) 45
Judah (southern kingdom)
    13–14, 17
  and Assyria 19–21
  and Deuteronomistic reforms
    20–3, 25
  and exile 9–11, 25
  and Greek empire 39–40
  post-exilic 30–1, 32–43
Judaism
  and Christianity 55–66, 71,
    74–8, 103
  and Ezra 35
  and modernity 186–91, 201–3,
    211–14, 235
  and Palestine 2
  Pharisaic 79–101
  Reform 201–4
  see also Hasidism; Kabbalah;
    Torah; Zionism
justification by faith 162–3
Justin Martyr 103–4

Kabbalah (inherited tradition)
    144–53, 169, 214, 236

Lurianic 169–73, 232, 233, 237, 242
and Torah 150–2, 171, 225
Kahane, R. Meir 213, 214
Kant, Immanuel 185, 202
Kara, Joseph 134
kavod (glory of God) 10, 90
kerygma (teaching) 118, 236
Kether Elyon (Supreme Crown) 147, 236, 239
kethuvim (Writings) 35–9, 90, 92, 236–7
King James Bible 165
King, Martin Luther Jr 181
kingdom of God/of heaven
  in Jesus movement 56–7, 60–61, 70–71
  in Jewish thought 46–7
Kook, R. Zvi Yehuda 212–13, 214
Krochmal, Nachman 203

laity, and *lectio divina* 129–30
Lane, Beldon C. 116–17, 262 n.50
lectio divina (sacred study) 126–54, 237
  and Hasidism 190
  and monasticism 127–8, 133, 136
  and rationalism 126, 136, 139–44

Levites 33
Leviticus (book) 25
Liberalism, Christian 195–7, 208
liberty, religious 175–6
literacy, spread 174
literal (plain) sense
  in Christianity 107–9, 112–13, 121, 129, 134–5, 139–41, 153
  in Judaism 27, 50, 52–3, 133–4, 141–4
  and kabbalah 151, 153, 171
  and Reformation 160–2, 168, 175, 177
literalism 2, 3, 229
  Christian 131, 197–201, 207–8, 216, 222–3
  Jewish 210–12, 214
literary criticism 218
Locke, John 185, 186
Logos 67, 237
  and exegesis 103–6, 109–11
  Jesus as 73–4, 103–6
  and Philo 49, 52
Loyola, Ignatius 158
Luke (gospel) 72–3, 77
Luria, Isaac 169–73, 188, 237
Luther, Martin 158–65, 173, 175, 225
  and canon 160, 165, 180

Maccabean wars 40–2
Maimonides, Moses 142–3

Malcolm X 181

Malkuth (kingdom) 148, 171, 237

Manasseh (king of Judah) 20, 22, 25

Marcion 66, 103

Mark (gospel) 69–70

Marsilio of Padua 153

Marx, Karl 206

maskilim (enlightened ones) 187, 201, 205, 237

Matthew (gospel) 70–72, 77

Maximus the Confessor 120, 137

Meir, R. 86–7, 88–9, 91, 93, 228

Mendelssohn, Moses 186–7, 235

Messiah (*meshiah*; anointed one) 45–6
  Jesus as 56, 58–60, 62, 67–8, 69
  in Judaism 29, 45, 214, 237

midrash 34, 79–92, 109, 133–4, 225, 229, *238*
  and compassion 82–3, 86–8, 125
  and *kabbalah* 144–5

miqra (summons) 82–3, 116, 217, 226, 229

Mishnah 93–7, *238*
  and Talmuds 97–101

Misnagdim 190, 205, 211, *238*

modernity

and fundamentalism 197, 199–201, 205–11

and Judaism 186–91, 201–2, 211, 235

and rationality 182, 183–5

and violence 206–7

Moleschott, Jakob 206

monasticism 116–17, 121, 127–8, 133, 136

monotheism
  of Christianity 61
  of Torah 16, 29, 58

Moody, Dwight 197

moral sense 107, 114–15, 127, 139, 144–5, 161

Moses 11–12, 14–15, 143
  and Israel 17
  and Jesus 71, 75
  and Mishnah 95–6, 100–101
  and Sinai covenant 62–3
  and Torah 11, 21–3, 33, 35, 64, 186

Moses of Leon 145

mystical sense 127, 144–7, 151

mysticism, Jewish 90, 92, 187–8, *see also* Kabbalah

mythos (myth) 50, 95–6, 147–9, *238*

Nahmanides 143–4

Nebuchadnezzar 40

and conquest of Judah 9, 17, 25

Netsakh (patience) 148, 171, 238

neviim (Prophets) 30, 35, 238

New Testament
canon 65–7, 76, 164, 165, 195
and Jews 76–7

Newton, Isaac 184–5

Nicholas of Lyra 153

North, Gary 216

Numbers (book) 25

oral tradition
and *midrash* 91
and Mishnah 93–7, 99
and Torah 12, 24, 164, 203

Origen 108–13, 117, 127, 226–7

ousia (divine essence) 52, 119, 238

'P' strand of Pentateuch 25–9, 33, 36, 52, 193–4, 225

Palestine, and Jesus movement 47–8, 54, 55

Pardes exegesis 144–5, 149–51, 232, 238

Pardes (paradise) 90, 144–5, 238

Paul of Tarsus 60–65, 66, 67, 77, 105, 157–8, 180, 200, 228
and Luther 160–161, 162

Pentateuch 239
authorship 143, 186, 192–3, 196

and national history 14–16, 19–23
see also Torah

peshat (literal sense) 144, 146, 239

pesher (deciphering) 226, 239
Christian 60, 63–4, 67–8, 72–3, 76, 85, 103
Qumran 43–4, 60, 63

Peter Lombard 132

Petrarch, Francesco 158

Pharisees 47
in the gospels 71–2, 77, 228
and mysticism 90
revival 78, 79–80
and temple 45, 80–81, 83–4
and Torah 44, 80–83

Philo of Alexandria 49–53, 107, 145, 227

Pierson, Arthur 198

Pietism 192

Pirke Avoth 93, 96

pistis (trust; faith) 63, 64, 73, 162, 239

Platonism
of Augustine 123
of Philo 49–53
polis (city state) 239

Pontius Pilate 46–7

printing, impact 157, 159–60, 174

proof texts 118, 157, 192, 222–3

prophecy, and Torah 41–2, 60, 63–4, 70
Protestantism, American 179, 197–200, 207–8, 215–17
Proverbs (book) 36, 92, 113, 117
Psalms (book), and Luther 160–161
Puritans, in New England 176–8

Q (gospel source) 66
Qumran sect 43–4, 60, 63
Qur'an 2, 6, 224

Rabin, Yitzhak 214
Rachamin (compassion) 148, 152, 171, 239
racism, 'scientific' 206
Rapture theory 200–201, 209, 215
Rashbam (R. Shemuel ben Meir) 134
Rashi (R. Shlomo Yitzhak) 133–6, 153
rationalism
    and Judaism 186–91, 202–3, 211
    and lectio divina 126, 136, 139–44
    and modernity 182, 183–5, 191, 194–9
Reconstruction movement 216–17
Reform Judaism 201–4

Reformation 158–67, 173–4
remez (allegory) 144–5, 151, 239
Renaissance 156–7, 183
revelation
    as ongoing 5, 35, 85, 89–90, 96, 145
    and reason 184, 186
    and science 167
    see also apocalypse
Revelation (book) 75–6, 160, 200, 207–9, 225, 228
Rig Veda 6, 228
righteousness, and Luther 161–2
ritual, and Hebrew Bible 34, 42, 203–4
Robertson, Pat 216
Robison, James 215
Roman Empire
    and Christianity 96, 102–3, 115
    collapse 120, 126–7, 129
    and conquest of Jerusalem 53–4, 64–5, 79
    and Jesus movement 55, 57
    and Judaism 46–7, 91–2, 96
Rosenzweig, Franz 217–18, 225–6
Rousseau, Jean-Jacques 185
Rushdoony, Rousas John 216

Saadia ibn Joseph 142

Sadducees 45

Samaria (capital of Israel) 19, 22, 58, 103

Schleermacher, Friedrich 194–5

scholasticism 141, 153, 156, 159

science, and the Bible 167–8, 174–5, 183–5, 195–9, 206, 209–10, 223

Science of Judaism school 202

Scofield, Cyrus 201, 208

Scofield Reference Bible 201

Scopes, John 210–11

Scriptures
and common hermeneutics 228
formation 34
see also Hebrew Bible; Mishnah; New Testament

Second Isaiah 29–30, 68, 71

sefer torah 21–3, 26, 38, 193, *239*

sefirah/sefiroth 239, 146–52, 171, *see also* Binah; Din; Hod; Hokhmah; Kether Elyon; Malkuth; Rachamin; Yesod

Seleucid empire 40

Sententiae 132–3

Sephardim 169–70, 186, *239*

Septuagint 48–9

Servant Songs 30, 68, 136

sex, ritual 17–18

shalom (wholeness) 7, 85, *240*

Shammai, R. 82, 95

Sharon, Ariel 216

Shekhinah *240*
Jesus as 73–5
in Kabbalah 148–50, 170, 172, 239, 240
in Pharisaic Judaism 72–3, 81–2, 87, 94
see also Holy Spirit

Shepherd of Hermas 66

Shor, Joseph Bekhour 134

Sifra 97

sin, original 126–7, 129, 137

slavery 179–81, 216, 223

sod 144–5, 150, *240*

sola scriptura 163–4, 165, 173–5, 181–2, *240*

Solomon, and Wisdom tradition 36

Soloveitchik, Haym 24

Song of Songs (book) 36–7, 39, 90, 92, 107, 114–15, 138–9, 150–1

Spain
and Jews 143, 169, 176, 186, *238*
and Muslims 131

Spinoza, Baruch 186, 192

spirituals 180–181

Suetonius (Gaius Suetonius Tranquillus) 56

synoptic gospels 67–73, 77, 160, *240*

Tabernacle Document 25–6
Tacitus, Publius Cornelius 56
Talmud (exegesis) 97–101, 222, 240
Tanakh 92, 93, 97–8, 104, 240
tanna; tannaim (scholars) 91, 240
targum (translation) 48
Temple, First
    as central to cult 10–11, 25
    destruction 9, 25, 65
    as Garden of Eden 7
Temple of Herod 46, 54, 55
    and gentiles 58
    and Jesus movement 56–7
    and Pharisees 80–81, 83–4, 93–5
    Roman destruction 64–5, 69–70, 92
Temple, Second 30–31, 32, 44–5
    and Hellenistic cult 40–41
    literature 43
Ten Commandments 15, 17, 23, 163
terrorism, and use of Qur'an 2
text (*textus*) 34, 105, 110, 222, 240
Theodore of Mopsuestia 107
theophany 23, 136, 240
theoria (contemplation) 115, 119, 120, 139, 240
Tifereth (grace) 148, 150, 152, 239, 240–241

tikkun (restoration) 170–172, 241
Toland, John 191
Torah 9–31
    and Babylonian exile 11
    and canon 25
    and Hasidism 188–90
    and Jesus 71–2
    and Jesus movement 57, 61–4
    and Kabbalah 150–152, 171, 225
    meaning 241
    and national history 13–14
    and oral tradition 12, 24, 96–9, 164, 203
    and Pharisees 80–81
    and prophecy 41–2, 60, 63–4, 70
    reverence for 4
    Roman ban on 91–2
    as Scripture 32–54
    study 34–5, 39–42, 72, 80–101, 204–5, 211
    and Wisdom literature 37–8, 241
    written text 21–5, 96–9, 226, 239
    see also midrash
Tosefta 96–7
tradition, and scripture 163–4
transcendence 2, 5–6
translations, vernacular 154, 164–5, 192

trepain 51
tribes of Israel 12–13, 14–15, 26
  lost 177–8
Trinity 119, 191
truth, and reason 183–4
Tyndale, William 154

United States
  and biblical literalism
    197–201, 207–8, 216–17
  and conservative
    Protestantism 179,
    197–200, 207–11, 215–17
  and manifest destiny 179
  and Reform Judaism 201–2
Urim and Thummim 34
Usha, rabbinic centre 92, 94,
  95

Valla, Lorenzo 157
Vater, Johann Severin 193
vernacular translations 154,
  164–5, 192
violence 3, 5, 131
  and the Bible 24, 28–30, 57,
    224–5
  and modernity 206–7, 217
  non-violence 28–30, 57, 175
  and Qur'an 2, 224
Vogt, Karl 206
Volozhiner, Hayyim 204
Vulgate (Latin translation) 121,

129, 132–3, 135, 156–7, 163

Waldman, R. Eleazar 213
Ward, Mrs Humphry 196–7
Warfield, Benjamin 199–200
Wars of Religion (1618–48) 176
Wellhausen, Julius 194
Whiston, William 191
William of Ockham 159, 161
Wilson, N. L. 227
Winthrop, John 177
Wisdom *see Hokhmah*
Wisdom literature 37–9, 92, 241
Writings *see kethuvim*
Wycliffe, John 153–4

Yahweh
  as divine warrior 16–19, 28–9
  exclusive worship 17–18, 29
  as one of many gods 16
Yavneh, as rabbinic centre
    79–92, 93
Yerushalmi (Jerusalem Talmud)
    97, 240, 241
yeshiva; yeshivoth (house of
    studies) 204–5, 211, 241
Yesod 148, 171, 239, 241

Zalman, Elijah ben Solomon
    190–191, 204
Zeir Anpin 171–2, 241–2
zimzum (withdrawal) 170, 242

Zionism
    Christian 215–16
    religious 212–14
    secular 206
Zohar 145–7, 150–152
Zunz, Leopold 203–4
Zwingli, Huldrych 158, 165–6,
    173, 225

INDEX OF BIBLICAL CITATIONS

Old Testament

Genesis
  1:6 268 n.28
  1:31 246 n.66
  2:5–17 246 n.63
  3 127
  3:8 260 n.19
  5:1 256 n.7
  9:25 271 n.52
  12:3 253 n.41
  15:6 252 n.39
  16 271 n.55
  16:11 254 n.79
  17:15–21 254 n.79
  20 260 n.23
  21:8–21 271 n.55

Exodus
  12:37 260 n.24
  13:21 261 n.26
  18 244 n.20
  19:4 270 n.50
  21:7–11 271 n.55
  24:3 245 n.37
  24:4–8 245 n.38
  24:9–31 244 n.20
  24:9 244 n.21
  24:11 244 n.21

  25–31 260 n.18
  29:45–6 246 n.54
  33:2 257 n.26
  33:23 262 n.62
  35–40 260 n.18
  40:34 246 n.56
  40:36–8 246 n.56

Leviticus
  13:47 256 n.17
  17–26 246 n.52
  19:2 246 n.59
  19:11 256 n.6
  19:33–4 246 n.62
  25–7 246 n.53
  25 246 n.61
  26:12 246 n.60
  35–8 246 n.53
  40 246 n.53

Numbers
  1:48–53 247 n.3
  3:5–40 247 n.3
  19:6 256 n.14

Deuteronomy
  1:1 265 n.34
  6:5 262 n.65, 263 n.68
  11:21 245 n.41
  12–26 245 n.40
  12:2–3 246 n.48
  21:23 86–7, 257 n.21

26:5–9 243 n.5
30:12 88, 257 n.25
30:15–17 270 n.45
32:8–9 244 n.13

Joshua
3 243 n.6
8:24–5 246 n.49
24 243 n.6
24:51 258 n.48

Judges
2:7 245 n.44
5:4–5 244 n.11
13:3–5 254 n.79

1 Samuel
9:9 247 n.10
15:3 276 n.59

1 Kings
5:9–14 248 n.16
8:27 245 n.43
13:1–2 246 n.45
22:8 247 n.10
22:13 247 n.10
22:19 247 n.10

2 Kings
21:2–7 245 n.34
21:10–15 246 n.50
22 245 n.36

23:4–20 245 n.39
23:10 245 n.34
23:11 245 n.34
23:15–18 246 n.45
23:25 246 n.45

Ezra
1:6 247 nn.7,9
1:9 247 n.9
1:10 247 n.8
10 248 n.12

Nehemiah
7:65 247 n.10
8:7–8 247 n.4
8:12–16 247 n.5

Job
7:12 246 n.65
9:8 246 n.65
26:12 246 n.65
38:7–11 246 n.65
42:3 248 n.17

Psalms
2 243 n.7
22:18 253 n.57
31:6 253 n.57
41:8 254 n.71
46:5–6 245 n.29
47 244 n.15
48 243 n.7, 244 n.15

68:18 245 n.35
69:9 252 n.35
69:21 253 n.57
71:2 267 n.13
72:1 267 n.12
82 244 n.14
84:12 245 n.35
87 243 n.7
89:2 84, 256 n.12
89:5–8 244 n.16
89:10–13 246 n.65
93:1–4 246 n.65
96 244 n.15
110 243 n.7
137 243 n.3
148 244 n.15
149 244 n.15
150 244 n.15
151 244 n.15

Proverbs
8:22 248 n.20
8:30–31 248 n.20
29:4–5 248 n.15

Song of Songs
1:2 261 n.43
3:1 264 n.25

Isaiah
2:1–6 270 n.48
2:1–4 277 n.78

2:2–3 252 n.27
2:10–13 245 n.29
6:1–9 245 n.26
6:6–7 249 n.37
6:11–13 245 n.27
6:13 245 n.28
7:14 245 n.31, 253 n.58
9:1 245 n.32
9:5–7 245 n.33
10:5–7 245 n.29
27:1 246 n.65
41:24 246 n.68
42:1–4 247 n.71
44:28 246 n.67
45:5 247 n.69
49:1–6 247 n.71
49:6 247 n.72
50:4–9 247 n.71
51:9–10 247 n.70
52:13 – 53:12 254 n.80
53:4 252 n.27
56:7 254 n.69
66:5 235, 275 n.53

Jeremiah
1:14 274 n.44
7:11 254 n.69
8:8–9 246 n.46
23:29 89, 257 n.31
25:11–12 248 n.34
31:31–3 277 n.76

Ezekiel
  1 243 n.1b
  1:1 249 n.37
  1:3 247 n.9
  1:24 249 n.37
  1:26–8 249 n.37
  3:1–3 11, 243 n.2
  14:14 248 n.28
  20:25–6 245 n.34
  22:30 245 n.34
  28:15 248 n.28
  40–48 243 n.3

Daniel
  1:4 248 n.29
  1:18 248 n.30
  7:13–14 248 n.33
  7:13 253 n.54
  7:25 248 n.31
  9:3 248 nn.34,35
  9:21 249 n.37
  9:27 254 n.68
  10:3 248 n.36
  10:4–6 249 n.37
  10:16 249 n.37
  11:15 274 n.44
  11:31 248 n.32
  11:35 249 n.38
  12:9–10 249 n.38

Hosea
  6:6 83–4, 244 n.22, 254 n.85,
    256 n.8
  11:5–6 245 n.23

Joel
  3:1–5 252 n.31

Amos
  1:3–5 245 n.24
  2:4–16 245 n.24
  5:24 245 n.25
  6:13 245 n.24

Habakkuk
  2:4 267 n.15
  3:4–8 244 n.11

Malachi
  1:6–14 247 n.1
  2:8–9 247 n.1

Apocrypha

Tobit
14:6 252 n.27

Ben Sirah
  24:1–22 248 n.18
  24:20 248 n.21
  24:21 248 n.22

24:23 248 n.19
24:28–9 248 n.23
24:33 248 n.26
35:1–6 248 n.24
35:7–11 248 n.25
50 256 n.10

New Testament

Matthew
1:22–3 253 n.58
3:1–2 249 n.51
5:1 254 n.81
5:3–12 251 n.11
5:11 254 n.77
5:17–19 251 n.13
5:17 254 n.76
5:19 254 n.82
5:21–39 254 n.83
5:29 260 n.16
5:38–48 251 n.11, 254 n.84
6:20 260 n.25, 261 n.29
7:12 252 n.16, 254 n.86
8:17 254 n.80
9:13 254 n.85
10:9 260 n.20
10:17–23 254 n.77
12:14–21 253 n.56
12:16 254 n.87
12:17 251 n.12
12:41–2 254 n.87
13:31–50 254 n.75

13:38-44 106, 260 n.10
17:5 262 n.52
18:20 254 n.89
19:21 261 nn.30,48
19:28 251 n.7
21:31 252 n.19
22:37–9 262 n.65, 263 n.68
23:1–33 255 n.108
24:9–12 254 n.78
24:30 253 n.54
24:36 262 n.52
26:26 173, 270 n.38
26:29 251 n.9
26:39 262 n.52
26:65 253 nn.54,56
27:17 251 n.4
27:22 251 n.4
27:25 255 n.107
27:33–6 253 n.57

Mark
1:14–15 249 n.53
1:15 254 n.74
2:21–2 253 n.64
4:3–9 253 n.63
5:12 251 n.4
8:17–18 253 n.63
8:27–33 251 n.3
11:15–19 254 n.69
12:30–31 263 n.68
13:1–2 252 n.17
13:5–27 254 n.67

13:9–13 253 n.62
13:14 254 n.68
13:26 253 n.54
13:33–7 253 n.64
14:21, 27 254 n.69
14:25 251 n.9
14:58–61 254 n.66
14:61–4 253 n.52
14:62 253 n.54
15:29 254 n.66
16:8 254 n.73
23:30–31 262 n.65

Luke
2:25 253 n.56
3:3–14 249 n.52
6:20–23 251 n.11
6:27–38 251 n.11
6:31 252 n.16
10:17 262 n.65, 263 n.68
14:27 131, 263 n.7
16:17 251 n.13
17:22 253 n.54
18:9–14 255 n.106
21:25 253 n.54
22:69 253 n.54
23:56 251 n.14
24:13–35 72–3, 254 n.90
24:53 251 n.8

John
1:1–14 253 n.55
1:1–5 255 n.91
1:30 255 n.92
2:19–21 255 n.99
3:1–21 255 n.109
3:8 268 n.24
5:10 262 n.66
6:32–6 255 n.102
6:51 261 n.28
6:60–6 255 n.95
7:34 255 n.98
7:37–9 255 n.101
8:12 255 n.101
8:19–21 255 n.98
8:57 255 n.100
8:58 255 n.103
11:47–53 255 n.109
15:12–13 255 n.93
15:18–27 255 n.94
18:2–3 255 n.109

Acts
2:14–21 252 n.31
2:46 251 n.8
4:32–5 251 n.10
8:1 252 n.20
8:18 252 n.20
8:32–4 253 n.56
9:2 252 n.20
10–11 252 n.23
11:19 252 n.20

11:26 252 n.24
15 252 n.22

Romans
  1:17 161, 267 n.15
  1:20–32 252 n.25
  4:22–4 253 n.40
  5:12–20 252 n.38
  8:9 252 n.32
  9:1–33 252 n.33
  12:9–13 251 n.11
  12:14 251 n.11
  13:6–7 251 n.12
  13:10 252 n.16
  13:13–14 121, 262 n.58
  15:3 252 n.35
  15:4 252 n.36

1 Corinthians
  1:22 252 n.18
  5:1–13 252 n.30
  6:7 251 n.11
  8:4–13 252 n.30
  10:1–4 261 n.27
  10:4 252 n.30
  12:27–30 263 n.73
  13:12 264 n.20
  15:20 251 n.5
  15:45 252 n.38

2 Corinthians
  3:9-18 252 n.37

Galatians
  1:1–16 252 n.28
  2:1–10 252 n.22
  2:11–12 251 n.15
  3:8 253 n.41
  4:16 252 n.32
  4:22–31 253 n.42
  5:3 252 n.22

Ephesians
  1:10 105, 259 n.6
  5:23–32 261 n.44
  6:5 271 n.53

Philippians
  2:6–11 253 n.53

Colossians
  1:15–20 263 n.73

1 Thessalonians
  1:9 252 n.30
  4:16 273 n.36

2 Thessalonians
  2:3–8 273 n.35

Hebrews
    1:2–4 253 n.55
    3:1–6 253 n.43
    4:12 – 9:28 253 n.44
    11:1 253 n.45
    11:32 253 n.46
    11:40 253 n.47

1 Peter
    2:23–4 253 n.56

2 Peter
    3:10 276 n.69
    3:15 253 n.49

1 John
    2:18–19 255 n.96
    3:12–13 255 n.94
    4:5–6 255 n.97
    4:7–12 255 n.93

Revelation
    16:14 208
    21:22–4 255 n.105

Indexes compiled by Meg Davies (Fellow of the Society of Indexers)